Connecting
Teacher
Leadership
and
School
Improvement

Joseph Murphy

Connecting
Teacher
Leadership
and
School
Improvement

CORWIN PRESS
A SAGE Publications Company
Thousand Oaks, California

For information:

Corwin Press
A Sage Publications Company
2455 Teller Road
Thousand Oaks, California 91320
www.corwinpress.com

Sage Publications Ltd.
1 Oliver's Yard
55 City Road
London EC1Y 1SP
United Kingdom

Sage Publications India Pvt. Ltd.
B-42, Panchsheel Enclave
Post Box 4109
New Delhi 110 017 India

Printed in the United States of America.

Library of Congress Cataloging-in-Publication Data

Murphy, Joseph, 1949-
Connecting teacher leadership and school improvement / Joseph Murphy.
  p. cm.
Includes bibliographical references and index.
ISBN 0-7619-3199-6 (cloth) — ISBN 0-7619-8830-0 (pbk.)
  1. Teacher participation in administration—United States. 2. School improvement programs—United States. 3. Educational leadership—United States. I. Title.
LB2806.45.M87 2005
371.1′06—dc22   2004022985

This book is printed on acid-free paper.

05   06   07   08   09   10   9   8   7   6   5   4   3   2   1

Acquisitions Editor:	Rachel Livsey
Editorial Assistant:	Phyllis Cappello
Production Editor:	Laureen A. Shea
Copy Editor:	Diana Breti
Typesetter:	C&M Digitals (P) Ltd.
Proofreader:	Penelope Sippel
Indexer:	Nara Wood
Cover Designer:	Lisa Miller

Contents

Preface

For much of the last quarter century, educators, policy-makers, and the general citizenry have been engaged in an unbroken quest to understand the school improvement equation. That is, there have been ongoing efforts, sometimes systematic and often ad hoc, to identify the factors that explain school performance and student achievement and to deepen our understanding of how they work, both as individual components and as parts of the system of schooling.

Research over these years has consistently underscored leadership as a critical theme in the school improvement narrative. Indeed, evidence from nearly every realm of investigation—beginning with effective school studies through the most recent work on comprehensive school reform—confirms leadership as an explanatory variable in schools where all students meet ambitious achievement targets.

Over that time, our understanding of leadership has deepened and become more complex. We have learned about the centrality of instructionally focused leadership and the importance of transformationally anchored leadership work. We have also learned that leadership is as much a property of the school and its culture as it is a dimension of administrative roles. The central place of teacher leadership in the school improvement play has been identified.

This book is designed to help the reader fully comprehend teacher leadership as a pathway to school improvement. We unpack teacher leadership into its core components and trace its evolution into a more mature reform concept. We reveal how teacher leadership fits into the larger array of school reform initiatives. We examine the ideological and empirical seedbed in which teacher leadership has been germinated. We investigate the larger forces underway in education that buttress efforts to promote teacher leadership in schools. And we review the engine or theory in action that powers the growing teacher leadership movement.

We are not salespersons for teacher leadership. Rather, we examine the teacher leadership phenomenon and explore how it can function as one, albeit an important, piece of equipment in the school improvement toolbox. By necessity, at times we assume a critical stance, exposing flaws in the formulation of the initiative and pointing out how, regardless of the health of the reform model itself, the environment sometimes provides only limited support for that potential to thrive.

In Chapter 1, we describe how emerging perspectives on teacher leadership represent a break with prevailing views of leadership built up around formal administrative roles. We recount how teacher leadership is both a catalyst for and an outcome of a shift away from a near-exclusive focus on hierarchical organizational systems and institutional views of schooling. We also parse the concept of teacher leadership into its prime elements and provide a definition. We trace the history of teacher leadership over time.

In Chapter 2, we expose the three major pillars buttressing the teacher leadership movement. We provide an analysis of the struggle to rebuild the organizational foundations of schooling, examining the dysfunctionalities of traditional hierarchical structures and investigating postindustrial organizational forms that privilege collective conceptions of leadership. We highlight the changing nature of leadership in these adaptive organizations, capturing the general storyline as well as the implications for those in formal leadership positions. We reveal how teacher leadership is nourished by reform initiatives that honor professionalism and by the ongoing struggle to promote high quality education for all youngsters.

As with all reform movements, teacher leadership is propelled by a specific power train, one that shares multiple properties with engines driving other professionally focused reform models, such as school-based decision making. In Chapter 3, we peel back the covering on that driveshaft to reveal its inner workings. We review how teacher leadership is expected to promote professionalization and to enhance the health of school organizations. We report how changes in these areas are believed to link with classroom and school improvements. We also present some caveats to hold onto while examining the hypothesized chain of benefits or theory of action fueling the teacher leadership movement.

In Chapter 4, we provide a brief portrait of teacher leaders. We offer a few words of caution about any attempt to craft a generic chronicle of this complex phenomenon. We provide a review of the limited research on factors motivating educators to assume the mantle of teacher leader and an overview of the central role of expertise in the teacher leadership narrative. We present some of the bedrock principles of teacher leadership. We provide an overview of the personal qualities that researchers often find associated with teacher leaders, as well as the essential skills often displayed by these educators. We also examine the nature of the tasks performed by teacher leaders.

In Chapter 5, we examine the variety of pathways to teacher leadership. We group these into two broad clusters: role-based pathways and community-based approaches. We organize the narrative around a set of variables (e.g., the embedded view of leadership) that allows us to illustrate and define each of the pathways.

In Chapter 6, we examine a collection of organizational conditions and a host of professional and cultural norms that can retard or promote the creation of a culture of shared leadership and constrain or enhance the activities of teacher leaders. We organize that analysis around the three broad topics of structure, support, and culture.

In Chapter 7, we explore the special role played by the building principal in locating, planting, and nurturing the seeds of teacher leadership. We discuss how the development of teacher leadership in general, and teacher leaders specifically, depends heavily on the quality of principal-teacher relationships. We emphasize the importance of principals arriving at new nonhierarchical understandings of leadership, including the willingness to share power widely among their teacher colleagues. We describe how recast organizational structures can be employed in the service of teacher leadership. We outline six key functions in which principals engage to promote teacher leadership: crafting a vision and delineating expectations for teacher leadership in the school, identifying and selecting teacher leaders and linking them to leadership opportunities, legitimizing the work of teacher leaders, providing direct support, developing the leadership skill set of teacher leaders, and managing the teacher leadership process at the school level.

In Chapter 8, we target professional development as a key ingredient that needs to be energized to bring teacher leadership to life in schools. We provide an analysis of the state of teacher readiness to assume the mantle of teacher leadership. We explore the elements of successful models for educating teacher leaders. We also unpack the skills and knowledge that anchor productive professional development experiences for teacher leaders.

In the final chapter, we introduce key issues that must be kept in mind as we move forward in our quest to link teacher leadership and school improvement. We raise some concerns and provide some challenges that, if met, could significantly enhance the viability of teacher leadership. Finally, we tease out some dilemmas associated with the motives that inform and the structures that buttress the teacher leadership movement, point out some thin spots in the teacher leadership tapestry, introduce a few caveats, and outline ways research on teacher leadership can be strengthened.

The book is designed to be of interest and use to a wide array of educators and other decision makers. It is intended to help teachers and principals bring teacher leadership to life in the service of school improvement. It is designed to facilitate the activities of educators at the district as they work on the school improvement agenda at the system level. It is also our hope that the teachers of future teachers and principals and those involved with professional development for sitting school educators will find the material herein to be helpful as we prepare colleagues for new forms of leadership. The book should be of assistance to school improvement researchers as they continue to deepen our understanding of ways to create more effective schools. In a similar vein, the book should be of interest to those colleagues who labor in the school reform vineyards, both those in the education and policy worlds.

About the Author

Joseph Murphy is Professor of Education and Associate Dean at Peabody College of Education at Vanderbilt University. He has also been a faculty member at the University of Illinois and The Ohio State University, where he was the William Ray Flesher Professor of Education.

In the public schools, he has served as an administrator at the school, district, and state levels, including an appointment as the Executive Assistant to the Chief Deputy Superintendent of Public Instruction in California. His most recent appointment was as the founding president of the Ohio Principals Leadership Academy. At the university level, he has served as Department Chair and Associate Dean.

He is past vice president of the American Educational Research Association and is the chair of the Interstate School Leaders Licensure Consortium (ISLLC). He is co-editor of the AERA *Handbook of Research on Educational Administration* (1999) and editor of the National Society for the Study of Education (NSSE) yearbook, *The Educational Leadership Challenge* (2002).

His work is in the area of school improvement, with special emphasis on leadership and policy. He has authored or co-authored fifteen books in this area and edited another eleven. His most recent authored volumes include *The Quest for a Center: Notes on the State of the Profession of School Administration* (1999), *The Productive High School* (2001), *Understanding and Assessing the Charter School Movement* (2002), and *Leadership for Literacy: Research-Based Practice, PreK–3* (2003).

Linda C. Holste
Premier Equestrian Person and Land Baroness

Good intentions and even strong efforts will fail in the absence of a strong conceptualization that informs and is informed by actions. So far, teacher leadership strategies are not being guided by strong conceptualization. (Fullan, 1994, p. 250)

Insofar as there are numerous examples of teacher leadership, it is appropriate that a theoretical model of teacher leadership be developed. (Strodl, 1992, p. 10)

PART I

Unpacking the Concept

CHAPTER ONE

Introduction to Teacher Leadership

There is significant progress being made in teacher leadership during the early years of the new century. (Katzenmeyer & Moller, 2001, p. 123)

States and local jurisdictions increasingly recognize teacher leadership as a strong and pervasive trend. (Clemson-Ingram & Fessler, 1997, p. 104)

For the last quarter century, the nation has witnessed a nearly unbroken chain of initiatives to reform the American PreK–12 educational system. These interventions have been germinated in a wide variety of ideological seedbeds. They have emerged in response to powerful changes underway in the larger economic, political, and social environments in which the schooling enterprise is nested. They have been undertaken to solve an assortment of problems and to meet a wide array of important objectives.

One significant line of work to strengthen our nation's schools emphasizes teachers assuming greater leadership of the organizations in which they work, or what has come to be known as teacher leadership. While teacher leadership in America's schools is not yet "a broadly accepted norm" (Urbanski & Nickolaou, 1997, p. 243) and while "teachers, in general, do not share a tradition of leadership" (Sherrill, 1999, p. 59), during the last 20 years "teacher leadership has become an established feature of educational reform in the United States" (Smylie, Conley, & Marks, 2002, p. 162). As we explain below, it differs from other improvement efforts in important ways, especially in the theory in action or reform engine that powers the reform. It varies in another critical way as well. Unlike many other reform endeavors, such as charter schools or school-based management, teacher leadership is often an embedded concept, one that appears as a defining strand in a larger reform effort rather than as a distinct strategy.

This book is designed to help the reader fully comprehend teacher leadership as a pathway to school improvement. Our jumping-off point is Snell and Swanson's (2000) observation that what is required in the field of "teacher leadership is a broader conceptualization of this phenomenon" (p. 3)—that "concerted efforts for the explication of conceptual underpinnings, implementation processes, and evaluation strategies are needed to make teacher leadership a genuine reform initiative, rather than another fad in the history of educational reform" (Yarger & Lee, 1994, p. 235). We also concur with Crowther, Kaagan, Ferguson, and Hann (2002) that a "massive" amount of work is required in "exploring the meaning of teacher leadership" (p. 18).

We are not salespersons for teacher leadership. Rather, it is our intention to examine the teacher leadership phenomenon and explore how it can function as one—albeit an important—piece of equipment in the school improvement toolbox. By necessity, at times we assume a critical stance, exposing flaws in the formulation of the initiative and pointing out how, regardless of the health of the reform model itself, the environment sometimes provides only limited support for that potential to thrive.

In this introductory chapter, we undertake two broad assignments. We explore prevailing concepts of leadership that often hinder the development of teacher leadership in schools. We also make our first pass at uncovering the meaning of this emerging construct. In Chapter 2, we investigate the impetus for the emergence of teacher leadership on the reform landscape. Chapter 3 focuses the analytic spotlight on the theory in action or reform engine that is powering the teacher leadership movement. After unpacking and describing the pieces and elements of teacher leadership, Chapter 4 presents a comprehensive model of this change strategy. Chapter 5 addresses methods to operationalize teacher leadership, moving from earlier and more discrete ideas (e.g., creating new roles) to later, more integrated and comprehensive formulations (e.g., reconfiguring the school as a learning community). Chapters 6 through 8 focus on getting the context right for teacher leadership to flourish. Overcoming organizational and professional dynamics that act as a drag on the change work is the purview of Chapter 6. Chapter 7 explores the critical role of the principal in helping teacher leadership take root and mature at the school level. It also offers strategies to help teachers and principals create productive relationships in the service of deepening the pool of leadership. Chapter 8 analyzes the significance of professional development for school staff in bringing alternative formulations and models of leadership to life. In the final chapter, we rescrub all the information to explore concerns that transect the teacher leadership movement. One lens is directed toward problems while a second is focused on the goal of reinforcing the architecture supporting teacher leadership.

THE STARTING GATE

In the literature on educational leadership little attention is given to the teacher as an educational leader in the school other than in the classroom. (Brownlee, 1979, p. 119)

The assumption has been that teaching is for teachers and leading is for administrators and managers of schools. (Lynch & Strodl, 1991, p. 2)

It is instructive to begin our analysis with a clear understanding of traditional perspectives and models of leadership in general and leadership in schools in particular—and to see how teacher leadership intersects with this work. Specifically, we start with the knowledge that throughout most of the last century, with its focus on hierarchical forms and institutional dynamics, "leadership has tended to be constructed as associated with ascribed authority and position" (Crowther & Olsen, 1997, p. 6): "leadership traditionally has been perceived to reside with school administrators where power flowed downward to teachers" (Yarger & Lee, 1994, p. 226). On the schooling scene, this has meant that (1) educational leadership has been defined in "hierarchical and positional conceptions" (Darling-Hammond, Bullmaster, & Cobb, 1995, p. 103), in terms of roles and the "positional authority" (Crowther, 1997, p. 5) of principals and superintendents; (2) "the system has not been organized to treat teachers as leaders" (Institute for Educational Leadership, 2001, p. 3); and (3) the leadership literature, in turn, "has focused almost entirely on those in formal school leadership positions" (Spillane, Halverson, & Diamond, n.d., p. 7). These understandings gave rise to views of leadership that were tightly connected to domains of responsibility, with the assignment of "school-wide leadership to principals and classroom leadership roles to teachers" (Clift, Johnson, Holland, & Veal, 1992, p. 878; Crowther et al., 2002).

The significant point here is not that teachers were unconnected to leadership but that such leadership was rarely acknowledged outside the realm of the classroom, teachers' role-based field of authority and influence as traditionally defined (Barth, 1988a). Because the work of teachers in terms of role and authority "has been seen as being composed of interactions with students in classes" (Griffin, 1995, p. 30), the expectation has been hardwired into the structure and culture of schools "that the only job of teachers is to teach students and to consider the classroom, at best, as the legitimate extent of their influence" (Urbanski & Nickolaou, 1997, p. 244). "The formal authority of teachers in schools remains carefully circumscribed. They exert extensive control over teaching in their classrooms and departments, but their formal influence rarely extends beyond that" (Johnson, 1989, p. 105).

This preoccupation with the hierarchical organizational system with its tenets of separation of management (leadership) from labor, chain of command, and positional authority has led to the crystallization of (1) forms of schooling in which "teachers are routed into traditional roles" (Kowalski, 1995, p. 247) and "teacher leadership is clearly not a common contemporary condition" (Barth, 1988b, p. 134)—models in which "few people have viewed these educators as a group in the same way as other leaders, i.e., principals" (Hatfield, Blackman, & Claypool, 1986, p. 20); and (2) a profession in which "teachers, even those who are already leaders, do not see themselves as leaders" (Hart & Baptist, 1996, p. 87). As a consequence, "there are almost no mechanisms by which teachers can emerge as leaders for the purposes of leading work on teaching, even when they have been acknowledged as exemplary classroom teachers" (Little, 1987, p. 510). Thus teachers are forced into "dependent roles" (Creighton, 1997, p. 5).

Not surprisingly, teachers have generally not been featured in school reform initiatives, except in the "cog-in-the-wheel role" (Griffin, 1995, p. 30) of implementing policy from above. They have been afforded very limited "opportunit[ies] to effect policy or restructure schools" (Manthei, 1992, p. 15; Lynch & Strodl, 1991) or to "participate in decision making about school improvement" (Wasley, 1991, p. 3)—"to effect meaningful change outside their classrooms or departments" (Johnson, 1989, p. 104). While the need for leadership has been a central ingredient in the school change and school improvement literature, consistent with the analysis above, historically that leadership has been associated with those in roles with positional authority over teachers (Heller & Firestone, 1994; Leithwood, Jantzi, Ryan, & Steinbach, 1997; Smylie, Conley, & Marks, 2002). Indeed, it is proposed that much of the reform activity of the last quarter century has actually solidified the traditional roles of administrators as leaders and teachers as followers (Crowther, 1997).

The theme of teacher leadership as a "seriously underdeveloped topic" (Crowther & Olsen, 1997, p. 6), both conceptually and in practice, is ribboned throughout this book. So too are analyses of the costs to the educational system and to teachers of the overreliance "on the accepted body of thought on educational leadership" (Crowther et al., 2002, p. 23) and prevailing models of schools as hierarchical organizations, especially theories that originate in the corporate and managerial system. We proceed from Suleiman and Moore's (1997) position that "the false assumption that teaching is for teachers and leading is for administrators has operated to the inutility of the public schools for a long time" (p. 6), that the sole emphasis on formal school leaders "at the center of educational leadership is ill directed" (Crowther et al., 2002, p. 49) and has real costs in terms of schooling outcomes.

We commence also from the proposition that "teacher leadership is essential to change and improvement in a school" (Whitaker, 1995, p. 76; Killion, 1996), that "genuine, long-lasting school change initiatives must derive from and involve teachers" (Kelley, 1994, p. 300), and that without teachers' "full participation and leadership, any move to reform education—no matter how well-intentioned or ambitious—is doomed to failure" (Lieberman & Miller, 1999, p. xi). In short, we argue for the necessity of challenging the underlying assumptions about existing roles for teachers and school administrators (Barth, 2001; Foster & Suddards, 1999; Rallis, 1990; Sergiovanni, 1991a, 1991b).

The scaffolding on which we construct our understanding of leadership is forged from "multiple sources and persons" (Crowther, 1997, p. 7). It arises in part from the stockpile of material on leadership roles but is inclusive of more than traditional administrative roles (Miller, 1992). That is, we advance beyond the view of "educational leadership as the domain of either a particular stratum of the educational system or the individuals within that stratum" (Crowther, 1997, p. 6). Our scaffolding is also erected, however, from our best understandings of leadership as (1) an organizational property, (2) a function or process, (3) an outgrowth of expertise, (4) an activity of a group, and (5) a dynamic of community, understandings that move us away from what O'Hair and Reitzug (1997) label "conventional leadership" (p. 65) and that permit the concept of teacher leadership to be positioned on center stage in the leadership play—insights that promote "a new type of leadership" (Katzenmeyer & Moller, 2001, p. 82) or "a new paradigm of leadership—one that recognizes the central place of teachers" (Crowther et al., 2002, p. 27).

DEFINITIONAL ISSUES

The issue of teacher leadership is devilishly complicated. And it doesn't help matters that the phrase itself is frustratingly ambiguous. (Wigginton, 1992, p. 167)

Even now, we are a long way from a common understanding of teacher leadership. Confusion about definitions . . . abound. (Katzenmeyer & Moller, 2001, pp. 4–5)

An Organizational Focus

There are almost no mechanisms by which teachers can emerge as leaders for purposes of leading work on teaching, even when they have been acknowledged as exemplary classroom teachers. (Little, 1987, p. 510)

Analysts emphasize either a "two-level concept" (Keedy, 1999, p. 787; Strodl, 1992) or a three-tiered model of teacher leadership (Murphy, 1991). Specifically, leadership can be linked to influence in three broad domains or "zones" (Ingersoll, 1996, p. 162): autonomy of teachers in their classrooms, the ability to shape school policies and practices, and control of the machinery of the profession writ large (e.g., licensure, certification) (Ingersoll, 1996; McCarthy & Peterson, 1989; Sizer, 1984). Leadership in each zone is seen somewhat differently; for example, it is often asserted that "teaching children and adolescents is quite different from leading and coaching teachers" (Berry & Ginsberg, 1990, p. 618).

While, by necessity, we touch on activity in zone one above, the focus of this book is on teacher leadership beyond the classroom, primarily at the school level. Our attention here does not gainsay the fact that "a classroom including a group of students and their class teacher is in itself a small social organization" (Cheng, 1994, p. 54), nor does it deny the importance of teacher leadership in classrooms (Berliner, 1986). Indeed, considerable effort has been devoted to describing student-based teacher leadership (see, for example, Cheng, 1994; Larkin, 1973; Reinoso, 2002; Vertiz, Fortune, & Hutson, 1985). Rather, it is simply an acknowledgment that our charge is to explore what is known about teacher leadership activities in the larger organization in which they work.

Newness

To make matters more complicated, teacher leadership is a fairly recent phenomenon. (Yarger & Lee, 1994, p. 233)

As we concentrate on the nature of teacher leadership beyond the classroom, certain inescapable conclusions emerge. To begin with, we find that teacher leadership defined in this way is a relatively new idea "in both research and practice circles" (Lieberman, 1992, p. 160). Certainly, prior to 1985 it is a difficult theme to observe, even employing powerful analytic lenses; "teaching and leadership [had] not been dealt with together much" (Lynch & Strodl, 1991, p. 2) before then. Indeed, given the overview in the previous section, one can see quite clearly why "the possibility that leadership might be a function of the work of teachers has only recently begun to be accorded serious consideration" (Crowther & Olsen, 1997, p. 7).

Because scholarship in the area "has only begun to emerge" (Silva, Gimbert, & Nolan, 2000, p. 779), there is "no well-established body of literature" (Wasley, 1991, p. 9) on teacher leadership and consequently "not much is known" (Fay, 1992a, p. 4) about the concept. Thus, even while the idea appears to have "burst upon the scene" (Lieberman, 1992, p. 160) and is something of a "hot topic" (Smylie, 1996, p. 573; Boles & Troen, 1996) today, it is instructive to remember that teacher leadership outside the classroom has rather shallow roots.

An Element in School Reform Models

> The second wave of educational reform . . . raised interest in new roles that give teachers more leadership responsibility. (Heller & Firestone, 1994, p. 1)

As we touched on in the first section and re-emphasize here, teacher leadership initially rode into play on the back of various broad-based reform movements, for example, school-based management and professionalization (Murphy, 1990a). Thus, while the concept sometimes assumed the leading role, it has more often been a supporting actor. For example, it is one of a series of critical elements in most models of site-based decision making (Monson & Monson, 1993; Murphy & Beck, 1995; Smylie, 1995).

At the same time, the idea of teacher leadership is often "caught in the collision . . . between two strategies for achieving reform: one resting on heightened involvement and commitment of participants and one relying on intensified control of participants' work" (Little, 1995, p. 50; Murphy, 1990a)—and more recently, we would add, the reliance on market forces to fuel improvement (Murphy, 1996, 1999, 2000c). It is also often difficult to tease out the extent to which teacher leadership is a causal variable in the school reform algorithm or a product of reform movements such as learning organizations and communities of practice.

Complexity

> I was struck . . . at how enormously complex teacher leadership roles are as they play out in practice. (Wasley, 1991, p. 154)

Contrary to much of the writing in this area, teacher leadership is not a simple concept. As a dimension of the larger dynamic of power redistribution in schools, it "is marked by substantial disagreement and confusion" (Ingersoll, 1996, p. 159). Teacher leadership positions are "full of problems and riddled with paradoxes" (Wasley, 1991, p. 155). And the more one moves from conceptual analysis to implementation—"to how teacher leadership roles play out in practice" (Wasley, 1991, p. 154)—the more visible this complexity becomes (Little, 1988).

Nesting teacher leadership within the plethora of changes required to bring it to life in schools only heightens the complexity (Manthei, 1992). Or to capture this idea in slightly different form, context is a critical variable here (Katzenmeyer & Moller, 2001; Little, 1995; Siskin, 1994). "The environment at the school and district" (Clemson-Ingram, 1997, p. 100) and state adds to both the richness of teacher leadership as well as the difficulty of neatly boxing up the concept (Kowalski, 1995).

Teacher leadership also means different things to different groups; for example, for teacher unions standing up for the rights of teachers as opposed to support-starved school principals looking for assistance in completing administrative tasks. There is also a good deal of within-group variability in how teacher leadership is portrayed; for example, for some teachers it is a path to career advancement while for others it is a vehicle to build professional community. It also varies depending on the reform vehicle to which it is attached; for example, as a dimension of school-based management versus an element of charter schools. Or as Miller, Moon, and Elko (2000) note, "teacher leadership is used widely among many different educational reform efforts" (p. 4). In a real sense, then, teacher leadership is like an evolving thread that appears in widely diverse locations and in a variety of shapes and colors in the school reform tapestry.

Definitions From the Literature

Clearly the whole issue of defining teacher leadership is problematic. (Wasley, 1991, p. 147)

Donaldson (2001) observes that as "we seek to understand how leadership can function to improve schools, we are exploring what leadership means" (p. 5). Certainly a reasonable place to begin is with the definition of the concept in the spotlight. Because of some of the issues explored in the preceding section (e.g., complexity, newness, context) and because "the subject of teacher leadership is cloaked in ambiguity" (Smylie, Conley, & Marks, 2002, p. 162), this is a less-than-straightforward task. Simply put, "variance makes it difficult to precisely define what is meant by the term 'teacher leaders'" (Kowalski, 1995, p. 251).

Teacher leaders are marked by an assortment of different names—"names that mean different things in different settings and refer to a broad array of actions" (Miller et al., 2000, p. 5). This variety is compounded by the fact that "when educators speak or write of teacher leadership they rarely define what they mean" (O'Hair & Reitzug, 1997, p. 67). "Confusion about definitions . . . of teacher leaders abound" (Katzenmeyer & Moller, 2001, pp. 4–5) and "the roles of teacher leaders are often ill-defined and misunderstood" (Johnson & Hynes, 1997, p. 107). The consequence is, of course, a significant measure of "ambiguity surrounding the term in the literature" (Crowther et al., 2002, p. 5), the use of the term "without a clear definition of what it means" (Childs-Bowen, Moller, & Scrivner, 2000, p. 28), and the near absence of "systematic conceptual definitions . . . of the variable in the [research] literature" (Smylie, 1996, p. 543). As Moller and Katzenmeyer (1996) remind us, the lack of anything approaching a "clear definition of teacher leadership also impedes its development" (p. 5) and results in "roles that remain ill defined and unclear to both researchers and teacher leaders" (Sherrill, 1999, p. 56; Fraser, 1991) themselves.

Acknowledging this reality, and the dynamics described above (e.g., complexity), it is still useful to uncover what existing efforts to define teacher leadership reveal, or fail to convey. We begin with a portrait of the broad array of "definitions of teacher leaders that abound in the literature" (LeBlanc & Shelton, 1997, p. 32)—13 to be exact—and then set about parsing out the critical elements found in that picture. We continue our quest to add conceptual depth to the construct of teacher leadership in Chapters 2 through 5 as well.

Teacher leaders, thus, are those teachers who influence the behavior of both students and adults in the school setting. (Brownlee, 1979, p. 120)

Teacher leaders were identified as those who reached out to others with encouragement, technical knowledge to solve classroom problems, and enthusiasm for learning new things. (Rosenholtz, 1989, p. 208)

Teacher leadership is defined as influencing and engaging colleagues toward improved practice. (Wasley, 1992, p. 21)

A teacher leader is a practicing teacher, chosen by fellow faculty members to lead them in ways determined by the context of individual school needs, who has formal preparation and scheduled time for a leadership role which, to preserve the teacher mission, calls for neither managerial nor supervisory duties. (Fay, 1992a, p. 8)

Teacher leadership is concerned with teachers helping teachers so that teachers can, in turn, better help students. Teacher leadership is helping teachers work together to establish and achieve the goals and objectives of the school. (Pellicer & Anderson, 1995, p. 22)

We characterize teacher leaders as individuals who are actively involved in promoting change, effectively communicate with multiple constituents, possess a global understanding of school and district organizations, and continue to grow professionally. (Harrison & Lembeck, 1996, p. 102)

Our definition of teacher leadership proposes that teachers are leaders when they are contributing to school reform or student learning (within or beyond the classroom), influencing others to improve their professional practice, or identifying with and contributing to a community of leaders. (Moller & Katzenmeyer, 1996, p. 5)

A transforming relationship between teachers, administrators, community, and concerned others who intend real educational reform grounded in shared consensus coupled with successful classroom application and research. (Suleiman & Moore, 1997, p. 6)

Teacher leadership is essentially an ethical stance that is based on views of both a better world and the power of teaching to shape meaning systems. It manifests in actions that involve the wider community and leads to the creation of new forms of understanding that will enhance the quality of life of the community in the long term. It reaches its potential in contexts where system and school structures are facilitative and supportive. (Crowther, 1997, p. 15)

Teacher leadership may be broadly defined as a professional commitment and a process which influences people to take joint actions toward changes and improved practices that enable achievement of shared educational goals and benefit the common good. (Forster, 1997, p. 88)

The concept of teacher leadership refers to a variety of roles for classroom teachers in staff development, management, and school improvement. (Clemson-Ingram, 1997, p. 95)

Teacher leadership includes: (a) modeling positive attitudes and enthusiasm; (b) devoting time to doing whatever it takes to make the school work better; (c) enhancing student learning through working with other teachers on improving pedagogy; and (d) being recognized, appreciated, respected, and/or valued for such efforts. (LeBlanc & Shelton, 1997, p. 33)

Teacher leadership generally refers to actions by teachers outside their own classrooms which involve an explicit or implicit responsibility to provide professional development to their colleagues, to influence their communities' or districts' policies, or to act as adjunct district staff to support changes in classroom practices among teachers. (Miller et al., 2000, p. 4)

Core Components

Although different terms are used and different aspects of teacher leaders are emphasized, these definitions highlight some core components of teacher leadership. (Yarger & Lee, 1994, p. 227)

Teacher leadership is about action that transforms teaching and learning in a school, that ties school and community together on behalf of learning, and that advances social sustainability and quality of life for a community. (Crowther et al., 2002, p. xvii)

Leadership has historically been defined across two axes, one representing a sense of vision about where an organization should be headed and a second capturing the relational work required to move organizational participants toward that end. In the assorted definitions provided above, these properties are qualified by data on enabling conditions and by information on attempts to distinguish a particular pattern of leadership (i.e., teacher leadership) from school leadership in general.

Turning to the *sense of vision,* we see in the above definitions a focus on three valued goals. First, there are indications that teacher leadership will promote "social sustainability and quality of life in the school community" (Crowther et al., 2002, p. xvii), that the endgame is the creation of a community of practice and new forms of understanding in that community. Next, we discern the goal of change, change which is the pathway to school reform and to improvements in classroom practice and enhanced "instructional performance" (Hart, 1995, p. 21). Finally, there are references to the more tangible outcomes of goal attainment and enhanced student learning.

What we do not see much in play here is the sense that the vision for the school is the product of the teacher leaders themselves. The end states are generally presented as givens, either professionally or organizationally. In contrast to the larger literature on leadership, the role of the teacher leader in defining that vision is muted (Heller & Firestone, 1994), either because of his or her place as one among many in the professional community of practice or because outcomes are organizationally predetermined.

The *relational component* of these definitions also provides interesting similarities to and differences from the larger corpus of scholarship on leadership. As in the more extensive body of work, influence forms the heart of the teacher leadership model (Corbett & Rossman, n.d.). However, unlike most, but not all, of the work on leadership, in "assuming new relationships with administrators and colleagues" (Hynes, Summers, & Socoski, 1992, p. 43) that power is exercised more indirectly and in more subtle ways. The strong (e.g., directing, telling) and even partially muted (e.g., facilitating, guiding) action verbs often associated with leadership give way to still softer conceptions of influence (e.g., reaching out, encouraging, collaborating) (Yarger & Lee, 1994).

Interspersed throughout the assortment of definitions provided above are references to *enabling conditions*, including elements that distinguish teacher leadership from administrative leadership. Whereas references to position, formal training, legal authority, and organizational expertise pepper writings on managerial leadership, descriptions of pedagogical knowledge and collegiality anchor the literature on teacher leadership (Darling-Hammond et al., 1995; Fay, 1992a, 1992b; Yarger & Lee, 1994). The definitions presented above also offer a variety of conditions that provide an enabling environment for teacher leadership to take root while setting it apart from prevailing views of administrative leadership. For example, the beliefs that a teacher leader must be someone who (1) is a practicing teacher, not someone who has left the classroom; (2) works and has influence outside his or her classroom; (3) does not engage in managerial and supervisory activities; (4) is chosen by teacher colleagues; and (5) wields considerable autonomy in undertaking his or her work can all be found in the definitional mosaic provided earlier. While these are not universally accepted premises, they do represent a concerted effort to delineate a distinct storyline for teacher leadership in the larger leadership narrative.

An Evolving Concept

To claim, as we have above, that the concept of teacher leadership outside the classroom is an emerging idea is not to gainsay the fact that teacher leadership as a general construct enjoys a long life (see Murphy & Beck, 1995; Smylie, 1995; Smylie & Denny, 1989); that is, in its broadest form it is hardly a "novel" (Livingston, 1992, p. 9; Hart, 1995) or a "new" (Suleiman & Moore, 1997, p. 2; Smylie & Brownlee-Conyers, 1992) idea. Indeed, as Gehrke (1991) discloses, "there have long been teacher leaders in schools" (p. 1). For example, teachers, as already observed, have always demonstrated considerable leadership in their individual classrooms (Crowther & Olsen, 1997). At the school level, they have also exercised informal leadership "of all kinds" (Strodl, 1992, p. 8; Fay 1992a; Hatfield, 1989). Finally, while "beyond the walls of the classroom teacher leadership roles have been limited in scope" (Livingston, 1992, p. 9), teachers have assumed "limited formal leadership roles in schools and school districts" (Smylie & Brownlee-Conyers, 1992, p. 150).

What is at the heart of this book, however, are analyses of efforts to enrich teacher leadership beyond these perspectives, to acknowledge its legitimacy outside the classroom and to deepen it as an organizational construct beyond informal and administratively determined and hierarchically anchored roles. When we talk about teacher leadership as a new idea, we do so in reference to this movement. Important elements of this expanded understanding include enhancing the importance of the leadership dimensions of teachers' work (Wasley, 1991); de-emphasizing "administrative prerogative" (Livingston, 1992, p. 9) in energizing teacher leadership (Suleiman & Moore, 1997); illuminating the educational dimensions, as opposed to the managerial aspects, of the work (Silva et al., 2000); highlighting "expanded visions of teacher leadership roles" (Smylie & Denny, 1989, p. 2); underscoring "substantially different working relationships among teachers and between teachers and administrators" (Smylie & Brownlee-Conyers, 1992, p. 151); featuring "the more global context of school change and improvement" (Stone, Horejs & Lomas, 1997, p. 60); and "plac[ing] teachers with administrators at the center of school and district decision making" (Smylie & Brownlee-Conyers, 1992, p. 151).

As we discuss more fully in later chapters, over the last 20 years we have witnessed the evolution of the idea of teacher leadership beyond the classroom through four overlapping phases, each of which features a relatively distinct footprint. The mid-1980s ushered in efforts to capture leadership for teachers by reshaping the structure of the school organization and the culture of the teaching profession, changing teaching from a single role to an assortment of differentiated assignments. Specifically, the period from the early to late 1980s saw the emergence of initiatives such as career ladders, differentiated teaching, mentor teaching plans, and performance-based compensation systems (Berry & Ginsberg, 1990; Yarger & Lee, 1994; Zimpher, 1988), interventions designed "to reconceptualize the nature of the teaching career" (Leithwood et al., 1997, p. 2). Not surprisingly, these early forays into teacher leadership were grafted onto the hierarchical organizational structure that had defined schooling for most of the 20th century and were grown from tenets of the centralized reform strategies in play at the time (Murphy, 1990a).

In the mid- to late 1980s, as empowerment ideology and decentralization strategies began to challenge the prevailing centralized perspectives on reform, a second strand of teacher leadership, this one featuring shared decision making and participatory governance, arrived on the educational scene (Murphy & Beck, 1995). This was supplemented by a third strain of teacher leadership, one in which new educationally anchored roles were created, "positions that capitalized on teacher instructional knowledge" (Silva et al., 2000, p. 780). The key point here is that these new opportunities moved teachers "away from management and toward pedagogical expertise" (p. 780).

Finally, with the development of community-grounded perspectives of schooling (e.g., schools as learning organizations), a frame for teacher leadership that highlighted not organizational roles or decision making responsibilities but the concept of a community of practice began to blossom. Leadership here was to be considered as a central element of the work of all teachers engaged in school improvement. Leadership was captured not in "hierarchical conceptions that slot[ted] individuals into different, limited functions that place[d] them in superordinate and subordinate relations to one another" (Darling-Hammond et al., 1995, p. 93), but in terms of "promoting the professionalization of all teachers" (Yarger & Lee, 1994, p. 227) and nurturing widespread collaboration (Silva et al., 2000).

CONCLUSION

Teachers who lead leave their mark on teaching. By their presence and their performance, they change how other teachers think about, plan for, and conduct their work with students. (Little, 1988, p. 84)

In this chapter, we provided an initial snapshot of the concept known as teacher leadership. We were particularly interested in laying the foundation for later analysis. In that regard, we described how emerging perspectives on teacher leadership represent a break with prevailing views of leadership built up around formal administrative roles. We also disclosed how these emerging understandings extend and deepen the types of leadership teachers have exerted in their classrooms and have enacted informally at the school level. We recounted how teacher leadership is both a catalyst for and an outcome of a shift away from a near-exclusive focus on hierarchical organizational systems and institutional views of schooling. We observed how teacher leadership draws energy from evolving perspectives on leadership as a function, a dynamic of community, and a product of pedagogical expertise.

We added to our foundation-building work by carefully parsing the concept of teacher leadership into prime elements. We described a three-tiered model of teacher leadership and explained that the focus in this book is primarily on activity at the school level. We noted that while the idea of teacher leadership enjoys a long history, attention to the domain of interest herein (i.e., leadership beyond the classroom) has only recently been afforded serious consideration. We divulged how the idea of teacher leadership has evolved over time and how it re-entered the school improvement narrative in the late 1980s as an element of sweeping school reform movements such as teacher professionalism and school-based management. We featured an assortment of commonly used definitions of teacher leadership and teased out core ingredients of those perspectives.

We close this chapter where we started. We begin by acknowledging that "both principal and teacher leadership have a significant influence on important features of the school" (Leithwood et al., 1997, p. 23). We then assert the need "to experiment with new organizational arrangements that offer new possibilities for improving the overall effectiveness of the teaching profession" (Whitaker, 1997, p. 15). Specifically, we honor the call "to look at teacher leadership carefully and critically" (Miller et al., 2000, p. 4), "to explore the importance of these previously under-recognized educational players" (Snell & Swanson, 2000, p. 2). To date, teacher leadership has not (1) "received much critical examination" (Brownlee, 1979, p. 120); (2) "been the subject of . . . deliberate attempts at analysis and development" (McCay, Flora, Hamilton, & Riley, 2001, p. 135); (3) been informed by work from a variety of "vantage points" (Smylie, 1995, p. 5); or

(4) been marked by much "systematic inquiry" (Leithwood et al., 1997, p. 21). As a result, "many unanswered questions linger" (Whitaker, 1997, p. 5) about teacher leadership. In the remainder of this book, we surface some of these key questions and provide information that leads us in the direction of more robust understanding and informed action.

Chapter Two

Forces Supporting Teacher Leadership

It is increasingly implausible that we could improve the performance of schools, attract and retain talented teachers, or make sensible demands upon administrators without promoting leadership in teaching by teachers. (Little, 1988, p. 78)

The model of top-down management with the principal at the "top" and the teachers at the "bottom" is outdated and ineffective. . . . This approach to management will become increasingly difficult to maintain. (Clemson-Ingram & Fessler, 1997, p. 96)

In this chapter, we expose the three major pillars buttressing the incipient teacher leadership movement. We begin with an analysis of the struggle to rebuild the organizational foundations of schooling, examining the dysfunctionalities of traditional hierarchical structures and investigating postindustrial organizational forms that privilege collective conceptions of leadership. We then highlight the changing nature of leadership in these adaptive organizations, capturing the general storyline as well as the implications for those in formal leadership positions. In the final section, we reveal how teacher leadership is nourished by reform initiatives that honor professionalism and by the ongoing struggle to promote high quality education for all youngsters.

RECONCEPTUALIZING SCHOOL ORGANIZATIONS

> Today's schools are organized in ways that support neither student nor teacher learning well. (National Commission on Teaching and America's Future [NCTAF], 1996, p. 15)

> Historically, schools have been hierarchical, bureaucratic, top-down organizations that have not encouraged teacher leadership. (Stone et al., 1997, p. 50)

While it is correct to maintain that calls for teacher leadership emanate directly from reformulations of school leadership, it is instructive to remember that "how we conceptualize organizational leadership is necessarily rooted in how we conceptualize organizations" (Ogawa & Bossert, 1995, p. 226). The two central points here are (1) that there has been a deluge of criticism about the ability of the traditional organizational structure to promote quality education for all youngsters and (2) that some insights about organizational forms that may be more productive—and more conducive to shared leadership—are taking shape. We explore each of these points in some detail below.

Critique of Traditional Organizational Forms

> The limits of the bureaucratic regulatory management model have been reached. (Wise, 1989, p. 302)

For some time now, "critics have argued that the reforms of the Progressive Era produced bureaucratic arteriosclerosis—and the low productivity of a declining industry" (Tyack, 1993, p. 3). There is an expanding feeling that the existing structure of administration, which has "changed only a little since the middle of the nineteenth century" (The Holmes Group, 1986, p. 6; NCTAF, 1996) and which discourages teacher leadership (Coyle, 1997) by "firmly fixing teachers on the bottom rung of [the] bureaucratic ladder" (Kelley, 1994, p. 301), is "obsolete and unsustainable" (Rungeling & Glover, 1991, p. 415). In particular, it is held that the management tools of the bureaucratic paradigm "misdirect the educational outcomes that schools seek to attain" (Wise, 1989, p. 301), that the "bureaucratic structure is failing in a manner so critical that adaptations will not forestall its collapse" (Clark & Meloy, 1989, p. 293). Behind this basic critique rests a central proposition: that "bureaucracies are set up to serve the adults that run them and in the end, the kids get lost in the process" (Daly, cited in Olson, 1992, p. 10). It is increasingly being concluded that the existing bureaucratic system of administration is "ineffective and counter productive" (Martin & Crossland, 2000, p. 4), that it has "led to teacher isolation, alienation, and disenchantment" (Pellicer & Anderson, 1995, p. 10; Elmore, Peterson, & McCarthey, 1996; Lynch & Strodl, 1991), and that it is "incapable of addressing the technical and structural shortcomings of the public educational system" (Lawton, 1991, p. 4).

More finely grained criticism of the bureaucratic infrastructure of schooling comes from a variety of quarters. There are those who contend that schools are so paralyzed by the "bureaucratic arteriosclerosis" noted above by Tyack (1993, p. 3) that "professional judgment" (Hill & Bonan, 1991, p. 65), "innovation" (Lindelow, 1981, p. 98), "morale" (David, 1989, p. 45), "creative capacity" (Snauwaert, 1993, p. 5), flexibility (Elmore et al., 1996), "autonomy" (Shakeshaft, 1999, p. 108), and responsibility, and "opportunities for continuing growth" (Howey, 1988, p. 30) have all been paralyzed (Bolin, 1989; Conley, 1989; Frymier, 1987; Sizer, 1984). Indeed, "many teachers . . . are forced to repress their leadership needs" (Fessler & Ungaretti, 1994, p. 211). Other reformers maintain "that school bureaucracies as currently constituted could [never] manage to provide high-quality education" (Elmore, 1993, p. 37) and that, even worse, "bureaucratic management practices have been causing unacceptable distortions in educational process" (Wise, 1989, p. 301), that they are damaging schooling by "interfer[ing] with best teaching" (Johnson, 1989, p. 105) and "getting in the way of children's learning" (Sizer, 1984, p. 206; Cuban, 1989; McNeil, 1988; Wise, 1978). These scholars view bureaucracy as a governance-management system that deflects attention from the core tasks of learning and teaching (Elmore, 1990b) and that inhibits the successful conduct of the teaching-learning act (Clark, 1987, p. 9).

Many analysts believe that bureaucracy is counterproductive to the needs and interests of educators within the school—"it is impractical, and it does not fit the psychological and personal needs of the workforce" (Clark & Meloy, 1989, p. 293); it "undermine[s] the authority of teachers" (Sackney & Dibski, 1992, p. 2); and it is "incompatible with the professional organization" (p. 4). They maintain that "the bureaucratic routinization of teaching and learning that has grown out of administrative attempts to control schools" (Fay, 1992b, p. 58) has neutered teachers (Frymier, 1987), undermined "the drawing power and holding power of strong collegial ties" (Little, 1987, p. 502), and "discourage[d] teachers from taking on additional responsibilities" (Creighton, 1997, p. 3). These reviewers contend that "it has become increasingly clear that if we want to improve schools for student learning, we must also improve schools for the adults who work in them" (Smylie & Hart, 1999, p. 421; Clark & Meloy, 1989).

Still other critics assert that bureaucratic management is inconsistent with the sacred values and purposes of education; they question "fundamental ideological issues pertaining to bureaucracy's meaning in a democratic society" (Campbell, Fleming, Newell, & Bennion, 1987, p. 73) and find that "it is inconsistent to endorse democracy in society but to be skeptical of shared governance in our schools" (Glickman, 1990, p. 74; see also Fusarelli & Scribner, 1993). They maintain that "if the primary purpose of public schools is to support democracy, then schools should be structured around a democratic model" (Katzenmeyer & Moller, 2001, p. 26).

As might be expected, given this tremendous attack on the basic organizational infrastructure of schooling, stakeholders at all levels are arguing that "ambitious, if not radical, reforms are required to rectify this situation" (Elmore, 1993, p. 34), and that "the excessively centralized, bureaucratic control of schools must end" (Carnegie Forum, cited in Hanson, 1991, pp. 2–3) and the "outmoded bureaucratic educational structure" (Pellicer & Anderson, 1995, p. 7) must be replaced. There is widespread agreement with the "idea that the 'command and control' approach to educational reform has taken us about as far as it can" (Frost & Durrant, 2003a, p. 173). Consequently, a variety of "groups are calling for major changes in the ways schools go about their work and the ways teachers are involved in their decision-making structure" (Lieberman, Saxl, & Miles, 1988, p. 148).

New Forms of Organization

One approach . . . is to rethink elements of that structure in response to evidence that the institution itself impedes the performance of those working within it. (Sykes & Elmore, 1989, p. 83)

It has long been part of the accepted wisdom in most sectors of the economy and the human services, certainly since the information age became a reality, that vertical hierarchy in organizations is giving way to horizontal informal sharing networks and collective decision-making. (Institute for Educational Leadership, 2001, p. 3)

New perspectives of schooling include methods of organizing and managing schools that are generally consistent with the "quiet revolution [in] organizational and administrative theory in Western societies" (Foster, 1988, p. 71). In the still-forming image of schools for the 21st century, the hierarchical bureaucratic organizational structures that have defined schooling since the onslaught of scientific management (Forster, 1997) give way to systems that are more focused on capacity building (Crowther et al., 2002) and that are more organic (Weick & McDaniel, 1989), more decentralized (Guthrie, 1986; Harvey & Crandall, 1988; Watkins & Lusi, 1989), and more professionally controlled (David, 1989; Houston, 1989; Weick & McDaniel, 1989), systems that "suggest a new paradigm for school organization and management" (Mulkeen, 1990, p. 105; Fay, 1992a). The basic shift is from a *"power over* approach . . . to a *power to* approach" (Sergiovanni, 1991b, p. 57). This model of change spotlights values of community and justice (Murphy, 2002).

In these redesigned, postindustrial school organizations, to which Louis and Miles (1990) have given the label "adaptive model" (p. 26), there are "very basic changes in roles, relationships, and responsibilities" (Seeley, 1988, p. 35): traditional patterns of relationships are altered (Conley, 1989; Rallis, 1990);

authority flows are less hierarchical (Clark & Meloy, 1989), for example, traditional distinctions between administrators and teachers begin to blur (Giroux, 1988; Petrie, 1990); role definitions are both more general and more flexible (Corcoran, 1989)—specialization is no longer viewed as a strength (Beare, 1989; Houston, 1989); because "organizational structures [will] promote authority based on ability" (Sergiovanni, 1991b, p. 62), leadership is dispersed and is connected to competence for needed tasks rather than to formal position (American Association of Colleges for Teacher Education [AACTE], 1988; Sykes & Elmore, 1989); and independence and isolation are replaced by cooperative work (Beare, 1989; Maccoby, 1989). Furthermore, the traditional structural orientation of schools is overshadowed by a focus on the human element (Crow, Hausman, & Scribner, 2002; Louis & Miles, 1990; Sergiovanni, 1991b). The operant goal is no longer maintenance of the organizational infrastructure but rather the development of human resources (Clark & Meloy, 1989; Mojkowski & Fleming, 1988; Schlechty, 1990): "developing teachers [trumps] developing efficient and effective structure" (Silva et al., 2000, p. 800). Building learning climates and promoting organizational adaptivity replaces the more traditional emphasis on uncovering and applying the one best model of performance (Clark & Meloy, 1989; McCarthy & Peterson, 1989). A premium is placed on organizational flexibility (Banathy, 1988) and purpose and values (Sergiovanni, 1990, 1992).

A new model for school management "will create a system driven by the educational needs of students and of society rather than by the imperatives of management accountability systems" (Wise, 1989, p. 310). It will grant that "shared power strengthens the organization" (Livingston, 1992, p. 11). Institutional perspectives no longer dominate the organizational landscape. Rather, schools are reconceptualized as communities (Barth, 2001; Sergiovanni, 1994), "professional workplaces" (Hart, 1995, p. 9), learning organizations (Conley, 1997), and "cooperative systems" (Hart, 1995, p. 10). Notions of schools as "democratic communities" (Katzenmeyer & Moller, 2001, p. 27) and "professional community-oriented images that challenge traditional bureaucratic conceptions of schools as organizations" (Smylie & Hart, 1999, p. 421) move to center stage. Ideas such as "community of leadership" (Barth, 1988b, p. 129), the "ethic of collaboration"

(Lieberman & Miller, 1999, p. 64), and the principle of care (Beck, 1994) are woven into the fabric of the organization. "The metaphor of the school as community" (Little & McLaughlin, 1993a, p. 189) is brightly illuminated (Beck & Foster, 1999; Sergiovanni, 1994).

The metaphors being developed for this new design for schools—for example, from principal as manager to principal as facilitator, from teacher as worker to teacher as leader—nicely portray these fundamental revisions in our understanding of social relationships and in our views of organizations and conceptions of management (Beck & Murphy, 1993). They reveal a reorientation in transformed schools from bureaucratic to moral authority and from bureaucratic control to professional empowerment, or control through "professional socialization, purposing and shared values, and collegiality and natural interdependence" (Sergiovanni, 1991b, p. 60). They also reveal an orientation toward accountability through professionalization, "rather than through micromanaging what the professional does" (Petrie, 1990, p. 24).

Under these new conceptions of school organizations, the need to recast leadership is palpable.

REDEFINING SCHOOL LEADERSHIP

These perspectives call for a broader conception of school leadership, one that shifts from a single person, role-oriented view to a view of leadership as an organizational property shared among administrators, teachers, and perhaps others. (Smylie & Hart, 1999, p. 428)

Multidirectional, interactive, and adjustive approaches to leadership provide a more authentic map for planning and development in education. (Hart, 1995, p. 17)

Teacher leadership draws considerable energy from the fact that in redesigned organizations "the idea of leadership is rapidly changing" (Bishop, Tinley, & Berman, 1997, p. 77). On the one side of the equation, there is a growing recognition that "if leadership is to be able to contribute to educational reform . . . it will be necessary to conceive of school leadership as something other than top-down hierarchy" (Angus, 1988, p. 34). On the other side, within this reforged understanding of leadership, the portrait of those in traditional leadership positions (i.e., principals and superintendents) is being repainted (Murphy, 1994b, 2002; Murphy & Datnow, 2003; Murphy & Hallinger, 1992; Murphy & Louis, 1994, 1999; Murphy & Shipman, 1999). The role is becoming "more consultative, more open and more democratic" (Early, Baker, & Weindling, 1990, p. 9). There is considerable evidence that power is being recast and influence is being passed on to teachers (Bredeson, 1989; Chapman, 1990). In the balance of this section, we explore these two dimensions of the reformulated conception of school leadership—the recasting of leadership writ large and the reforming of the role of principals and superintendents in the service of the new understanding of leadership.

Recasting Leadership

Leadership is now being dramatically reframed. (Caine & Caine, 2000, p. 7)

Creating more effective schools requires a significant change in patterns of leadership. (Louis & Miles, 1990, p. 19)

Two themes ribbon the current leadership literature in education. One is "that traditional models of leadership imported from business and industry fall short of the type of leadership required in schools and school districts" (Killion, 1996, p. 64; Sergiovanni, 1990). A second is that "the theoretical orientations that have grounded research on leadership in school organizations" (Pounder, Ogawa, & Adams, 1995, p. 565) leave a good deal to be desired. In short, "the models of school leadership that dominate worldwide are weary, worn, and inadequate" (Crowther et al., 2002, p. xvi). Specifically, academics and practitioners alike increasingly acknowledge that role-based leadership strategies have "dangerously polarized our assumptions about who is responsible for and capable of providing leadership for schools" (Donaldson, 2001, p. 39) and "have been essentially unable to meet the complex challenges associated with school change" (Copland, 2003, pp. 31–32).

Concomitantly, there is a growing belief that "the times are ripe for widening the lens in search of a model of school leadership that is both more productive for schools and more sustainable for those who aspire to lead" (Donaldson, 2001, p. 5), that "rethinking leadership in schools is a crucial first step in moving toward shared, ongoing, and sustainable school improvement" (Copland, 2003, p. 4). There is an acknowledgment that "increasing professionalism, redistributing authority, and increasing collegial interaction redefine school leadership" (Keedy, 1999, p. 787). There is a recognition that emerging conceptions of leadership "stress the need to enable, entrust, and empower personnel" (Bishop et al., 1997, p. 77) and that "successful organizations depend on multiple sources of leadership" (Childs-Bowen et al., 2000, p. 28; Marks & Printy, 2003). There is an understanding that teachers' "full participation in the work of leadership is necessary for high leadership capacity" (Lambert, 2003, p. 32) and to sustain the leadership of those in formal roles (Donaldson, 2001). In short, "current efforts to redefine leadership are rooted in notions of distribution" (Copland, 2003, p. 5; see especially Elmore, 2000; Sergiovanni, 1984; Spillane, Diamond, & Jita, 2000; Spillane et al., n.d.), in the recognition that "leadership permeates organizations rather than residing in particular people or formal positions of authority" (Smylie et al., 2002, p. 167; Ogawa & Bossert, 1995; Rallis, 1990).

The concept of leadership that buoys teacher leadership is one that is nonhierarchical in nature, that is neither predominantly position- or authority-based (Ogawa & Bossert, 1995; Sykes & Elmore, 1989)—one in which "leadership is not . . . confused with official position or with exercise of authority" (Foster, 1986, p. 177). Collectively, it bestows less emphasis "upon formal role in the system" (Copland, 2003, p. 2) and less stress on the notion of "legitimate power" (Crowther et al., 2002, p. 23). The new understanding of leadership in play here is "based on expertise" (Keedy, 1999, p. 787) and moral suasion (Fullan, 2004; Greenfield, 1988). Leadership "escapes the role trap" (Pounder et al., 1995, p. 566); it is "authoritative rather than authoritarian" (Forster, 1997, p. 87).

Leadership is defined, at least in part, as an "organizational characteristic" (Hart, 1995, p. 17), "quality" (Ogawa & Bossert, 1995, p. 225), "phenomenon" (Smylie, 1995, p. 6), or "property"

(Smylie & Hart, 1999, p. 435). "The capacity to lead is not principal-centric . . . but rather embedded in various organizational contexts" (Copland, 2003, p. 6), contexts that formal leaders help create (Firestone, 1996; Rallis, 1990). Leadership is no longer seen as a "zero-sum game" (Pounder et al., 1995, p. 566). Leadership in schools "is not a function of individuals . . . rather it has to do with the mixture of organizational culture and the density of leadership competence among and within many actors" (Copland, 2003, p. 4). "This perspective signals a shift of leadership as the prerogative of an individual to leadership as an organizational property" (Smiley & Hart, 1999, p. 435); "leaders can come from many places and assume many forms" (Crowther et al., 2002, p. 26).

Leadership as an organizational property assumes different forms as the viewing prism is turned. In lieu of a focus on roles and positions, some analysts highlight "responsibilit[ies]" (Silva et al., 2000, p. 782), tasks, and "functions that must be performed if the organization is to . . . perform effectively" (Firestone, 1996, p. 396; Spillane et al., n.d.). Other reviewers spotlight a set of "shared qualities" (Copland, 2003, p. 8). At the heart of all these perspectives is the understanding that "leadership is more collective in nature than individual" (Elmore, 2003, p. 204); "that is, leadership inheres not in the individual characteristics and traits of people in positions of authority, but in the way authority and responsibility are focused, defined, and distributed in organizations" (p. 204). Leadership is cast as a "broad concept, separated from person, role, and a discrete set of individual behaviors" (Copland, 2003, p. 5), especially from those at the top of the organization (Spillane et al., n.d.). It is viewed "as dispers[ed] . . . across education" (Silva et al., 2000, p. 782): "school leadership practice is constituted in the dynamic interaction of multiple leaders . . . and their situation around particular leadership tasks" (Spillane et al., n.d., p. 6).

This recast conceptualization of leadership is based on research that "suggest[s] that people in many different roles can lead and thereby affect the performance of their schools" (Pounder et al., 1995, p. 586), "that shared power strengthens the school as an organization" (Stone et al., 1997, p. 50, Heifetz & Laurie, 1997), and that "the accomplishments of a proficient and well-organized group are widely considered to be greater than the accomplishments of isolated individuals" (Little, 1987, p. 495; Retallick & Fink, 2002; Uline & Berkowitz, 2000). Leadership as a shared construct (Chenoweth & Everhart, 2002; Marks & Printy, 2003; Smylie & Hart, 1999) replaces overreliance on hierarchy and bureaucracy (Harrison & Lembeck, 1996) and acknowledges that multiple people "have the opportunity to contribute in meaningful ways" (Wasley, 1991, p. 57):

> The logic of distribution indicates that school leadership overall is ultimately enhanced by the different knowledge and skills brought by a variety of people and by the commitments that are developed among those who perform leadership tasks together. (Smylie et al., 2002, p.177)

The DNA of shared or distributed leadership—or leadership as an organizational quality—is interactive in design and relational in form (Smylie & Hart, 1999). In the "postheroic era of leadership" (Hart, 1995, p. 10; Fullan, 2004), "collective relationship is replacing the person as the kernel of leadership" (Donaldson, 2001, p. 42), and the "reality of leadership as an interactive rather than a unidirectional process" (Hart, 1995, p. 25) is affirmed: "leadership is embedded not in particular roles but in the relationships that exist among the incumbents of roles" (Ogawa & Bossert, 1995, p. 235). Leadership "depends more on connections with rather than authority over" (Uline & Berkowitz, 2000, p. 437). The "idea of leadership as relatedness" (Crowther et al., 2002, p. 27) or the tenet that "leadership is a form of relationship among people" (Donaldson, 2001, p. 40), in turn, shifts the focus "away from the individual and toward the interaction patterns among individuals" (Forster, 1997, p. 85). The spotlight is on "interpersonal networks" (Donaldson, 2001, p. 7). The focus is on interactions—"the interact, not the act, becomes the basic building block of organizational leadership" (Ogawa & Bossert, 1995, p. 236).

Reforming Formal Leadership Positions

> The traditional roles of principals . . . are changing and will continue to be reshaped, redefined and restructured. (Bredeson, 1991, p. 1)

What has been the traditional role of the principal appears to be changing. (Christensen, 1992, p. 6)

An obvious corollary from the above analysis is that deeper and more nuanced understandings of leadership require a transformation in our conception of school administration, that leaders in formal positions will need to look and act differently (Brunner, Grogan, & Björk, 2002; Crow et al., 2002). Because "changing our metaphors is an important prerequisite for developing a new theory of management and a new leadership practice" (Sergiovanni, 1991b, p. 68), we explore this change under the three metaphors of administrator as servant leader, organizational architect, and moral educator (Murphy, 1992, 2002).

Administrator as Servant Leader

If there is an all-encompassing challenge for educators in formal leadership positions, it is to lead the transition from the bureaucratic model of schooling, with its emphasis on minimal levels of education for many, to a post-industrial adaptive model, with the goal of educating all youngsters well. At the same time, "school leaders will have to adjust their own definition of what it means to be a school leader" (Hallinger, 1990, p. 76).

The leadership challenge for administrators is quite complex (Goldring & Greenfield, 2002; Louis & Murphy, 1994). Not only must they accept the mantle of leadership—changing from implementers to initiators, from a focus on process to a concern for outcomes, from risk avoiders and conflict managers to risk takers—but they must also adopt leadership strategies and styles that are in harmony with the central tenets of the heterarchical school organizations we described above. They must learn to lead not from the apex of the organizational pyramid but from the nexus of a web of interpersonal relationships (Chapman & Boyd, 1986)—with people rather than through them (Beck, 1994). Their base of influence must be professional expertise and moral imperative rather than line authority (Fullan, 2004). They must learn to lead by empowering rather than by controlling others (Heifetz & Laurie, 1997), or as Barth (1988b) puts it, "perhaps the most important item in the list of effective principals is the power to relinquish [decision-making authority] so that the latent, creative powers of teachers may be released" (p. 138). Leadership becomes "a support function for teaching rather than a mechanism for the control of teaching" (Bolin, 1989, p. 88). Servant leaders will understand that the "world can and will go on without them. Leaders don't create . . . transformations, but rather they know how to place the props carefully and wisely on the educational stage so as to be so inviting that individuals are enticed to transform themselves" (Collins, 1990, p. 34).

Servant leadership will differ from more traditional views of leadership in a number of other ways as well. "Such concepts as purposing, working to build a shared covenant" (Sergiovanni, 1989, p, 33), and establishing meaning—rather than directing, controlling, and supervising—are at the core of this type of leadership: "empowering leadership is based on dialogue and cooperative, democratic leadership principles" (Bolin, 1989, p. 86). Enabling leadership also has a softer, less heroic hue (J. T. Murphy, 1989, 1991). It is more ethereal and less direct: "symbolic and cultural leadership are key leadership forces" (Sergiovanni, 1989, p. 33). There is as much heart as head in this style of leading (Moorman, 1990; Roberts, 1990). It is grounded more upon teaching than upon informing (Heifetz & Laurie, 1997; Lam, 1990), more upon learning than upon knowing (Barth, 1988b; Deck, 1990), and more upon modeling and clarifying values and beliefs than upon telling people what to do (Bredeson, 1989; National Association of Elementary School Principals [NAESP], 1990; Petrie, 1990). Its goals include "ministering" (Sergiovanni, 1991b, p. 335) to the needs of organizational members rather than gaining authority over them, and creating "new structures that enable the emergence of leadership on a broad basis" (Sykes & Elmore, 1989, p. 79). It is more reflective and self-critical than bureaucratic management (Bates, 1984; Foster, 1984; Louis & Murphy, 1994).

Administrator as Organizational Architect

As we have documented throughout this book, there is considerable agreement that existing organizational structures and arrangements contribute to the problems that currently confront schools, that these conditions either support or cause the educational negligence that often characterizes the schooling enterprise.

What is clear from this analysis is that if schooling is to be reformed and new patterns of leadership are to take root, then the organizational and governance structures of the current system will need to be systemically reconfigured. Leaders will face the great challenge of helping define and breathe life into these new forms of governance, organization, and leadership. The work will be neither easy nor comfortable. Furthermore, because "the prospect is for a continuous prospect of reconstruction" (Sirotnik, 1989, p. 104), they will need to "build with canvas" (Sergiovanni, 1989, p. 34).

In becoming organizational architects, those in formal leadership positions must replace a traditional focus on stability with a focus on change (Goldring & Rallis, 1993; Hallinger, 2003; Louis & Miles, 1990). They will need to function less as classical managers and more as change agents (Kanter, 1983; Kotter, 1996). Tomorrow's leaders will need to disavow tenets of organizing consistent with bureaucracies (controlling, directing, supervising, evaluating, etc.) and embrace those principles associated with heterarchies (cooperation, empowerment, community, participation, etc.) (Brunner et al., 2002; Rinehart, Short, Short, & Eckley, 1998; Smylie et al., 2002).

The specific challenge, then, is to use these new principles of organization in service of the creation of adaptive and organic forms for schooling (Heifetz & Laurie, 1997). These new structures need to promote the development of a professional workplace (Firestone, 1996).

> Our analysis suggests that people who create organizational designs for schools should construct forms that aid the articulation and development of professional values, since these values are sources of guidance when people process nonroutine information. Our review also suggests that organic organizational forms are better designs both for developing values and for clarifying vague causal structures than are mechanistic forms. Since organic forms also encourage the development of substitutes for leadership, they encourage professional development as well as utilize current skills and attitudes. (Weick & McDaniel, 1989, p. 350)

Even more important, construction of new forms must advance from blueprints based on our best knowledge of student learning (Sykes & Elmore, 1989). We now know that "the organization of schooling appears to proceed as if we had no relevant knowledge regarding the development of children and youth" (Goodlad, 1984, p. 323). Thus the "main challenge facing educational leaders is . . . to reconstruct conceptions of authority, status, and school structure to make them instrumental to our most powerful conceptions of teaching and learning" (Elmore, 1990b, p. 63).

Administrator as Moral Educator

As we have documented in a variety of venues (e.g., Murphy, 1992, 1999c, in press), both the educational and value dimensions of leadership have atrophied since the formative era of school administration when superintendents were thought of as philosopher-educators. Throughout most of this century, the field has gravitated toward conceptions of leadership based on scientific images of business management and social science research. There is an expanding acknowledgment of "the pathology of such an approach to educational administration" (Bates, 1984, p. 264) and a growing belief that to prepare administrators to lead based on the tenets of post-hierarchical organizations, the pendulum must swing back (Greenfield, 1995).

The metaphor of the administrator as moral educator takes on many forms. At its root are two fundamental beliefs: that "the deep significance of the task of the school administrator is to be found in the pedagogic ground of its vocation" (Evans, 1991, p. 17), and that "the new science of administration will be a science with values and of values" (T. Greenfield, 1988, p. 155). Moral leadership acknowledges that "values and value judgments are the central elements in the selection, extension, and day-to-day realization of educational purpose" (Harlow, 1962, p. 67) and that "deeply educative and pedagogic interest in the lives of children and young people" (Evans, 1991, p. 17) is critical to administering schools. Thus at the most basic level, there is an emerging consensus that "educational administration must find its mission and purpose in the purpose of schooling generally" (Foster, 1988, p. 69) and that with a postindustrial "reformation of the purpose of education a reconceptualization of school administration [is] in order" (Parker, 1986, p. 59).

As moral educators, administrators in formal positions of influence will need to become much more heavily invested in "purpose-defining" (Harlow, 1962, p. 61) activities and in "reflective analysis and . . . active intervention" (Bates, 1984, p. 268) than simply in managing existing arrangements. This means that "persons wishing to impact society as school leaders must be motivated by a set of deep personal values and beliefs" (Spaedy, 1990, p. 157), by a "guiding set of academic and social values that can provide a rudder" (Wimpelberg, 1990, p. 177); "they must also have a view of the future that is significantly different from how schools have been" (Spaedy, 1990, p. 157). In short, they must have a "critical spirit" (Foster, 1989, p. 17) and visionary powers (Culbertson, 1988) and "bring to their enterprise a certain passion that affects others deeply" (Sergiovanni, 1991b, p. 334). They must view their task more as a mission than a job (Fullan, 2004), "as a meaningful calling of the highest order" (Roberts, 1990, p. 134); "they must develop strong commitments to important things and model them persuasively" (Moorman, 1990, p. 101); "the task of the leader is to create a moral order that bonds both leader and followers to a set of shared values and beliefs" (Sergiovanni, 1989, p. 34). Therefore, moral leadership means that administrators must use their personal platforms to "engage participants in the organization and the community in reinterpreting and placing new priorities on guiding values for education" (Moorman, 1990, p. 98) and in reconstructing "structures so that they celebrate the intended educational purposes of the school community" (Bates, 1984, p. 268).

The pedagogic dimensions of moral leadership are also becoming more clearly defined. Administrators must provide "students with a more complex and demanding educational experience than ever before" (Shakeshaft, 1990, p. 148). At the same time, they must reach a large portion of the students who have not experienced success even under less demanding standards and expectations. To accomplish this, formal school leaders in a postindustrial society will need to be much more committed to education and invested in children than they have been previously (Murphy, 2002). Because the challenge for leaders will be "to refocus the structure [of schooling] on some new conception of teaching and learning" (Elmore, 1990b, p. 63), they will need to be more broadly educated in general (Culbertson, 1988) and much more knowledgeable about the core technology of education in particular

(Brunner et al., 2002; Kochan, Bredeson, & Riehl, 2002). "Instructional and curricular leadership must be at the forefront of leadership skills" (Hallinger, 1990, p. 77) and administrators must "maintain a focus on teaching and learning in the school" (p. 76). In a rather dramatic shift from earlier times, school and district administrators will be asked to exercise intellectual leadership not as head teachers, but as head learners (Barth, 1986, 1988a).

The belief that the activities of administrators are deeply intertwined with critical and ethical issues is central to the metaphor of administration as moral educational leadership (Beck & Murphy, 1994; Beck, Murphy, & Associates, 1996; Riehl, 2000; Starratt, 1991). In tangible terms, it suggests changing schooling to be responsive to the needs of historically disenfranchised and undereducated pupils rather than attempting to mold children to fit currently dysfunctional organizational forms (Greenfield, 1990); it calls for us to examine current arrangements from a critical viewpoint (Larson & Murtadha, 2002).

The centrality of values for administrators is clearly evident in the call for leadership of the school community (Beck & Foster, 1999; Furman & Starratt, 2002). In their role as transformative leaders (Hallinger, 2003; Leithwood, 1992; Leithwood, Jantzi, & Dart, 1991; Leithwood, Jantzi, Silins, & Dart, 1992; Leithwood, Jantzi, & Fernandez, 1994; Marks & Printy, 2003), school heads are being asked to nurture the development of learning, professional, and caring communities based on the values of "reflective inquiry and democratic participation" (Foster, 1988, p. 71; Bolin, 1989; Kochan et al., 2002). In developing "communities of learning" (Zeichner & Tabachnich, 1991, p. 9), formal leaders promote an atmosphere of inquiry (Copland, 2003). They "must be curious and inquiring about schooling practices and effective learning conditions, and they must instigate curiosity and inquiry among others" (Roberts, 1990, p. 135). These "leaders will need to know how to find, interpret, and use important information to weave plausible scenarios of future conditions that will challenge educators" (Achilles, Brubaker, & Snyder, 1990, p. 16). They "must develop the capacity to reflect on their practice" (Deck, 1990, p. 50) and promote self-inquiry among other members of the school community. Particular attention must be given to examining organizational values that provide meaning to community activity (Driscoll, 1990; Sergiovanni, 1991b). Our earlier comments about the administrator as head learner are relevant here as well.

In developing democratic, professional communities, leaders must operate from moral authority based on ability (Angus, 1988), commitment to the values of the school (Sergiovanni, 1991b) and "to serving the best interests of the children in their schools" (Greenfield, 1990, p. 74), and "courageous tenacity" (Sanford, 1990, p. 145) or "the courage to persist in what is right" (Moorman, 1990, p. 101). In working with others, they must widen the circle of participation in schools (Blackman, 1990; Collins, 1990), focus on collaboration and shared decision making (Furman & Starratt, 2002), enhance "the feelings of self-efficacy among . . . organizational members so that they can work to develop new organizational forms and functions based on the emerging needs of our culture and society" (Deck, 1990, p. 49), and encourage "others to be leaders in their own right" (Sergiovanni, 1991b, p. 335); "this expanded vision of leadership is accessible and cooperative" (Lam, 1990, p. 86).

Finally, in facilitating the development of a caring community (Beck, 1994), "school leaders need to demonstrate the ethic of care to all members of the school community" (Astuto, 1990, p. 4). They can bring this about by (1) attending to the "human factor" (Frank, 1990, p. 69) or "human infrastructure" (Cunningham, 1990, p. 13) directly—by "concentrat[ing] on people first" (Sergiovanni, 1991b, p. 52); (2) "valuing each of them as ends [and by being] alert to their unique qualities and needs" (Moorman, 1990, p. 101); (3) "ministering" to their needs "by furnishing help and being of service" (Sergiovanni, 1991b, p. 35); and (4) "developing people as human resources" (Vazquez, 1990, p. 174)—"by building capabilities of people . . . and by encouraging them to develop the ways and means for using their capabilities" (Sergiovanni, 1989, p. 39; Beck & Foster, 1999).

THE CHANGING CALCULUS OF SCHOOL IMPROVEMENT

> Teacher leadership has become a defining characteristic of recent efforts to professionalize teaching and reform schools. (Smylie, 1995, p. 3)

> Teacher leadership is now a key element in improving the teaching profession and school reform. (Stone et al., 1997, p. 49)

Consistent with our earlier analysis, we also find that teacher leadership has drawn strength from efforts to recalibrate school improvement in the United States, efforts that are shifting the calculus of change from a nearly exclusive reliance on centralized, government-directed measures to initiatives that legitimize decentralization and professionalism. At the outset of the reform movement beginning around 1980, attempts at change featured centralized controls (Murphy, 1990a; Murphy & Adams, 1998), "a tightening of the organization and an increased supervision and evaluation of both teachers and students" (Sedlak, Wheeler, Pullin, & Cusick 1986, p. 175). The attack on the supposed problems with schooling assumed that the conditions of schooling contributing to poor student outcome measures were attributable to the poor quality of the workers and to the inadequacy of their tools, and that they were subject to revision through mandated, top-down initiatives—especially those from the state. Using the bureaucratic model to institute improvement proposals led, in turn, to the emphasis in early reform efforts on policy mechanisms such as prescriptions, tightly specified resource allocations, and performance measurements that focused on repairing components of the system and raising the quality of the workforce by telling employees how to work. The notion of teacher leadership was conspicuous by its absence from this wave of educational reform. Or, as Maeroff (1988) asserts, "the teacher role [was] ignored in the recommendations for improving schools" (p. 1).

No sooner had the ink dried on these early reform measures than they came under attack. A wide variety of scholars and practitioners found the entire fabric of the wave reform agenda to be wanting (see, for example, Boyd, 1987; Chubb, 1988; Cuban, 1984; Sedlak et al., 1986; Sizer, 1984). Finding the earlier suggestions inadequate at best and wrongheaded at worst, reformers clamored for fundamental revisions in the ways analysts approached school improvement. The muted voice of teachers (Creighton, 1997)—"too long silent and isolated in classrooms" (Wasley, 1991, p. 5)—and the overreliance on those in formal leadership roles to carry the reform freight (Chenoweth & Everhart, 2002; Pellicer & Anderson, 1995) were seen as especially problematic (Smylie et al., 2002). There was an expanding recognition that these elements of the early reforms "undermined teacher professionalism" (Frost & Durrant, 2003a, p. 175) and "inhibit[ed] sustained school reform" (Crowther et al., 2002,

p. 29). Concerns were increasingly voiced that these centralized reforms not only lacked the energy to power improvement but may have actually been an obstacle in the path toward enhanced student performance.

New ways to formulate school improvement began to surface, new forms that grew from a different philosophical seedbed than the one that nourished the early round of change efforts. Teachers were now "perceived as part of the solution to school revitalization" (Keedy, 1999, p. 785; Snell & Swanson, 2000). Reformers began to assert that educational improvement was (and is) contingent on empowering teachers to work more effectively with students (Carnegie Forum on Education and the Economy, 1986; The Holmes Group, 1986; Pellicer & Anderson, 1995). More and more people began to discern "the tremendous potential of teacher leaders" (Smyser, 1995, p. 131) and to hold "teacher leadership qualities as necessary elements for redesigning schools for success" (Wynne, 2001, p. 1).

> Recent calls for reconsidering this relatively tightly controlled view of teacher work have caused many school and university practitioners to think about what teachers can contribute to school improvement and effectiveness. (Griffin, 1995, p. 30)

The belief "that teachers need[ed] to assume leadership if efforts to improve education [were] to succeed" (Hinchey, 1997, p. 233; Silva et al., 2000)—that teacher leadership was "essential for successful school reform in a knowledge-based society" (Crowther et al., 2002, p. 29)—began to take root (Stone et al., 1997). Analysts who turned their gaze on school change increasingly maintained that school reform would be dead on arrival "unless teachers [were] recognized as full partners in leading, defining, and implementing school improvement efforts" (Fessler & Ungaretti, 1994, p. 211); "school improvement efforts [would] succeed or fail to the degree that teachers [were] engaged as partners in the process" (Stone et al., 1997, p. 60). In particular, educators suggested that "by using the energy of teacher leaders as change agents, the reform of education [stood] a better chance of building momentum" (Katzenmeyer & Moller, 2001, p. 2). They also concluded that teacher quality would be more likely to improve (Childs-Bowen et al., 2000; Wasley, 1991) and that school reforms had "a better chance of penetrating the classroom and contributing to achieving better results in student learning if teacher leadership [could] be nurtured and strengthened" (Urbanski & Nickolaou, 1997, p. 250), "that without teacher leadership the changes and improvement desired in student learning [could] not be achieved" (Snell & Swanson, 2000, p. 2).

The major policy mechanism employed in these new reforms is "power distribution"—a perspective that

> assume[s] that schools can be improved by distributing political power among the various groups who have legitimate interests in the nature and quality of educational services. Reforms that seek to reallocate power and authority among various stakeholders are based on the belief that when power is in the right hands, schools will improve. (Association for Supervision and Curriculum Development, 1986, p. 13)

Unlike the strategy employed in the earlier era of reform, this change model is designed to capitalize on the energy and creativity of teachers at the school site level. Underlying the ideology of these more recent reform initiatives is the assumption that the problems in education can be ascribed to the structure of schooling—"that the highest impediment to progress is the nature of the system itself" (Carnegie Forum on Education and the Economy, 1986, p. 40).

It is not surprising, therefore, that the focus of improvement shifted to the professionals who populated schools and the conditions they needed to work effectively, including basic changes in the organizational arrangements of schooling—a shift from mechanistic, structure-enhancing strategies to a professional approach to reform and from "regulation and compliance monitoring to mobilization of institutional capacity" (Timar & Kirp, 1988, p. 75). Nor is it surprising that reformers who considered the basic structure of schools as the root of education's problem should propose more far-reaching and radical solutions than their predecessors, who believed that the current system could be repaired (Boyd, 1987; Perry, 1988).

More directly to the topic at hand, we note that the reform dynamics outlined above "created a window of opportunity for teacher leaders" (Wilson, 1993, p. 24). That is, "new leadership roles for teachers occurred, in large part, in reaction to the regulatory bureaucratically oriented educational reforms of the late 1970s and early 1980s" (Smylie, 1996, p. 522) and that the concept itself was "born out of a 'second wave' of reform" (Berry & Ginsberg, 1990, p. 617; Odell, 1997) developed in response to earlier initiatives (Smylie & Denny, 1989; Murphy, 1990a). "Creating change through enhancing teachers' roles as leaders" (Conley & Muncey, 1999, p. 46) was thus both a reaction to the failed framework of centralized control as well as a central plank in alternative reform strategies (Boles & Troen, 1996).

While teacher leadership sometimes held center stage by itself, more often than not it was "connected with several interrelated educational reform themes" (Forster, 1997, p. 84). It has been both a spur to the acceptance of these reform strategies (e.g., school-based management) (Murphy & Beck, 1995) as well as a "key element" (Smylie, 1996, p. 521) and a "central component of the latest educational reform efforts" (Snell & Swanson, 2000, p. 2; Fay, 1992b; Hart, 1995). That is, the reforms themselves, in turn, have "spurred the development of teacher leaders" (Moller & Katzenmeyer, 1996, p. 2; Bliss, Fahrney, & Steffy, 1995) and have caused teachers "to exercise more leadership outside the classroom than traditionally has been expected of them" (Leithwood et al., 1997, p. 2). Or, as Teitel (1996) affirms, "the current reform movements ask classroom teachers to take on significant new leadership roles" (p. 150) and "require a new type of leadership from professional educators" (Conley, 1997, p. 330).

The broadest and most powerful reform stream that has carried teacher leadership to prominence is the "professionalization of teaching" (Forster, 1997, p. 84) movement—a "call for dramatically different approaches to educational change" (Livingston, 1992, p. 10) and "an emphasis on moving on to more professional models of school organization and management" (Conley & Muncey, 1999, p. 46; Stone et al., 1997; Wise, 1989). The first of two tributaries of rationale here spotlights the macro, occupational level (Berry & Ginsberg, 1990; Wasley, 1991) and underscores the importance of teacher leadership "as a means of reforming the teaching profession" (Lieberman, 1987, p. 400). Teacher leadership is viewed as a conduit for the emergence of (1) "a new paradigm of the teaching profession"

(Crowther et al., 2002, p. 3)—a "true profession" (Pellicer & Anderson, 1995, p. 12; Lieberman & Miller, 1999; Rallis, 1990) and (2) "a professional model of teaching" (Katzenmeyer & Moller, 2001, p. 40)—conditions, it is held, that are essential for "the preservation of the public school tradition" (Wise, 1989, p. 309; Maeroff, 1988) writ large. The logic here is that "teachers must assume leadership if teaching is ever to become accepted as a profession" (Hinchey, 1997, p. 233). Or, as Katzenmeyer and Moller (2001) assert, "a professional model of teaching points to the need for teacher leadership" (p. 43) and "teacher leadership has become synonymous with the drive toward greater professionalism for teachers" (McCay et al., 2001, p. 137). The essence of the change here is a shift in the attempt to address issues of quality control "by substituting quality control over personnel for quality control over service delivery" (Wise, 1989, p. 304)—a "shift from hierarchical to peer control of teaching" (Firestone, 1996, p. 401) and the "transformation of teaching from an occupation to a profession" (Berry & Ginsberg, 1990, p. 617). The change features "a variety of roles for teachers, which provide teachers with greater opportunities to influence both practice and change in schools" (Stone et al., 1997, p. 49).

A second parallel but somewhat distinct tributary of rationale was introduced earlier—the micro level and more instrumental argument "that unless teachers are . . . supported as professionals, schools will not be able to sustain change through school reform efforts" (Wynne, 2001, p. 1). That is, unless we create a teaching profession, our ability to restructure schools and "improve schools on behalf of student learning" (Wasley, 1991, p. 18) will be crippled (Pellicer & Anderson, 1995; Stone et al., 1997; Wasley, 1991), that "teacher leadership is a critical component" (Stone et al., 1997, p. 50) or "crucial element of school improvement" (Smylie et al., 2002, p. 162). Thus professionalism is "held out with the promise that [it] will produce more successful solutions to problems of students learning and student socialization" (Little, 1988, p. 82; Hallinger & Richardson, 1988).

Teacher leadership is also buttressed by a set of values or "reform imperatives" (Fay, 1992b, p. 57) that are at the heart of postbureaucratic reforms in general and teacher professionalism specifically. The most visible of these is "empowerment" (Katzenmeyer & Moller, 2001, p. 23; Johnson, 1989) or "professional autonomy" (Wasley,

1991, p. 20), the focus on "empower[ing] school staff by providing authority" (David, 1989, p. 52)—on overcoming "the high degree of powerlessness among professional staff" (Hallinger & Richardson, 1988, p. 242) through the "shift of a major portion of responsibility for leadership from principals to teachers" (Pellicer & Anderson, 1995, p. 14). The assumption is that formal alterations in decision-making structures will lead to real changes in the involvement, voice, and autonomy of local stakeholders (Chapman, 1990; Dellar, 1992; Sackney & Dibski, 1992). Or, more specifically, that "decentralized schools alter the educational power structure" (Wohlstetter & McCurdy, 1991, p. 391). A second premise is that this augmented autonomy and authority provide the requisite context for change, "that school autonomy is a prerequisite for a school to be effective" (Robertson & Buffett, 1991, p. 3; see also Chubb, 1988). "With adequate authority at the school level, many important decisions affecting personnel, curriculum and the use of resources can be made by the people who are in the best position to make them (those who are most aware of problems and needs)" (Clune & White, 1988, p. 3; Jandura & Burke, 1989). The final premise at work here is "the assumption that change in the venue of decisions will alter one or more of the major components that determine the kind of decision that emerges from the decision-making process" (Weiss, 1993, p. 2). More specifically, "there is a significant relationship between providing authority to employees at the work site and achieving the organization's ultimate goal" (Duttweiler & Mutchler, 1990, p. 30). That is, by relying on "a matrix of authority vested in many people rather than a strict hierarchy of authority and power vested in the principal" (Hart, 1995, p. 11; Katzenmeyer & Moller, 2001) and by "extending teachers' decision-making power into schoolwide leadership activities" (Boles & Troen, 1994, p. 6) and "schoolwide decision making and policy development" (Griffin, 1995, p. 30; Hatfield, Blackman, & Claypool, 1986), students will learn more effectively (Brown, 1992; Hannaway, 1992; Wagstaff & Reyes, 1993; Wohlstetter, 1990).

Other values also nourish second wave reforms such as school-based management and restructuring that features teacher leadership. While "professionalism empowers teachers" (Rallis, 1990, p. 192), the development and use of a "specialized knowledge base" (Wasley, 1991, p. 16) that is widely shared by teachers (Elmore, 1996)—an emphasis on "knowledge-based work" (Clemson-Ingram & Fessler, 1997, p. 99)—brings professionalism to life (Conley, 1997). Emerging understandings of reform as processes that privilege community (Rogus, 1988), "collaboration and collegiality" (Wasley, 1991, p. 18; Jandura & Burke, 1989), and a "collaborative culture" (Lieberman, 1992, p. 164) and "social contexts in which knowledge can be created, transferred and transposed" (Frost & Durrant, 2003a, p. 175) are also significant. So too are commitments to democratization in the workplace (Barth, 1988a; Furman & Starratt, 2002) and to the principle of building schooling on "the consent of the governed" (Clark, 1987, p. 40)—an affirmation of "schools as communities in which all members have voice and are allowed the space to fulfill their human potential and exercise leadership" (Frost & Durrant, 2003a, p. 176).

CONCLUSION

Others who have traced the foundations of teacher leadership in the U.S. have highlighted a series of tangible problems such as teacher shortages (Christensen, 1987; Wasley, 1991); administrative overburden (Copland, 2003; Rallis, 1990); the need to plan for the "next generation of administrators" (Jandura & Burke, 1989, p. 11); the increasing complexity of schools (LeBlanc & Shelton, 1997); the failure of many, if not most, formal school leaders to successfully assume the reigns of instructional leadership (Hallinger & Richardson, 1988; Howey, 1988); and the flatness of the teaching career (Christensen, 1987), with its absence of opportunities for recognition (LeBlanc & Shelton, 1997). We agree that these problems support the teacher leadership movement. At the same time, we believe that the roots of teacher leadership extend below these pressure points. In this chapter, we attempted to explore these more fundamental sources of the teacher leadership phenomenon. We found and described three such roots in considerable detail: (1) the struggle afoot in education to rebuild the organizational foundations of schooling; (2) the evolving nature of leadership in postindustrial organizations; and (3) the recalibration of school improvement work and the legitimization of new forms of school reform.

CHAPTER THREE

Teacher Leadership

A Theory in Action

Benefits to the school, to the teacher, and to the students make investing in teacher leadership a sound investment. (Katzenmeyer & Moller, 2001, p. 16)

The development of teacher . . . leaders . . . promises hope for sustained changes within educational institutions. (Johnson & Hynes, 1997, p. 113)

Teacher leadership is . . . a necessary condition for renewed professionalism and ultimately for the improvement of educational practices that affect children. (Miller, 1992, p. 126)

A variety of reform analysts maintain that the teacher leadership movement is ripe with "transformative potential" (Hinchey, 1997, p. 233) and with "multiple effects" (Howey, 1988, p. 30). They foresee potential benefits flowing to teachers—to individual teachers (Miller, 1988; Walters & Guthro, 1992), "to other teachers" (Smylie & Denny, 1989, p. 4), and to the "larger teaching force" (Wasley, 1991, p. 25) or to the "teaching profession" (Crowther et al., 2002, p. 69); to individual schools and to the youngsters in them (Hart & Baptist, 1996; Rettalick & Fink, 2002); and to the system of public education writ large (Boles & Troen, 1996). That is, teacher leadership is a "sustainable measure that can greatly benefit all schools" (Feiler,

Heritage, & Gallimore, 2000, p. 69). These reformers declare that "the potential for substantial change and improvement in teaching and learning, student success, and collegial relations is clear" (Fay, 1992a, p. 10) and "obvious" (Crowther et al., 2002, p. 69). They assert that "teacher leadership [is] recognized as a major resource to the school community" (Darling-Hammond et al., 1995, p. 94) and as "a 'win-win' situation because both students and teachers benefit" (LeBlanc & Shelton, 1997, p. 33); "through leadership . . . teachers can make a major difference to the personal and interpersonal capacities of themselves and their colleagues, to pupils' learning, and to the organizational structures and cultures of their schools" (Frost & Durrant, 2003a, p. 178). These scholars maintain that teacher leadership contains "both moral (it is more humane and more democratic) and programmatic (it works better and produces better results)" (Hynes et al., 1992, p. 49) potential for school reform, that it allows school assets, especially teachers, "to be better utilized for the benefit of the entire school community" (Rowley, 1988, p. 16), and that it is an especially fruitful "means for better achieving the operational tasks and goals of the school organization" (Hatfield et al., 1986, pp. 21–22).

SOME CAUTIONS

The creation of teacher leadership opportunities may well depend in nearly all cases on the conditions present in individual school buildings. (Conley, 1997, p. 334)

This link between parallel leadership and improved outcomes is tenuous, substantiated only by case study research at this juncture. (Crowther et al., 2002, p. 43)

Overall, the research indicates that these teacher leadership initiatives did little to support school level improvement. (Smylie et al., 2002, p. 166)

Before we explore the "policy logic" or "descriptive assumptions" (Smylie, 1995, p. 4) about how the above-noted benefits are to be garnered, it is important to introduce some of the caveats that temper this embedded logic in action (Malen, Ogawa, & Kranz, 1989). We begin with a reminder. At this point in the analysis, we are simply identifying the supposed benefits of teacher leadership and welding them together into a coherent framework. We are not testing these claims here. This is of significance because when we illuminate the empirical findings on the various links in the model, we will expose some troubling conclusions. To begin with, while "the ultimate value of teacher leadership is improvement of prac-tice and increasing student performance" (Katzenmeyer & Moller, 2001, p. 34; Wynne, 2001) and while "the prospects for teacher leadership remain dim if no one can distinguish the gains made for students" (Little, 1988, p. 100), empirical evidence on these cru-cial issues is "limited in quantity" (Leithwood et al., 1997, p. 4) and "equivocal" (Smylie, 1996, p. 554): "more teacher leadership has been advocated over the last decade for several reasons but without much evidence that it has the potential its advocates claim" (Leithwood & Jantzi, 1998, pp. 25–26; Schmoker & Wilson, 1994). While "a great deal of effort has been placed on designing and implementing diverse programs across contexts, little atten-tion has been given to the evaluation of programs" (Yarger & Lee, 1994, p. 233). More troubling still, the empirical evidence that is available is "mixed" (Little, 1988, p. 87; Ingersoll, 1996; Wasley, 1991) and negative implications of teacher leadership have been uncovered (Crow & Pounder, 2000; LeBlanc & Shelton, 1997; Smylie, 1996), at least in the form of opportunity costs associated with the exercise of teacher leadership (Little, 1987; Smylie, 1996). Scholars also caution that teacher leadership initiatives "might make things worse by diverting teachers' attention, wast-ing their time, or creating divisive distinctions among them" (Johnson, 1989, p. 109). Even when positive, the results are often "modest" (Griffin, 1995, p. 38) and even then are often of "limited practical guidance" (Little, 1988, p. 87); that is, "we know rela-tively little about the specific mechanisms by which collegial rela-tions among teachers operate to the benefit of students" (Little, 1987, p. 494). In short, "the assumptions that undergird most of the teacher leadership initiatives" (Zimpher, 1988, p. 54) are not automatic; they "are not easily attained" (p. 54), especially when the focus is on "assigning formal leadership roles to teachers" (Darling-Hammond et al., 1995, p. 91; Odell, 1997; Wasley, 1991).

It is also instructive to acknowledge that because the benefits of teacher leadership can flow to individuals, to organizations, and to systems, the unit of gain needs to be carefully delineated— more so than is often done in the existing literature. Context issues also suggest caution in digesting assertions about the assumed advantages of teacher leadership. For example, the type of teacher leadership initiative matters. Benefits from early-era programs, such as career ladders and other formal role-based models of teacher leadership, are often quite distinct from later initiatives to create learning organizations and communities of practice (Darling-Hammond et al., 1995; Hart, 1994).

Likewise, the source and depth of initiatives need to be considered in analyses of the benefits and costs. So too does the organizational context (Conley, 1997). For example, in her case studies, Wasley (1991) found that

> the context in which each of the people worked had a significant impact on the teacher leader's ability to influence the practice of others—one role could not easily be transported to another place without giving careful thought to the impact of the place and its culture. (p. 145)

As we discuss in greater detail in the concluding section of the book, the role of the formal leaders in the organization, especially the presence or absence of transformational leadership, can have a profound influence on whether the theory powering teacher leadership functions as hypothesized. Contexts in which leadership across actors is exercised in a "coordinated manner" (Smylie, Wenzel, & Fendt, 2003, p. 152) also appear to be more effective than when teacher leadership is grafted onto existing arrangements. So too do situations in which a broad-based system of leadership shapes the activities performed by multiple actors (Smylie et al., 2002) versus contexts in which "individual role-based models of teacher leadership" (p. 181) are employed. The place of the individual teacher in the leadership equation is significant as well. Because "teacher leaders are approachable and influence primarily through their personal power" (Katzenmeyer & Moller, 2001, p. 7), teacher leaders who are recognized by their peers as master teachers maneuver more effectively as leaders than do less-well-regarded colleagues

(Childs-Bowen et al., 2000; Uline & Berkowitz, 2000; Zimpher, 1988).

EMBEDDED LOGIC

When teachers are enlisted and empowered as school leaders, everyone can win. (Barth, 1988b, p. 132)

Teacher leadership may make both independent and, with leadership from other sources, additive or multiplicative contributions to school improvement and outcomes for students. (Smylie et al., 2002, p. 177)

Teacher leadership might be most valuable as a means to enhance the professional growth and development of teachers, and as a means to revitalize their teaching and their interactions with their colleagues in ways that enhance student learning and increase the capacity of the school to adapt and improve. (Conley, 1997, p. 332)

The DNA ladder or "logic of benefits" (Smylie, 1992, p. 53) chain that defines teacher leadership is long and complex. For organizational purposes, we divide it into three sections—the professionalization of teaching, the strengthening of the school organization, and the promotion of classroom and school improvement—all linked together in reciprocal relationships (see Figure 3.1).

Professionalization

Teacher leaders become owners and investors in the school rather than mere tenants. They become professionals. (Barth, 2001, p. 449)

Empowerment and Ownership

Examined with one turn of the analytic prism, we see that teacher leadership works by strengthening the professional nature of teaching, both for individual educators and for teaching as an occupation (Midgley & Woods, 1993; Stone et al., 1997).

Figure 3.1   The Embedded Logic of Teacher Leadership

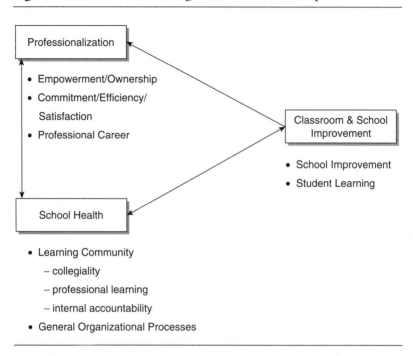

From this angle, teacher leadership is about "rais[ing] teachers' sense of empowerment" (Klecker & Loadman, 1998, p. 367; Wall & Rinehart, 1997), about "expand[ing] . . . professional status" (Smylie & Denny, 1989, p. 4) and "supporting local autonomy" (Whitaker, 1997) and "control" (Christensen, 1987, p. 106) so that teachers can "realize their professional worth" (Katzenmeyer & Moller, 2001, p. 16): "substantial evidence exists that the new teacher leadership roles alter authority relationships in schools and school districts and increase the amount of teachers' influence over curricular and instructional, as well as administrative, matters" (Smylie, 1996, p. 574). As teacher leaders, "teachers gain responsibility for areas traditionally reserved for administrators—instruction, assessment, rules and procedures, and major decision making" (Lieberman & Miller, 1999, p. 22). "Professional status" (Smylie & Denny, 1989, p. 2) is elevated.

A key assumption here is that this autonomy and authority provide the requisite context for change, "that school autonomy is a prerequisite for a school to be effective" (Robertson & Buffett,

1991, p. 3; see also Chubb, 1988): "with adequate authority at the school level, many important decisions affecting personnel, curriculum, and the use of resources can be made by the people who are in the best position to make them (those who are most aware of problems and needs)" (Clune & White, 1988, p. 3). Another premise at work here is "the assumption that change in the venue of decisions will alter one or more of the major components that determine the kind of decision that emerges from the decision-making process" (Weiss, 1993, p. 2). More specifically, "there is a significant relationship between providing authority to employees at the work site and achieving the organization's ultimate goal" (Duttweiler & Mutchler, 1990, p. 30)—"if schools have greater autonomy, students will learn more" (Wohlstetter, 1990, p. 2).

The next piece of the design tells us that "the goal of this teacher empowerment is to improve the quality of the educational experience by creating ownership in those responsible for teaching and learning" (Stone et al., 1997, p. 50). Thus, the opportunity to wield significant influence over school-level decisions is supposed to enhance widespread participation of teachers in the activities of the school (Clune & White, 1988). This "broad-based involvement in decision making" (Conley, 1991, p. 37)—what Burke (1992) refers to as the "participation in the formulation of collective viewpoints" (p. 39)—promotes a general "sense of ownership" (Etheridge, Valesky, Horgan, Nunnery, & Smith, 1992, p. 10; Barth, 1988b; Lindelow, 1981) by members of the school community, "a greater stake in seeing those decisions succeed" (Rothstein, 1990, p. 22), and staff ownership for the results of those decisions (Short & Greer, 1989), namely, "increased ownership and responsibility" (Smylie, 1996, p. 563).

The ownership link of the logic chain of benefits takes on enhanced power in light of the widely held belief that "change requires ownership" (David, 1989, p. 46). Thus ownership is the fulcrum for school improvement efforts and an essential element in the equation to "sustain and deepen reforms" (Copland, 2003, p. 3).

Commitment/Efficacy/Satisfaction

Woven throughout the literature on teacher leadership is the premise that empowerment and ownership work to improve organizational processes and outcomes through their influence on three important bridging variables—commitment, efficacy, and satisfaction/motivation. To begin with, it is regularly claimed that "members of the school community . . . [will] be more committed to decisions if they participate in making them" (Rothstein, 1990, p. 6)—that "people will show a greater level of support . . . for educational decisions in which they have meaningfully partici- pated" (Burke, 1992, p. 39). Teacher leadership represents a promising antidote to "drift and detachment" (Duke, 1994, p. 255). It reduces alienation (Carnoy & MacDonell, 1990) and promotes a sense of connectedness (Short & Greer, 1989), which, in turn, nurtures commitment to organizational decisions (Duttweiler & Mutchler, 1990; Smylie, 1992) and to the organiza- tion itself (Smylie & Denny, 1989). Commitment, in turn, leads teachers to work harder to implement decisions (Imber, 1983; Rothstein, 1990; Smylie, 1992) and to take greater responsibility for activities (Burke, 1992; Katzenmeyer & Moller, 2001).

Efficacy is another pattern highlighted in the teacher leader- ship mosaic—specifically, the belief that teacher leadership will enhance teachers' "individual and collective" (Smylie et al., 2002, p. 170) sense of efficacy (Lieberman, 1992; Morris & Nunnery, 1994; Smith, 1993), "professional confidence" (Duttweiler & Mutchler, 1990, p. 35; Rallis, 1990), and "self esteem" (Wasley, 1991, p. 25)—all of which are expected to enable teachers "to feel that they are better able to promote change" (Smylie et al., 2002, p. 169) and to produce stronger school results (Burke, 1992). As Katzenmeyer and Moller (2001) propose,

> this sense of efficacy encourages teachers to move the locus of control for student results back into the teaching profession and to place less blame on factors beyond their control, such as the students' home environments. If teachers feel confi- dent in their abilities to be leaders, they will assume responsi- bility for the learning of all students. This single outcome from teacher leadership can affect teaching and learning throughout the school. Linking teacher leadership to efficacy in their classrooms can help teachers understand how they can touch the lives of more students. (p. 32)

Finally, the elevated levels of commitment and efficacy result- ing from autonomy and empowerment at the core of teacher lead- ership will, it is suggested, enhance the motivation, morale, and satisfaction of teachers (Keiser & Shen, 2000; Smylie, 1996). "Access to new roles . . . will motivate teachers to perform better" (Hart, 1990, p. 504) and leadership activities that "tap the talent, competencies, and enthusiasm of teachers . . . [will] help maintain their internal motivation for teaching" (Hart & Baptist, 1996, p. 87). "Improved teacher morale" (Keiser & Shen, 2000, p. 118) will also become visible (LeBlanc & Shelton, 1997; Katzenmeyer & Moller, 2001). In the chain of logic in Figure 3.1, teacher leadership is also seen as a method "to enhance satisfaction" (Conley, 1997, p. 331; Leithwood et al., 1997). Because empowerment is "both engaging and satisfying" (Uline & Berkowitz, 2000, p. 429; Ingersoll, 1996), schools that operationalize teacher leadership, it is argued, are places where "teachers are more satisfied with their work" (Moller & Katzenmeyer, 1996, p. 1; Barth, 1988b) and exhibit a heightened sense of energy (Barth, 2001; LeBlanc & Shelton, 1997).

Professional Career

There are indications in the research that the power of teacher leadership is mediated through heightened professionalism (Crowther et al., 2002; Troen & Boles, 1994; Yarger & Lee, 1994)—the sense that teacher leadership promotes the development of teaching as a career rather than simply as a job (Hart, 1994). Teacher leadership, it is argued, fosters "professional recognition [and] professional involvement" (Little, 1987, p. 497) and "professional opportunities" (Hatfield, 1989, p. 11). This appears to hold when considering the profession as a whole—that is, "it causes everyone to see teaching as a more valued and prestigious profession" (Troen & Boles, 1994, p. 283; see Fullan, 1994, for an alternative perspective)—and the careers of individual teachers (Hart, 1990, 1995; Hatfield et al., 1986; Smylie, 1996). Teacher leadership is also judged to be a productive vehicle "to create a more professional workplace in schools" (Hart, 1995, p. 9) and "more professional working conditions for teachers" (Stone et al., 1997, p. 52). It is anointed as a strategy to "dramatically reshape the . . . status of the teaching profession" (Crowther et al., 2002, p. 10). The quality of the workforce is upgraded, it is asserted, while the array of rewards and recognitions "to attract and retain the most talented teachers in the profession" (Smylie,

1996, p. 521) is expanded. That is, teacher leadership is presented "as a means to provide greater rewards and recognitions to capable teachers" (Hatfield et al., 1986, p. 22).

School Health

> The more teachers share leadership, . . . the more they come to perceive the school as a community. (Harrison & Lembeck, 1996, p. 114)

> Teacher leadership and teacher professional development are inextricably linked. (Doyle, 2000, p. 14)

> Teacher leadership has unlimited potential in making a real difference in the pace and depth of school change. (Katzenmeyer & Moller, 2001, p. 102)

Reviewers hypothesize that teacher leadership promotes important organizational outcomes, such as student learning, by strengthening the health of schools as organizations. On this front, they discern two trends: the emergence and reinforcement of elements of learning communities and improvements in general organizational processes, such as decision making and change.

Learning Organizations

Those closest to the teacher leadership movement believe that it will be a catalyst in creating communities of professional practice that, in turn, will foster enhanced learning for youngsters. They maintain that as teacher leadership takes root in schools, cooperation, cohesion, collaboration, and collegiality will expand (Fay, 1992b; Hart, 1994; Morris & Nunnery, 1994)—although these gains are hardly automatic (Hart, 1994; Little, 1990). These analysts aver that teacher leadership encourages the development of a "more democratic, communal, or communitarian school system for schools and schooling" (Hart, 1995, pp. 10–11) as well as the emergence of "caring community culture[s]" (O'Hair & Reitzug, 1997, p. 71). Teacher leadership, it is asserted, helps "remove barriers between teachers and administrators" (Hynes et al., 1992, p. 49) and "reduce[s] the amount of teacher isolation often found in schools" (Manthei, 1992, p. 2). It supports "increased cooperation between teachers and administrators" (Smylie & Denny, 1989, p. 11) and development of an "interconnected conception of what it means to teach" (Uline & Berkowitz, 2000, p. 432). Teachers come "to define themselves in relation to . . . how they work with their . . . colleagues" (p. 432). Because "the opportunities for participating in the leadership of schools . . . are the means to break the isolation of teachers [and] engage them in collective efforts" (Lieberman et al., 1988, p. 152), they promote the development of "solid relationships" (LeBlanc & Shelton, 1997, p. 38) among teachers.

An important subtheme holds that community development via teacher leadership nurtures democracy (Barth, 2001; LeBlanc & Shelton, 1997). In turn, benefits in terms of "helping students understand how a democratic society works" (Blegen & Kennedy, 2000, p. 5) are sometimes featured in the DNA chain of logic leading from teacher leadership to enhanced student performance.

When teachers [feel] valued as members of a coherent community, and empowered as decision makers, they [are] able to empower their students by offering them choices and by including them in decisions affecting their own instruction. (Miller, 1992, p. 128)

An essential component of the hypothesis concerning the development of learning communities is the assertion "that teacher leadership is inextricably connected to teacher learning" (Darling-Hammond et al., 1995, p. 89). It is argued that "teacher leadership provides an inevitable and fecund occasion for teacher growth" (Barth, 2001, p. 444; Whitaker, 1997; Wasley, 1991) and a catalyst for the emergence of "a learning culture" (Darling-Hammond et al., 1995, p. 96), that "the strongest benefit of teacher leadership is professional learning" (Stone et al., 1997, p. 56). Embedded in the writing in this area is a sense that "emphasis on teacher leadership will focus energy on more career development activities for teachers" (Lynch & Strodl, 1991, p. 1), that it will result in "improvements in staff development opportunities" (Smylie & Denny, 1989, p. 10) and "new opportunities for professional development" (Stone et al., 1997, p. 51) as well as a belief that "professional learning" (Smylie, 1995, p. 4) and "intellectual growth" (O'Hair & Reitzug, 1997, p. 71) will follow.

Teacher leadership is proposed as "an avenue for the professional growth" (Manthei, 1992, p. 1) of those exercising teacher leadership as well as for their peers in the school (Darling-Hammond et al., 1995; Smylie, 1996): "teacher-leaders are not only making learning possible for others but, in important ways, are learning a great deal themselves" (Lieberman et al., 1988, p. 164). Or, as Wigginton (1992) reports, "the most persuasive reason of all for encouraging and nourishing the potential leaders is the impact that such efforts have on our personal and professional growth" (p. 171): "the primary benefit is that we are recognizing teacher leadership as a resource [for] teachers' own professional and personal development" (Hart & Baptist, 1996, p. 98).

Finally, learning communities mediate valued organizational outcomes by inculcating "an increased sense of responsibility and accountability" (Boles & Troen, 1996, p. 52; Katzenmeyer & Moller, 2001)—an improvement-centered sense of accountability (Lieberman, 1992) and a strong internal locus of responsibility. Teacher leadership substitutes hierarchical models of accountability with "shared" (Hallinger & Richardson, 1988, p. 237), "collaborative" (Stone et al., 1997, p. 50), "collegial" (Boles & Troen, 1994, p. 14), "collective" (Smylie et al., 2002, p. 178), and professionally anchored understandings of responsibility—with frameworks in which teachers feel personal responsibility for their efforts (Darling-Hammond et al., 1995) and are "accountable to each other" (Troen & Boles, 1994, p. 284) for the work they are doing. Teacher leaders also "help to breed a continuous process of evaluation: not the evaluation that makes judgments that offer little help for improvement" (Lieberman, 1992, p. 162).

General Organizational Processes

In the teacher leadership benefits framework, professionalization is linked to classroom and school improvement by a bridge of improved organizational operations. A variety of scholars in this area profess that teacher leadership creates an environment in which "the professional values of teachers . . . have greater play in the formal decisions of school officials" (Johnson, 1989, p. 109), a professional climate (Smylie & Denny, 1989) in which there is "more shared decision-making" (Hynes et al., 1992, p. 48). This, in turn, infuses stronger knowledge into the school's deliberative processes (Rallis, 1990). Burke (1992) observes that this increased involvement serves to broaden dialogue and establish a "more diverse information base" (p. 39; Broyles, 1991) for decision making and produces "more informed stakeholders through shared experience of people with a range of perspectives and expertise" (p. 39).

As a consequence, analysts aver, "teacher leaders . . . contribute to an improvement in the school's decision-making process" (Leithwood et al., 1997, p. 24), and "schools benefit from better decisions" (Barth, 2001, p. 445), with quality being determined by the match of decisions to the needs of the students (Weiss, Cambone, & Wyeth, 1991), creativity (Barth, 2001), acceptability (Wagstaff & Reyes, 1993), and relevance and workability (Burke, 1992). The result is that these *better decisions* "lead to school improvement and increased student learning" (Hart, 1995, p. 16; Rallis, 1990).

Teacher leadership is also often associated with *enhanced creativity:* "traditional thinking is challenged [and] new ways of rethinking old concepts occur" (LeBlanc & Shelton, 1997, p. 33). Teacher leadership promotes the "exam[ination] and test[ing] of new ideas, methods, and materials" (Little, 1987, p. 502). The collaboration that results from teacher leadership "breaks teachers out of . . . common 'ruts,' allowing them to see the 'big picture' that comes by looking at the school through broader lenses" (LeBlanc & Shelton, 1997, p. 33). The ensuing "stimulus to innovation is powerful" (Darling-Hammond et al., 1995, p. 98; Smylie & Denny, 1989), with the likelihood that distributed leadership may help teachers "exercise more creativity by working closely with colleagues and administrators" (LeBlanc & Shelton, 1997, p. 33) and "may promote the development and adoption of innovations" (Smylie, 1996, p. 575). Barth (2001) nicely sums up the logic here as follows:

> We are most likely to find rich conceptions of a better school
> and inventive ways to attain it when teachers step into leader-
> ship roles and articulate for the public and for the profession
> just what school and teaching might become. (p. 447)

Advocates for teacher leadership propose that decisions made under this organizational framework will be *more responsive* to the needs of the local community than is the case under a more centralized management framework (Epps, 1992), "that stimulation of such leadership . . . is likely to improve the capacity of schools to respond to the needs of students" (Darling-Hammond et al., 1995, p. 89). As Lawton (1991) informs us, "the key indictment here is that bureaucracy's lack of response, its commitment to uniformity and standardization, and its susceptibility to political rather than economic forces result in an inability to respond appropriately" (p. 7). Bryk (1993), in turn, argues that "enhanced democratic activity at the local level can be an effective antidote to unresponsive societal institutions" (p. 5). Teacher leadership can promote enhanced attention to targeted instructional strategies and conditions, promoting a high degree of responsiveness (Mojkowski & Fleming, 1988). With the coming leadership of teachers, our schools can adapt to meet the needs of youngsters going to school in this increasingly unpredictable world. As schools become "more responsive to community and student needs" (Lindelow, 1981, p. 126), as they "focus attention on issues central to improving the performance of . . . particular student population[s]" (Duttweiler & Mutchler, 1990, p. 42), flexibility moves center stage and diversity and variety become the norms (Sackney & Dibski, 1992). Thus it is the contention of many that teacher leadership will "enable school communities to shape distinctive forms of school life" (Bryk, 1993, p. 14).

A defining message in the literature in this area is that teacher leadership works by *building "institutional capacity"* (Smylie, 1995, p. 4) for the organization to function effectively (Crowther et al., 2002; Frost & Durrant, 2003b; Whitaker, 1997). Expanding capacity is portrayed in terms of "increas[ing] human capital" (Moller & Katzenmeyer, 1996, p. 1), of enhancing teacher expertise or teacher knowledge (Keiser & Shen, 2000; Morris & Nunnery, 1994). It is also discussed in terms of doing a better job of tapping into and organizing that expertise (Hatfield et al., 1986; Smylie & Denny, 1989) to "accomplish more" (Whitaker, 1997, p. 10)—to energize a "school resource" (Hart, 1995, p. 11) "for school improvement" (Stone et al., 1997, p. 57): "teacher leadership enables schools to draw on their teachers' expertise and experience" (Doyle, 2000, p. 15); "expanded opportunities for leadership will bring much needed, but often overlooked, expertise into play" (Hallinger & Richardson, 1988, p. 242). In addition to expanding the "talent bank from which to draw" (Whitaker,

1997, p. 12), teacher leadership works by making more efficient use of human resources. It is expected to do a better job than traditional ways of doing business by meshing the energy of "all who engage in renewal at the building level" (Candoli, 1991, p. 34). This, in turn, allows school staffs to "define and solve problems more effectively" (Conley, 1991, p. 36).

A special dimension of capacity building ribboned throughout the literature attends to attracting and holding teachers, the proposition that teacher leadership helps build expertise by *retaining good teachers* at the school level by preventing the knowledge drain that occurs when teachers leave the profession (Lynch & Strodl, 1991; Smylie, 1995, 1996). Because it is asserted that "the lack of leadership opportunities contributes to . . . attrition" (Katzenmeyer & Moller, 2001, p. 32), "the creation of new leadership roles for teachers hold[s] the promise of creating the new challenges and opportunities that some of our best teachers need if they are to remain in the profession" (Rowley, 1988, p. 16). Indeed, "new kinds of leadership roles for teachers [can] strengthen the incentives to . . . stay in the profession" (Wasley, 1991, p. 21) and can foster collegiality that, in turn, can "ease the strain of staff turnover" (Little, 1987, p. 502). And new "teacher leadership opportunities can promote teaching as a more desirable career and help to retain outstanding teachers for the complex tasks of school change" (Katzenmeyer & Moller, 2001, p. 32).

Concomitantly, it is suggested that teacher leadership increases capacity by attracting bright new teachers who normally would not enter the profession (Smylie et al., 2002). In short, the theory proposes, "talented people [will] be attracted to and remain in the profession" (Stone et al., 1997, p. 52; Hart, 1995). "Opportunities for teachers to lead will attract more able people to the profession. And by engaging teachers in leadership activities, the very able, empowered, ennobled, and challenged will choose to remain in teaching" (Barth, 1988b, p. 134).

Finally, perhaps the most distinct link in the chain of logic on organizational conditions is that teacher leadership will *promote change* at the school level (Smylie et al., 2002), that "teacher leadership holds the potential for significant school change" (Katzenmeyer & Moller, 2001, p. 20; Conley, 1997; Lieberman, 1992). In fact, some claim that the "evidence of teacher leadership" (Brownlee,

1979, p. 120) can best be seen in "teachers' influence in bringing about change in a school" (p. 120). Teacher leadership fosters change, supporters aver, by "hasten[ing] the pace of change" (Urbanski & Nickolaou, 1997, p. 253; Troen & Boles, 1994), by encouraging action when performance declines (Murphy & Beck, 1995), by "overcoming resistance to change" (Katzenmeyer & Moller, 2001, p. 33), by making implementation of decisions more probable (Datnow & Castellano, 2002; Short & Greer, 1989), by creating "powerful change agents for school development" (Smylie et al., 2003, p. 154), by sustaining "momentum on a school's improvement efforts . . . during changes in formal, administrative leadership" (Katzenmeyer & Moller, 2001, p. 7), and, more comprehensively, by promoting the development of a culture of continuous improvement (Copland, 2003).

The starting point here "is the notion that school revitalization will not happen, and certainly not be sustained, without teacher leadership" (Crowther et al., 2002, p. 70), that if "teachers are not able to join in leading . . . change, the changes will not take place" (Urbanski & Nickolaou, 1997, p. 254). It follows, therefore, that "creating new leadership positions for teachers can play an important role in bringing about substantive change in schools" (Rowley, 1988, p. 13), that "the prospects for improving education in America's schools can be significantly improved if policy makers nurture, support, and multiply the emerging opportunities for teachers to provide leadership in that endeavor" (Urbanski & Nickolaou, 1997, p. 254). Or, in its strongest form, "teacher participation in leading may be the most critical component of the entire process of change" (Lieberman, 1992, p. 159).

Classroom and School Improvement

Teacher leaders are the strongest link for transforming teaching practices. (Doyle, 2000, p. 4)

Teacher leadership . . . improves professional practice. (Stone et al., 1997, p. 58)

Teacher leadership is vital to the improvement of student achievement. (McKeever, 2003, p. 84)

Classroom Teaching

An important link in our chain of benefits logic highlights the "connection between teacher leadership in the school and what happens in classrooms" (Miller, 1992, p. 123)—"on whether or not the ways of working affect life in classrooms, the ways that teachers and students go about teaching and learning" (Griffin, 1995, p. 30). In the absence of much accumulated data, and in the face of somewhat "equivocal findings" (Smylie, 1996, p. 575), advocates assert that teacher leadership is expected to have a substantial impact on the core technology of schooling, that under shared leadership teaching practices "change significantly" (Boles & Troen, 1994, p. 11). They aver that teacher leadership is "required if there is to be any lasting and meaningful change in teaching and learning" (Doyle, 2000, p. 12) and any substantial alignment of the key pedagogical and curricular elements of schooling (Crowther et al., 2002). Analysts suggest that because "teacher leaders seem to position themselves on the cutting edge of the pedagogical frontier" (Rosenholtz, 1989, p. 66), "developing successful teacher leaders enables the creation of strong professional cultures that are essential for changing norms of teachers' teaching practices" (Doyle, 2000, p. 14). Teacher leadership, they claim, fosters important changes in the ways teachers teach (Darling-Hammond et al., 1995) and nurtures "considerable change in teacher practice schoolwide" (Smylie et al., 2002, p. 169). Reviewers often suggest that "leadership opportunities will bring out the very best in teachers; and the very best from teachers will bring out the very best in their students" (Barth, 1988b, p. 134), that teacher leadership leads to "improv[ed] teacher performance" (Smylie et al., 2002, p. 165), that is, "improved teaching" (Conley & Muncey, 1999, p. 46; Wasley, 1991).

Improved teaching, in turn, is expected to produce an array of benefits in the instructional program, all of which materialize through "the improvement of learning conditions" (Hallinger & Richardson, 1988, p. 230). "Curricular and instructional program development" (Smylie & Denny, 1989, p. 4) is enhanced and the "adoption of curricular and instructional innovations" (Smylie, 1996, p. 576) is improved—changes that result in "improv[ed] curriculum offerings" (Stone et al., 1997, p. 58). It is also hypothesized in our benefit chain that these "new structures for teaching and learning [will] better meet the needs of students"

(Hart, 1990, p. 504). "Higher standards" (Yarger & Lee, 1994, p. 235) materialize and are supported by a new emphasis on "schoolwide approaches to pedagogy" (Crowther et al., 2002, p. 39). "New frames for thinking about teaching" (Darling-Hammond et al., 1995, p. 93) are introduced.

School Improvement and Student Learning

The conviction that teacher leadership is a "very promising issue for the improvement of schools" (Barth, 1988b, pp. 145–146) is fairly well ingrained in the literature on teacher leadership (Hart & Baptist, 1996; Stone et al., 1997; Wasley, 1991). In fact, teacher leadership is often presented as "an instrument of school improvement" (Smylie et al., 2002, p. 164) and sometimes as "a pre-condition for school improvement" (Datnow & Castellano, 2003, p. 5): "as teacher leaders emerge, so do the answers for school improvement" (Harrison & Lembeck, 1996, p. 115). In a similar vein, teacher leadership is often connected to more effective schools (Smylie et al., 2003) and "improve[d] school performance" (Stone et al., 1997, p. 51). Finally, at the far end of the logic chain, analysts discern the benefit of enhanced student learning (Darling-Hammond et al., 1995). There is a belief that shared leadership "should produce youngsters that learn more" (Copland, 2003, p. 27): "most importantly, teacher leadership benefits the students in the building" (Katzenmeyer & Moller, 2001, pp. 85–86).

CONCLUSION

As with all reform movements, teacher leadership is propelled by a specific power train, one that shares multiple properties with other professionally focused reform models such as school-based decision making. In this chapter, we peeled back the covering on that driveshaft to reveal its inner workings. We reviewed how teacher leadership is expected to promote professionalization and to enhance the health of school organizations. We further reported how changes in these areas are believed to link with classroom and school improvements. We also presented some caveats to hold onto while examining the hypothesized chain of benefits or theory of action fueling the teacher leadership movement.

CHAPTER FOUR

The Skills, Attributes, and Knowledge of Teacher Leaders

By studying teacher leaders we are finding out that there are skills and abilities that help make a more effective leader. (Lieberman, 1992, p. 163)

Colleagues are more easily influenced if the teacher leader exhibits behavior they advocate. (Katzenmeyer & Moller, 2001, p. 8)

Exemplary teaching is the foundation of teacher leadership. (Snell & Swanson, 2000, p. 10)

I n this chapter, we provide a brief portrait of teacher leaders. In the introductory section, we offer a few words of caution about any attempt to craft a generic chronicle of this complex phenomenon. We then provide a review of the limited research on factors motivating educators to assume the mantle of teacher leader and an overview of the central role of expertise in the teacher leadership narrative. We close by presenting some of the bedrock principles of teacher leadership. The second part of the chapter overviews the personal qualities that researchers often find associated with teacher leaders, as well as the essential skills often displayed by these educators. In the final section, we turn our attention to the nature of the tasks performed by teacher leaders.

INTRODUCTORY NOTES

Teacher leadership is characterized by remarkable diversity and in that diversity resides complexity. (Crowther et al., 2002, p. 31)

Teacher leadership can take many forms. (Fessler & Ungaretti, 1994, p. 213)

A Cautionary Note of Analysis

We want to resist the popular view that teacher leadership can be defined by identifiable personal or professional attributes. (Crowther et al., 2002, p. 31)

While our intention in this chapter is to furnish a general description of teacher leaders, it is important to remember that there is a great deal of diversity in the reasons teachers assume these roles as well as in the qualifications they possess and the tasks they perform. Thus, while our analysis provides a solid composite of a teacher leader, each teacher leader will require a unique portrait. Individuals are different. So too is each "individual's work environment" (Smylie, 1992, p. 55).

It is also necessary to point out that "behavioral and trait approaches to leadership" (Crowther et al., 2002, p. 32) are incomplete. They tend to ignore the situational and context dimensions of leadership. They devote insufficient attention to the cognitive, moral, and collaborative aspects of leadership (Yukl, 2002). They also "deny the capabilities of individuals whose characteristics and talents lie in areas other than those identified" (Crowther et al., 2002, p. 32).

Finally, while a good portrait is instructive, it provides insufficient information about the process of painting. In this case, it does not translate automatically into guidelines on how to identify and select teacher leaders (Yarger & Lee, 1994). At the same time, we know that "knowledge, skills, and attitudes are important for teacher leadership" (Katzenmeyer & Moller, 2001, p. 13). With appropriate safeguards in place, an understanding of these qualities and skills can be quite informative.

Motivation and Expertise

> It seems that those who become teacher leaders need not only good technical skills, but legitimacy from their own ranks as well. (Lieberman, 1987, p. 402)

Somewhat surprisingly, systematic exploration of the motivations of those seeking and/or accepting teacher leadership roles and functions is nearly conspicuous by its absence from the literature in this area. There is a sense that "teachers assume leadership roles primarily because of personal, intrinsic reasons" (Stone et al., 1997, p. 59). Or alternatively, as Smylie (1996) concludes, "there is little evidence to suggest that they seek these roles for the status or extrinsic rewards associated with them" (p. 574): "external reasons for mentoring, such as financial gain or a request from an administrator, were the least influential motivators" (Manthei, 1992, p. 13). In general, teachers are motivated to take on leadership responsibilities because of "dissatisfaction with current curriculum and conditions of work" (Smylie, 1996, p. 546), "to satisfy their need for professional growth and stimulation" (Manthei, 1992, p. 16), "to be catalysts for other teachers' learning" (Smylie, 1996, p. 546), "to change and improve what exists" (Manthei, 1992, p. 13), and "to contribute to their profession" (p. 16).

A number of researchers have ascertained that expertise is "the first essential dimension of teacher leadership" (Snell & Swanson, 2000, p. 13). The starting point is the finding that "teacher leadership require[s] some power base, some source of authority that allows leaders to influence others" (Wasley, 1991, p. 48). The middle ground is occupied by the evidence that "teacher leaders seem to have influence . . . through their relationships with colleagues" (Keedy, 1999, p. 797). The capstone conclusion is that it is expertise, as distinguished from authority or from position, that provides the basis for that influence and permits educators to function as teacher leaders (Snell & Swanson, 2000).

According to scholars in this area, more extensive teaching experience in general and in one's current school (Brownlee, 1979) and additional years of formal education (Brownlee, 1979; Stone et al., 1997) are elements of the expertise equation. So also are knowledge of "subject matter" (Yarger & Lee, 1994, p. 228), "instructional skills" (Brownlee, 1979, p. 121), and mastery of classroom management techniques (Brownlee, 1979). In short, expertise is connected to "skill in teaching" (Berry & Ginsberg, 1990, p. 620). Or, as Wilson (1993) captures it, "in the eyes of their colleagues, leadership skills with students is what uniquely qualifies some teachers as leaders in their schools" (p. 25).

Expertise is connected to the capacity to hold "a broader view of the classroom, the school, and the society" (Lieberman, 1987, p. 402) and is linked to an understanding of current issues and reform directions (Snell & Swanson, 2000). Thus in addition to a robust understanding of children and curriculum, expert teachers possess a solid knowledge of the school as a workplace and of the community (Collinson & Sherrill, 1997). Expertise is also linked to "a commitment to ongoing learning" (Snell & Swanson, 2000, p. 10).

Principles of Teacher Leadership

Such roles might prove beneficial if those to be mentored had some influence in the design of the role and the relationship. (Wasley, 1992, p. 53)

Context is a critical variable. (Lieberman, 1987, p. 403)

A careful reading of the literature reveals that the teacher leadership movement is scaffolded on a set of potent guiding principles, principles that define and give meaning to collaborative leadership and serve as a template to assess efforts to promote shared leadership in schools. We present eight of these standards below.

1. Teacher leadership is grounded in classrooms (Fay, 1992b; McLaughlin & Yee, 1988; Wasley, 1991). "Teachers who aspire to lead must be able to display their own mastery of classroom challenges" (Little, 1988, p. 89).

2. Effective teaching is a prelude to teacher leadership. "One cannot be an effective teacher leader if one is not first an accomplished teacher" (Odell, 1997, p. 122), and "teaching, learning, and leadership are inextricably linked" (p. 122).

3. Teacher leadership is collaborative work (Lieberman, 1987; Suleiman & Moore, 1997). "Teachers are interested in leadership opportunities that allow them to collaborate with their colleagues" (Wasley, 1992, p. 54), and they "thrive best in an atmosphere of cooperation and collaboration" (Fay, 1992b, p. 59).

4. Teacher leadership is community anchored. It "is demeaned by a hierarchical viewpoint" (Fay, 1992b, p. 59), and it works best when it is "characterized by a professional rather than a bureaucratic orientation" (Lieberman, 1987, p. 403).

5. Teacher leadership is a service function (Little, 1985). It is grounded in "respect for the teachers [one] serves" (Fay, 1992b, p. 70); it focuses on facilitation and is "dominated by a 'helping stance'" (Lieberman, 1987, p. 403).

6. Teacher leadership is co-constructed, it is a co-learning process (Kilcher, 1992). "For teacher leadership to work, the source of power and authority [has] to be granted to the leaders by their colleagues—those they wish to lead" (Wasley, 1992, pp. 52–53). "Only with such authorization will the leaders actually have the potential to change practice" (p. 54).

7. Context is important (Lieberman, 1987). Situational dynamics have broad influence on teacher leadership initiatives and teacher leadership work (Kilcher, 1992). Teacher leadership can only be understood "in the broader contexts of teachers' work and workplaces" (Smylie, 1995, p. 5).

8. Teacher leadership makes a difference. "Teacher leaders are more likely to change classroom practices than other teachers" (Johnson & Hynes, 1997, p. 108), "improv[ing] instruction and thereby improv[ing] student achievement" (Creighton, 1997, p. 3).

TEACHER LEADERSHIP SKILLS

Teachers who have a wide array of skills, broad knowledge, a healthy attitude about service to others, and enthusiasm and willingness to serve have the greatest success as leaders. (Killion, 1996, p. 69)

> As they developed high levels of skill in each of these domains [expertise, collaboration, reflection, and empowerment], teachers emerged as leaders. (Snell & Swanson, 2000, p. 19)

> The most important factors for teacher leadership reside within teachers themselves. (Yarger & Lee, 1994, p. 228)

Keeping in mind the previously highlighted caveat about the dangers of attempting to generate an inclusive and universal list of qualities and skills possessed by teacher leaders, it is none-theless instructive to examine the personal characteristics and competencies that characterize these educators. On the personal qualities side of the equation, teacher leaders are often distin-guished by well-defined dispositions and values. While maintain-ing membership in the school community, they display a proclivity "to challenge the status quo" (Boles & Troen, 1996, p. 48) and a "willingness to take risks" (Yarger & Lee, 1994, p. 228; Smylie, 1996). Teacher leaders "seek challenge, change, and growth" (Wilson, 1993, p. 24); they "enjoy learning as adults" (Manthei, 1992, p. 13), "seeking out ongoing opportuni-ties to enhance and refine their craft" (Snell & Swanson, 2000, p. 7; Wasley, 1991). They demonstrate "a disposition toward inquiry" (Collinson & Sherrill, 1997, p. 59) and act from a "sense of empowerment" (Snell & Swanson, 2000, p. 17). They are reflec-tive about their teaching and their leadership (Katzenmeyer & Moller, 2001). Teacher leaders are known for their commitment to hard work (Leithwood et al., 1997; Wilson, 1993), passion (Snell & Swanson, 2000), "positive vision" (Manthei, 1992, p. 13), conviction (Crowther et al., 2002), and "enthusiasm and sense of optimism" (Crowther et al., 2002, p. 12). They emanate a discernable sense of efficacy, a strong sense of confidence "in their ability to make a difference in student learning" (Snell & Swanson, 2000, p. 7), and a belief that they "can make a differ-ence in children's lives" (Collinson & Sherrill, 1997, p. 59). They are also dedicated to making a difference in the lives of their col-leagues (Snell & Swanson, 2000). Teacher leaders are "marked by commitment to rigor and high expectations for themselves" (Snell & Swanson, 2000, p. 7) and "demonstrate how personal convic-tion can create a potent force for growth and change" (p. 17). They manifest "a genuine commitment to the work of colleagues and the school" (Leithwood et al., 1997, p. 23). They express a "willingness to be responsible for one's own actions" (Yarger & Lee, 1994, p. 228; Leithwood et al., 1997) and an obligation to personal accountability (Killion, 1996).

Teacher leaders are often distinguished by a set of qualities that make leadership via expertise rather than formal authority possible. They are authentic (Crowther et al., 2002), secure (Brownlee, 1979), open and confident (Smylie, 1996), self-actualized (Snell & Swanson, 2000), and trustworthy (Lieberman et al., 1988), spending personal resources "gaining the trust of people in their buildings" (p. 153) and "building rapport" (p. 153). Teacher leaders are reflective, devoted to improvement "by using reflection as a vehicle toward change" (Snell & Swanson, 2000, p. 7). They tend toward collaboration and are often "characterized by a high degree of collegiality and cooperation" (Snell & Swanson, 2000, p. 7) and a commitment to "make themselves available to other teachers as a resource or an advocate" (Wilson, 1993, p. 24). They display marked tendencies toward "sensitivity and receptivity to the thoughts and feelings of others" (Yarger & Lee, 1994, p. 228; Berry & Ginsberg, 1990), toward "consideration for others" (Crowther, 1997, p. 13) and "supportive[ness] of colleagues" (Wilson, 1993, p. 24; Leithwood et al., 1997). Teacher leaders exhibit an orientation toward the "value of stewardship" (Killion, 1996, p. 68) and "possess an appreciative orientation to others" (Leithwood et al., 1997, p. 19).

On the other side of the equation, a variety of analysts have addressed the skills found in the toolkits of teacher leaders. Representative examples follow. O'Connor and Boles (cited in Killion, 1996) list seven key competencies:

- understanding of politics, power, and authority
- skill in managing interpersonal relationships
- communication skills
- understanding of group dynamics
- presentation skills
- organizational skills
- ability to change (p. 68)

Hatfield et al. (1986) provide the following "blend of professional/personal attributes" (p. 19):

- adept in dealing with people
- skilled in communications (oral and written)
- flexible, patient, objective
- competent in the subject field and respected by their peers
- organized
- committed to the role (p. 19)

And Lieberman and her colleagues (1988) conclude that teacher leaders tend to be fluent in six skill domains:

- building trust and rapport
- organizational diagnosis
- dealing with the process
- using resources
- managing the work
- building skills and confidence in others (p. 153)

When we combine the information from these scholars and test that composite against the research of other analysts in this field, beyond "the essential dimension" (Snell & Swanson, 2000, p. 10) of expertise discussed above, four broad domains of skills emerge: visioning, interpersonal, collaborative, and management skills. Snell and Swanson (2000) maintain that vision is "essential for teacher leadership, for without a vision of the goals toward which one is striving . . . one cannot be effective in achieving them" (p. 10). One aspect of visioning, according to Crowther and his associates (2002), is the facility to articulate "clear views [about] a better world" (p. 11) for education and for youngsters. Another component is an "understanding of school and district operations" (Harrison & Lembeck, 1996, p. 113), the capacity to "acquire an appreciation for teachers, principals, and the community as a whole" (Killion, 1996, p. 69). Thus vision includes a distinct strand of local insight, "matching local needs and capabilities" (Lieberman et al., 1988, p. 158) and "solv[ing] problem[s] in context" (Katzenmeyer & Moller, 2001, p. 88).

"Strong interpersonal skills" (Snell & Swanson, 2000, p. 3), or "the ability to work well with . . . colleagues" (Leithwood et al., 1997, p. 20), are also at the core of teacher leadership (Berry & Ginsberg, 1990; Childs-Bowen et al., 2000). Indeed, Lieberman (1987) asserts that "the key skills of people who play these [teacher leadership] roles turn out to be in the areas of social interaction" (pp. 402–403), and Yarger and Lee (1994) aver that the "ability . . . to work with colleagues distinguishes effective teachers of teachers from effective teachers of children" (p. 229):

> These interpersonal skills, in interaction with personal characteristics, allow teacher leaders to earn the trust and respect of their peers and to guide and influence a colleague's instructional activities and decisions . . . and to collaborate with their colleagues on instructional improvement. (p. 229)

Indispensable elements here include communication skills, especially the capacity "to communicate proactively, confidently, assertively" (Crowther, 1997, p. 12), and clearly with adults (Yarger & Lee, 1994). Teacher leaders often demonstrate fluency in "communicating with multiple constituents" (Harrison & Lembeck, 1996, p. 113). One way they communicate is by being "visible in the school" (Leithwood et al., 1997, p. 21). Another important proficiency is the ability to bring out the best in others. For example, in her landmark study on teacher work, Rosenholtz (1989) found that "teacher leaders suggest and inspire ideas and discourse, drawing others upward to higher places" (p. 66). Adeptness at solving problems, resolving conflicts, negotiating rough terrain, and leading diverse participants to shared decisions is often found in the interpersonal toolkits of teacher leaders (Lieberman et al., 1988; Smylie, 1996; Yarger & Lee, 1994). Teacher leaders also exhibit skills in "build[ing] trust and rapport" (Lieberman, 1987, p. 403). They know "how to be strong, yet caring and compassionate" (Leithwood et al., 1988, p. 150).

Closely linked to the engagement of interpersonal capacities is the third skill domain, collaborative proficiencies. In general, "both survey and case study research find that lead . . . teachers use collaborative and facilitative approaches in their work" (Smylie, 1996, p. 546), that they are "proactive in their search for and creation of opportunities for collaboration" (Snell & Swanson, 2000, p. 13). One skill here is "modeling collegiality as a mode of work" (Wasley, 1991, p. 25). Another is employing "interactive talents . . . to develop networks of support" (Crowther, 1997, p. 12), in "build[ing] alliances and networks in many forms" (p. 14). "Developing a critical mass" (Miller et al., 2000, p. 7) of support for change is an essential collaborative skill. So too is "building support among administrators" (p. 7). Collaboration privileges cooperation over competition and transparency and accessibility over privacy; it signals that collective work offers real promise of solving complex problems (Snell & Swanson, 2000).

"Administrative skills" (Boles & Troen, 1996, p. 55) incorporates a final set of proficiencies that define teacher leaders. Lieberman et al. (1988) hold that to manage work teacher leaders need a "blend of skills, including managing time, setting priorities for work, delegating tasks and authority, taking initiative, monitoring progress, and coordinating the many strands of work taking place in their schools" (p. 158). Often featured here are skills in confronting and overcoming troublesome barriers, both structural and human (Crowther, 1997; Miller et al., 2000), and in "building supportive structures" (Lieberman et al., 1988, p. 159) to accomplish important ends. Skills in securing and using resources often characterize teacher leaders (Miller et al., 2000). Lieberman and her colleagues (1988) also confirm that a set of skills they label "organizational diagnosis—an understanding of the school culture and the ability to diagnose it—is critical if a leader is to have the basis for knowing how and where to intervene to mobilize people to take action and begin to work together" (p. 155).

TEACHER TASKS

> Teacher leaders are exemplars in their classrooms, effective coaches of their peers, and change agents who contribute to school, district, state, and national educational reform. (Snell & Swanson, 2000, p. 4)

> An analysis of these tasks seems to line up closely with the general tasks of teaching. (Hatfield, 1989, p. 13)

Teacher leaders can complete assignments from a nearly limitless portfolio of potential work. Indeed, research on this issue over the last 20 years has shown that teacher leaders are "involved in a wide variety of school activities" (Hatfield et al., 1986, p. 13) and a "wide range of functions" (Leithwood & Jantzi, 1998, p. 98):

"the large number of all-encompassing responsibilities of teacher leaders is one of the major conclusions of this study" (Hatfield et al., 1986, p. 20).

It is also interesting at the outset to note two essential generalizations about the nature of teacher leadership work. First, the "teacher" concept in teacher leadership is firmly rooted in the role of teaching: "the similarity in teaching tasks and the focus of teacher leaders . . . pointedly reflect[s] an extension of role not a different role" (Hatfield, 1989, p. 13). Second, the "leader" concept in teacher leadership shares considerable space with work in the area of leadership in general (Troen & Boles, 1994).

Our aim here is not to furnish a full accounting of all teacher leadership responsibilities. Rather, in order to complete our portrait, we lay out a broad framework of areas in which teachers maneuver in bringing their leadership roles to life, acknowledging at the outset that the specific tasks of any teacher leader can only be known in the context of his or her own school. We begin by outlining "frameworks" of teacher leadership functions developed by scholars in this area. We close by repackaging that work around a two-dimensional conceptualization: facilitating teacher work and completing essential tasks in the service of school improvement.

Frameworks in the Teacher Leadership Literature

Listed below are general models of teacher leadership tasks from leading scholars in this domain, presented in chronological order. In "an extensive study of school-based teacher educators" (Hatfield, 1989, p. 6), Cooper (cited in Hatfield, 1989) identifies the following leadership responsibilities:

Curriculum development

Support systems

Resources

Personnel issues and inservice (p. 6)

From their comprehensive analysis of over 50 activities undertaken by teacher leaders, Hatfield and his team (1986) offer the following "descriptors" (p. 16):

Staff development and consultation responsibilities

Curriculum improvement responsibilities

Administration responsibilities

Policy and planning responsibilities

Evaluation responsibilities (pp. 16–17)

Based on their research, Smylie and Denny (1989) outline four "general descriptions of the types of roles" (p. 5) for teacher leaders:

Being a resource for other teachers and administrators

Planning and leading staff development activities

Leading and assisting in the development of curricula and instructional strategy, and

Serving as a linkage among teachers and administrators (p. 5)

Berry and Ginsberg (1990), in turn, categorize teacher leadership work as follows:

Classroom teaching

Mentoring and coaching other teachers

Appraising the performance of other teachers

Professional development

Peer reviews of school practice, and

Building-level decision making (p. 618)

Strodl (1992) provides an especially useful three-dimensional framework of teacher leadership, focusing on facilitative activities, concept development, and leadership tasks. Employing a somewhat different frame, Rossman (1995, cited in Katzenmeyer & Moller, 2001) furnishes us with the following cluster of roles for teacher leaders:

The "moral steward," who acts on the belief that the purpose of education is to ensure each child's right to reach his or her full potential

The "constructor," who makes sense of the subjects taught, the craft of teaching, and the development of children

The "philosopher," who uses professional commitment to shape the experience of schooling for children

The "facilitator," who enacts the learner-centered classroom, where children integrate their own knowledge construction with that of their peers

The "inquirer," who asks critical questions about what students should learn and have learned

The "bridger," who blurs the boundaries between the classroom and the community

The "changemaker," who advocates for constructive change (pp. 22–23)

Boles and Troen (1996) list five areas of teacher leadership:

Pedagogical innovation

Preservice teacher education

Curriculum development

Research

Governance (p. 51)

From their comprehensive investigation, Leithwood and his colleagues (1997) provide a typology of teacher leadership activity around nine practices:

Performs administrative tasks

Models valued practices

Formal leadership responsibilities

Supports the work of other staff

Visible in the school

Teaching responsibilities

Confronts issues directly/makes hard decisions

Shares leadership with others

Personal relationships (Table 3)

Taking still a different path in his review of the literature, Barth (2001) describes "10 areas in which teacher leadership is essential to the health of a school" (p. 1):

Choosing textbooks and instructional materials

Shaping the curriculum

Setting standards for student behavior

Deciding whether students are tracked into special classes

Designing staff development and inservice programs

Setting promotion and retention policies

Deciding school budgets

Evaluating teacher performance

Selecting new teachers

Selecting new administrators (pp. 1–2)

A Synthetic Design

With a remarkable consistency, teacher leaders identified their roles primarily in terms of helping and supporting fellow teachers within their buildings. (Smylie & Denny, 1989, p. 7)

Teachers are involved in many leadership activities including program-related meetings, school district and building-level decision making, curriculum development, and instructional initiatives. (Strodl, 1992, p. 8)

When we draw an analytic magnet across the scholarship on teacher leadership tasks, activities, functions, and responsibilities, most of the work clusters into two broad related categories: helping teacher colleagues and facilitating school improvement. In the first domain, which is in many ways foundational for the second, teacher leaders work "to create and sustain positive working relations with their colleagues" (Ainscow & Southworth, 1996, p. 233). They "become vehicles for empowering" (Berry & Ginsberg, 1990, p. 618) peers (Snell & Swanson, 2000), laboring diligently to actualize what Ainscow and Southworth (1996) label the "principle of participation" (p. 233), namely, "drawing together the staff" (p. 234) and "facilitat[ing] collaboration on activities and encourag[ing] information sharing" (Hatfield et al., 1986, p. 16).

Perhaps the central dynamic of "providing help and support" (Smylie & Denny, 1989, p. 7) for teacher colleagues is role modeling (Doyle, 2000)—"these teachers . . . lead by example" (Ainscow & Southworth, 1996, p. 233), they are "role models who facilitate the development of those around them" (Boles & Troen, 1996, p. 48). Through their own work, they "reveal to others new ways of doing things" (Rosenholtz, 1989, p. 64) and "a collaborative way of working" (Ainscow & Southworth, 1996, p. 233). They endeavor to "create and sustain a collaborative and collegial atmosphere" (Doyle, 2000, p. 16), "a trusting atmosphere where fellow teachers can try new teaching practices" (p. 15). They "promote change" (Harrison & Lembeck, 1996, p. 112)—or, more specifically, they "positively influence the willingness and capacity of other teachers to implement change in the school" (Leithwood et al., 1997, p. 5)—and they confront the barriers that stand in the way of change efforts (Crowther et al., 2002).

While teacher leaders exercise an array of responsibilities in facilitating school improvement, three broad domains stand out: administrative tasks, staff development activities, and curriculum and instructional functions. To begin with, over the years researchers have consistently reported that administrative tasks are a central element of teacher leadership (Doyle, 2000; Leithwood et al., 1997; Wasley, 1991). On the one hand, given the central place of administrative work in school-level leadership in general, this conclusion is neither surprising nor troubling. On the other hand, as is the case with principal leadership, when administrative responsibilities consume teacher leaders or become disconnected from "educational" leadership, either from the natural turn of events or from the manipulations of formal school leaders, this conclusion is more problematic (Wasley, 1991). A key dimension of the management domain of teacher leadership work, then, is using administration in the service of enhanced learning and teaching and improved organizational performance.

Katzenmeyer and Moller (2001) report that "many teacher leaders step into roles in which they work with colleagues as staff developers" (p. 39). Indeed, teacher leadership for school improvement comes to life when teachers assume responsibility for professional development (Hatfield et al., 1986). Here, teacher leaders take on the tasks of "identify[ing] school and individual teacher growth needs, identifying available resources to assist in meeting those needs" (Fessler & Ungaretti, 1994, p. 216), "offering professional learning experiences, and evaluating the outcomes of teacher development" (Childs-Bowen et al., 2000, p. 30). They are often active in educating preservice teachers (Fessler & Ungaretti, 1994; Troen & Boles, 1994), "induct[ing] new teachers into the school" (Leithwood et al., 1997, p. 5), and serving as "mentors to new faculty" (Katzenmeyer & Moller, 2001, p. 39) and "peer coaches" (Fessler & Ungaretti, 1994, p. 216) to more experienced colleagues. These educators also lead by (1) exercising influence over decisions about professional development and by facilitating professional learning opportunities (Katzenmeyer & Moller, 2001); (2) as noted earlier, modeling the importance of professional development through their own actions (Harrison & Lembeck, 1996; Smylie, 1996); and (3) engaging in informal counseling (Doyle, 2000).

Finally, teacher leaders often assume responsibilities for and perform tasks designed to strengthen the school's curricular and instructional program and learning and teaching in classrooms (Boles & Troen, 1996; Wasley, 1991). They often provide "curriculum assistance in subject specialties . . . and leadership of school-wide . . . curriculum programs" (Hart, 1990, p. 509). Teacher leaders "have an important role to play as curriculum developers" (Fessler & Ungaretti, 1994, p. 217). They also often are "heavily engaged in . . . instructional improvement activities" (Hatfield et al., 1986, p. 15), including "consultations on instructional techniques" (Hart, 1990, p. 509).

We close here by noting that there are certain leadership functions that cut across these three dimensions of "leading for school improvement." One that is ribboned throughout the literature is conducting research with colleagues on the curricular and instructional program (Boles & Troen, 1996; Fessler & Ungaretti, 1994). A second is assuming responsibility for group meetings and "participating in building-level decision making" (Smylie & Denny, 1989,

Table 2). A final cross-cutting function is acting as a "conduit for communication" (Doyle, 2000, p. 34), engaging as a "liaison between the district leaders, principals, and their teachers by communicating each other's needs" (p. 16).

CONCLUSION

In this chapter, in broad strokes we provided a portrait of teacher leaders. With caution about generalizing too freely and with a firm understanding of the limitations of relying only on skills and tasks to define teacher leadership, we nonetheless were able to highlight some commonalities and recurring patterns in our mosaic of teacher leadership. We laid out core principles on which the teacher leadership movement is built. We uncovered a bundle of personal qualities that researchers often find in their studies of teacher leaders. And we reported that there are distinct functions and patterns of tasks often associated with the work of teacher leaders.

CHAPTER FIVE

Pathways to Teacher Leadership

A wide range of efforts to support, acknowledge, reward, or better use teachers' abilities has been attempted from career ladders and merit pay proposals that have aimed to identify outstanding teachers, to differentiated roles like mentor teachers and lead teachers, to the creation of professional networks and other learning communities. (Darling- Hammond et al., 1995, p. 87)

There have been two basic schools of thought regarding approaches to the creation of teacher-leadership roles. One has focused on developing formal programs such as mentor teachers or career ladders. . . . An alternative is to develop teacher leadership on an ad hoc basis. (Conley, 1997, p. 334)

Our thinking about teacher leadership is changing. Since the mid-1990s there has been a shift away from individual empowerment and role-based initiatives toward more collective, task oriented, and organizational approaches to teacher leadership. (Smylie et al., 2002, p. 165)

I t should be clearer as we move more deeply into our analysis that teacher leadership is a complex concept and one that covers a fair portion of the reform landscape. Or, as we capture that reality in this chapter, there are a variety of pathways to teacher leadership. "Opportunities for teacher leadership . . . come from many sources" (Smylie & Brownlee-Conyers, 1992, p. 150) and "from an array of . . . programs and policies" (Smylie, 1996, p. 521); they "have developed in a number of different ways" (Smylie & Denny, 1989, p. 2). Over the last quarter century, "school districts and state departments have experimented with various types of teacher leadership" (Stone et al., 1997, p. 51; Hallinger & Richardson, 1988). As a consequence, "several models have emerged for developing teacher leaders" (Wynne, 2001, p. 1). For organizational purposes, we group these opportunities and models into two broad pathways: role-based strategies and community-based approaches. We organize the narrative around a set of variables that allows us to illustrate and define each of the pathways (see Table 5.1).

Table 5.1   Pathways to Teacher Leadership

	Role-Based Strategies		Community-Based Strategies	
Domains	Teacher Career Strategies	Broadening Administrative Structures and Roles	Shared Leadership	Communities of Practice
Architecture	structural/hierarchical/ institutional		organic/communal/cultural	
View of Leadership	individually based		organizational property/ professional phenomenon	
Focus	management/administrative		instruction and learning	
Foundation	administrative prerogative		community product	
Influence Base	legitimacy/control		expertise/social capital	
Scope	targeted work/limited		distributed/generalized	
Nature of Work	activities performed by those in formal roles		work as ingrained in teacher role of all	
Accountability	to administrators (bureaucratic)		to colleagues (professional)	
Nature	formal/competitive		informal/ingrained/cooperative	
Dynamic	planned		emergent	
Expression	from the point, organizational		from a web of relationships	
Duration	limited		ongoing	
Relationships	thin/separation from peers		deep/collaborative	
Impact	minimal		unknown	

ROLE-BASED STRATEGIES

> The teacher leadership initiatives of this period were closely associated with role-based theories and models of individual work redesign and job enhancement. (Smylie et al., 2002, p. 165)

It should come as no surprise to learn that when policymakers, school administrators, and advocates for teacher professionalism began their struggle to forge an ideology of shared leadership and models of teacher leadership, they turned to the knowledge base and organizational frameworks that dominated schooling at the time. That is, they cobbled together an understanding of teacher leadership from raw material culled from prevailing views of leadership and organizations. Given the dominance of the hierarchically anchored organizational designs and the bureaucratically grounded conceptions of leadership that we described in great detail in earlier chapters, it is understandable that role-based models comprised the major pathway to actualize teacher leadership in schools throughout the nation for much of the 1980s and early 1990s.

Initiatives undertaken to foster teacher leadership were constructed using "institutional" (McLaughlin & Yee, 1988, p. 23) and "organizational" (Smylie et al., 2002, p. 165) blueprints. Thus when teacher leadership began to move toward center stage with the arrival of the restructuring and professionalization reform agendas of the mid-1980s, "one prominent suggestion was to capitalize on school-level positions that—at least in name, if not always practice—already present[ed] opportunities for teacher leadership" (Little, 1988, p. 96). And research confirms that teachers themselves began to "define teacher leadership in terms of traditional roles with which they were familiar—union representatives, department heads, and committee chairs" (Wasley, 1991, p. 52). Thus initial efforts in this area focused on "assign[ing] teachers to formal leadership roles within schools" (Odell, 1997, p. 120)—formal roles such as "lead/master/mentor teachers and the forms of differentiated teacher staffing including career ladders" (p. 120).

Types of Programs

During the past several years a wide variety of new jobs have been created to supplement the work of the superintendent, principal, and . . . coordinators. (Hatfield et al., 1986, p. 1)

A key feature of career ladders is the differentiation of teacher roles to provide opportunities for teacher leadership. (Fessler & Ungaretti, 1994, p. 220)

As can be seen in Table 5.1, two overlapping designs are featured in the role-based pathway to teacher leadership: career-based strategies and "broadened school leadership structure[s]" (Little, 1995, p. 49). While the concepts of differentiated staffing and career-based models of teacher leadership enjoy an extensive history (Christensen, 1987; Fessler & Ungaretti, 1994), they became central characters in the school reform play in the mid-1980s with the release of the Holmes Group (1986) and Carnegie Forum (1986) reports. Career approaches to teacher leadership attack "the unstaged nature of . . . teaching" (Rowley, 1988, p. 16). They create "upward movement" (McLaughlin & Yee, 1988, p. 26), "vertical progress" (Fessler & Ungaretti, 1994, p. 220), and "staged careers" (Johnson, 1989, p. 95). These strategies provide "a hierarchical, institutionally structured notion of a career" (McLaughlin & Yee, 1988, p. 26)—as opposed to the existing "horizontal" (p. 25) and "incredibly flat career structure" (Berry & Ginsberg, 1990, p. 617)—that is "individually constructed and experienced (McLaughlin & Yee, 1988, p. 26). "Such models provide for differentiated roles for teachers as they move up a ladder of responsibility and leadership" (Fessler & Ungaretti, 1994, p. 220). For example, the Holmes Group (1986) proposed the development of a three-phase career of instructor, professional teacher, and career professional (pp. 8–9). The Association of Teacher Educators (1985, cited in Christensen, 1987) developed a model that "includes the steps of teacher, associate teacher, senior teacher, and master teacher" (p. 101). The Rochester, New York, school district implemented a "four-tier profession" (Urbanski & Nickolaou, 1997, p. 250) of intern teacher, resident teacher, professional teacher, and career teacher (p. 250). Fessler and Ungaretti (1994) introduced the extra step of "clinical faculty member" (p. 221), positions that "provide an opportunity for teachers to connect to university teacher education programs" (p. 221; Morris & Nunnery, 1994).

Under differentiated staffing, "teachers assume leadership roles with increasing responsibility, higher pay, and greater, more flexible accountability" (Rallis, 1990, p. 197). A key issue here is that all these career-based "approaches provide specific strategies for empowering teachers for leadership" (Fessler & Ungaretti, 1994, p. 220) and "outlets for leadership in such areas as mentoring, teacher-led inservice and staff development, and teacher research" (p. 214), responsibilities we delineated in considerable detail in the last chapter.

Efforts to broaden leadership structures, in turn, focus on connecting teachers to new or expanded roles, roles which appear as nodes on the organizational chart. The focus is less on the "hierarchically arrayed positions" (Broyles, 1991, p. 3) that define career-based efforts to develop teacher leadership and more on establishing "a richer pool of professional opportunities" (p. 3) for teachers, on "enlarg[ing] teachers' roles and responsibilities beyond their regular classroom assignments" (Smylie & Denny, 1989, p. 4). For example, Fessler and Ungaretti (1994) assert that "modest adaptations of role structures that provide opportunities for teacher leadership include the creation of such positions as team leaders, grade-level leaders, and chairs of staff development committees" (p. 220). Efforts here include reenergizing "existing legitimized leadership roles for teachers" (Conley, 1997, p. 336), such as the department head (Little, 1995), as well as bringing new leadership roles on line, such as school reform facilitators (Berends, Bodilly, & Kirby, 2002; Datnow & Castellano, 2002; Smylie et al., 2002). By and large, broadened roles line up nicely with the teacher leadership tasks that we described in Chapter 4. Conley (1997), Jandura and Burke (1989), and Killion (1996) provide especially helpful taxonomies of role-based teacher leadership (see also Hynes et al., 1992; Stone et al., 1997; Yarger & Lee, 1994). As an example, Conley (1997) describes the following teacher leadership roles:

- club sponsor/coach/student leadership advisor
- protégé to a mentor
- peer observer/peer coach
- chair or member of committee or site council

- department (or division) chair/coordinator
- lead teacher
- association representative
- teacher researcher
- staff developer
- curriculum developer
- educational entrepreneur
- reflective practitioner
- administrative intern
- mentor (pp. 335–343)

Role-Based Scaffolding

These positions are creations of, and quickly blend into, the bureaucratic hierarchy. (Forster, 1997, p. 84)

Efforts to create new, more professional places for teachers to work and students to learn have attended primarily to the structural features of school organizations. (Smylie & Hart, 1999, p. 421)

Table 5.1 captures the infrastructure supporting both role-based and community-grounded pathways to teacher leadership. It is at this level of analysis that the dynamics of the different approaches can be seen most clearly. We begin with the observation that the architecture of role-based approaches to teacher leadership is structural in form, that it is institutionally and organizationally focused (Hart, 1995). It reflects a "hierarchical orientation" (Livingston, 1992, p. 12) and underscores the importance of "formal roles and positions" (Snell & Swanson, 2000, p. 3). It acknowledges that many "of the suggestions for teacher leadership positions are hierarchical in nature" (Wasley, 1991, p. 22). Role-based designs represent a type of "division-of-labor model" (Firestone, 1996, p. 411; Forster, 1997), an approach in which "several roles perform functions . . . in a discrete manner" (Firestone, 1996, p. 411). In the role-based pathway, teachers often "occupy legitimate, paid leadership positions" (Miller, 1988, p. 181). The "bureaucratic forms of teacher leadership [often] . . . simply create a few more slots in an already isolating and compartmentalized structure" (Darling-Hammond et al., 1995,

p. 103). Teachers, in effect, are "require[d] to fit the designated leadership mold" (p. 95). Teacher leaders often "become little line supervisors" (Livingston, 1992, p. 12).

Deeply embedded in the framework of role-based teacher leadership is an individually grounded conception of leadership (Smylie & Hart, 1999), one that depends on "individual empowerment" (Smylie et al., 2002, p. 163). As with other formal leadership positions in the organizational structure, "development has focused at the level of the individual teacher leader" (Smylie & Denny, 1989, p. 2). Leadership is a property of individual educators, not an element of the school as an organization (Smylie et al., 2002). Teacher leaders are generally isolated (Forster, 1997). They regularly work alone (Boles & Troen, 1994). While there is a broad conception of the work to be accomplished, considerable attention is lavished on management responsibilities and administrative tasks (Forster, 1997; Smylie & Denny, 1989), on "running the system." There is often a good deal of "administrative and quasi-supervisory" (McLaughlin & Yee, 1988, p. 24) work in role-based models of teacher leadership.

Role-based teacher leadership is founded on administrative prerogative (Smylie, 1995; Wasley, 1991): leadership roles often "exist at the prerogative of the principal" (Stone et al., 1997, p. 51). Teachers are "formally appointed to new roles" (Darling-Hammond et al., 1995, p. 88). Traditional views of teachers as implementers rather than as initiators generally hold (Darling-Hammond et al., 1995). Teachers are still seen as objects rather than as agents (Johnson, 1989). For example, Wasley (1991) has documented a "disturbing silence in the voice of the teachers these [leadership] roles are intended to support" (p. 150) in regard to the "design, selection, and evaluation of these positions" (p. 150). There is generally a direct and primary line of responsibility from teacher leaders not to peers but to formal school leaders (Wasley, 1991). Influence and accountability follow the organizational chart. Power is not derived from other teachers, and bureaucratic rather than professional accountability dominates. By design, the scope of work for any given teacher is limited (Sherrill, 1999). Role-based pathways tend to target select numbers of teachers (Berry & Ginsberg, 1990), "to provide special privileges to a few" (Darling-Hammond et al., 1995, p. 104). "The authority of the vast majority of teachers [is] assumed not to change" (p. 88).

There is considerable formality associated with role-based teacher leadership (Hart, 1995), with responsibilities often being captured "through contractual agreement" (Hallinger & Richardson, 1988, p. 240) and work being linked to "formal roles or positions" (Snell & Swanson, 2000, p. 3). Role-based teacher leadership is more planned than emergent. Teacher leadership responsibilities are often "bestowed on some teachers for a given period of time under limited circumstances" (Forster, 1997, p. 82). Leadership is exercised "from the point," organizationally rather than collegially. Since competition rather than collaboration defines these role-based designs (Little, 1988), relationships with teacher colleagues are often shallow (Stone et al., 1997). Indeed, "teachers assuming these new roles usually find themselves set apart from their peers" (Forster, 1997, p. 84; Livingston, 1992). Finally, evidence of positive impact, especially for career-based approaches is thin (Berry & Ginsberg, 1990; Crow & Pounder, 2000). Or as Smylie and his colleagues (2002) sum up the narrative here, "the evidence on the effectiveness of the individual empowerment, role-based teacher leadership initiatives of the 1980s and early 1990s is equivocal at best" (p. 165).

COMMUNITY-BASED STRATEGIES

> Even though the idea of teacher leadership has been around for quite some time, our thinking about its form, its function, and its role in school improvement has evolved considerably. In the past 10 years several new approaches to teacher leadership have emerged. (Smylie et al., 2002, p. 163).

> The essence of teacher leadership is found in leadership *acts* rather than in leadership roles. (O'Hair & Reitzug, 1997, p. 67)

In this section, we describe the second pathway to teacher leadership, a pathway that "extends the definition of teacher leadership" (Boles & Troen, 1994, p. 27) and incorporates "alternative forms" (p. 27), one that "moves past the idea of leadership as manifested in individuals occupying formal positions to more dynamic, organizational views of leadership" (Smylie et al., 2002, p. 167), to what we label "community-based strategies." Here we find that the concept of teacher leadership is "reconfigured to be inclusive" (Darling-Hammond et al., 1995, p. 98). It is anchored in the belief "that all individuals in the school community have knowledge that can contribute to and enhance the work of the school" (O'Hair & Reitzug, 1997, p. 70) and that "teacher leadership needs to apply to all teachers in all schools" (Odell, 1997, p. 122). That is, there are a variety of opportunities for teachers to exercise leadership (Childs-Bowen et al., 2000; Lieberman & Miller, 1999). While space limitations preclude the individual treatment of each of the two community-based, teacher leadership strategies (shared leadership and communities of practice), we do expose the scaffolding that supports these perspectives collectively.

Community-Based Scaffolding

There is growing attention to other less positional, less structured, emergent forms of teacher leadership. (Smylie, 1995, p. 4)

We are interested in the exercise of leadership beyond the boundaries arising from hierarchical models of organization and traditional views of teachers' roles. (Frost & Durrant, 2003a, p. 174)

As was the case in the discussion above, we turn to Table 5.1 to help expose the pillars on which community-based strategies of teacher leadership are constructed. We begin by recounting that "most attention and . . . research on teacher leadership are focused on formal leadership roles" (Buckner & McDowelle, 2000, p. 36; O'Hair & Reitzug, 1997). That is, "we usually think of teacher leadership as a formal process" (Whitaker, 1995, p. 78) and as "traditional, officially defined, prestructured, 'add-on' leadership positions" (Darling-Hammond et al., 1995, p. 90). We also observe, however, that the architecture here encourages "new forms of teacher leadership" (p. 87) and strategies that are "organic instead of formalistic" (Fullan, 1994, p. 245; Broyles, 1991). Community-based teacher leadership blueprints acknowledge that "the realities of practice for teacher leaders are much more challenging and complex" (Sherrill, 1999, p. 57) than earlier reform models suggested. Designers here express a wariness about "empowerment proceed[ing] along one very narrow axis" (Greer, 1989, p. 297), of creating "new hierarchies that . . . simply mimic the current administrative structures" (Johnson, 1989, p. 109). They steer clear of defining teacher leadership in ways that "establish hierarchical, patriarchal model[s]" (Fay, 1992a, p. 17), "create artificial, imposed formal hierarchies" (Darling-Hammond et al., 1995, p. 87), and privilege "bureaucratic forms of teacher leadership" (p. 103; Berry & Ginsberg, 1990).

Community-based teacher leadership strategies "shift our attention away from individual and role-based conceptions of leadership" (Smylie et al., 2002, p. 172). There is a shift in focus "beyond the person and the role" (p. 172) and from the "formal empowerment of individual teachers" (Odell, 1997, p. 121) to "leadership tasks, behaviors, and functions" (Smylie et al., 2002, p. 172) and to "the importance of the teaching context and organizational development of schools" (Odell, 1997, p. 121). As a consequence, "teacher leadership is not experienced in isolation but rather is linked with development in schools" (Zimpher, 1988, p. 54). The center of interest is less about "moving into a few administratively designated leadership positions and more on enlarging other professional roles" (Boles & Troen, 1994, p. 22). Attention is directed to the "exercise of leadership on the part of those who do not necessarily hold power or authority by virtue of their formal position" (Frost & Durrant, 2003a, p. 174).

Analysts of this pathway explore how leadership functions are "carved out by multiple individuals in different roles in redundant, mutually reinforcing" (Smylie et al., 2002, p. 173) ways. They "redefine teacher leadership as a fundamental principle and function of the teaching role" (Forster, 1997, p. 86). Teacher leadership is formulated as "more than a role; it is a *stance*, a mind-set, a way of being, acting, and thinking as a learner within a community of learners" (Darling-Hammond et al., 1995, p. 95; O'Hair & Reitzug, 1997). The idea of the "school as a center of inquiry" (Lieberman & Miller, 1999, p. 74) trumps hierarchy. "Institutional [and] structural" (McLaughlin & Yee, 1988, p. 24) issues and "organizational and production metaphors" (Livingston, 1992, p. 14) are pushed into the background. In community-grounded approaches to teacher leadership, "teachers assume leadership naturally as part of a more professional conception of work" (Darling-Hammond et al., 1995, p. 88): "Teacher leaders . . . emerge as a matter of course in informally structured positions along with a communi-tarian social system for schools" (Odell, 1997, p. 121). The calcu-lus shifts from filling roles to "creat[ing] an interactive community of teachers collaborating for improvement and experimentation in their schools" (Boles & Troen, 1996, p. 48), to "creating collabora-tive work cultures" (Fullan, 1994, p. 247) and "community-related approach[es] to enhancing teaching and learning" (Griffin, 1995, p. 37).

Leadership is viewed as an organizational property and a professional phenomenon, as both "distributed performance on tasks or functions" (Smylie et al., 2002, p. 173) and "as an organization-wide resource of power and influence" (p. 173). The focus on "a designated leader or two" (Uline & Berkowitz, 2000, p. 439) gives way to more "collegial" (Griffin, 1995, p. 37), "collective" (Boles & Troen, 1994, p. 21), and collabora-tive and team-based designs (Barth, 2001): "leadership functions as a collective as opposed to an individual enterprise" (Smylie, 1995, p. 5). There is an "ascendancy of collective will . . . over individual autonomy with regard to matters of professional prac-tice" (Little, 1995, p. 52). In community-anchored pathways, "leadership is defined less by the actions of single leaders than by a set of leadership tasks shared across a broad segment of a school community" (Smylie et al., 2002, p. 171).

The focus here, more so than in role-based strategies, is on issues of learning and teaching rather than on administrative activities and management functions (Odell, 1997; Rosenholtz, 1989); it is less "managerial in nature" (Forster, 1997, p. 87). There is a recognition that "to professionalize teaching is not to make it something other than teaching" (Johnson, 1989, p. 110). Teacher leadership here "means that teachers work with teachers and focus their time and energy on the investigation of challeng-ing instructional strategies" (Wasley, 1991, p. 170).

Community-based approaches to teacher leadership operate from a different foundation as well. These strategies acknowledge that "the processes used to select teacher leaders are important" (Wasley, 1991, p. 150). Indeed, "perhaps the most important issue deals with who creates [and] selects . . . teacher leaders" (p. 145). This pathway recognizes the weaknesses of administra-tive appointments, "the incongruity between those selecting and those being represented/benefiting from the actual role"

(Hatfield et al., 1986, p. 18), as well as the fact that "teachers are [generally] unresponsive to top-down efforts to improve their instruction through administratively created teacher leadership positions" (Wasley, 1991, p. 160). The community-based pathway builds from a more extensive foundation than the administrative prerogative that often defines role-based approaches to teacher leadership (Hatfield et al., 1986). In community-based approaches, we often find that "teacher leadership emerges and grows rather than being appointed or assigned" (Darling-Hammond et al., 1995, p. 100). When more formal approaches are employed, teachers play a key role in developing that work and selecting those colleagues who will perform it (Katzenmeyer & Moller, 2001).

The influence that powers teacher leadership has less to do with legitimate authority connected to role than with expertise (Fessler & Ungaretti, 1994), experience (Duke, 1994), and "passion for teaching" (Katzenmeyer & Moller, 2001, p. 6). Or, as Little (1995) remarks, community-based strategies "establish the importance of subject expertise as a warrant for teacher leadership" (p. 55). The authority of teacher leadership "cannot rest on the basis of formal positionality and, instead, must stem from credibility as expert classroom practitioners" (Snell & Swanson, 2000, p. 4). Thus personal power bases—the type of power that "is the result of the actions of the individual" (Katzenmeyer & Moller, 2001, p. 25)—are heavily underscored while positional power bases—"power a person receives through formal authority" (p. 25)—are downplayed. Influence is often expressed in a "subtle, quiet, and behind the scene" (Duke, 1994, p. 266) manner. Servant leadership (Pellicer & Anderson, 1995) and leading by example or modeling (Silva et al., 2000; Snell & Swanson, 2000; Wasley, 1991)are highly visible in community-based approaches to teacher leadership.

As should be clear from the analysis presented above, the scope of work in the community pathway is different than in the role-based pathway. In the latter designs, we observed that the scope of work was quite focused and limited to a "few designated teacher leaders" (Odell, 1997, p. 120), that it was circumscribed and possessed an exclusive quality. In community-based designs, "there is an awareness that all teachers can assume leadership responsibilities" (Hart & Baptist, 1996, p. 98) and efforts are made to "engage all teachers in leadership activities" (Katzenmeyer & Moller, 2001, p. 29). In these designs, "leadership is configured to be inclusive . . . and is available to significantly more teachers" (Boles & Troen, 1994, p. 21; Forster, 1997; Suleiman & Moore, 1997): "teacher leadership is more inclusive in that the need to encourage all teachers to be 'change agents' is addressed, whether or not they have . . . a formal role" (Frost & Durrant, 2003a, p. 176). Community-based approaches "redefine the job of teaching as one in which all teachers engage in decision making" (Darling-Hammond et al., 1995, p. 88). Teacher leadership "becomes a more normative role for all teachers in the school" (Odell, 1997, p. 121). Schools become "leadership-dense organizations" (Lieberman & Miller, 1999, p. 46).

Consistent with this analysis, we find that in community-based strategies work tends to be as much "natural and informal" (Odell, 1997, p. 121) as it is captured in a "set of formal roles" (Snell & Swanson, 2000, p. 3); it is emergent, voluntary, and informal (Katzenmeyer & Moller, 20001; Lieberman, 1992; Wasley, 1991). Teachers "assume leadership naturally as part of a more professional conception of teaching work" (Darling-Hammond et al., 1995, p. 88). Work is "collaborative" (LeBlanc & Shelton, 1997, p. 44) and collective rather than individualistic and competitive (Dana, 1991; Faye, 1992a; Mitchell, 1997). Teacher leadership work is as much about "promoting inquiry" (O'Hair & Reitzug, 1997, p. 69) as it is about furnishing answers. Leadership is seen "as a central role of teaching" (Forster, 1997, p. 89). As a consequence, "the 'normal' role of the teacher is expanded" (Darling-Hammond et al., 1995, p. 87). The web of relationships in schools with community-based teacher leadership designs is richer and more complex. Relationships tend to be more inclusive and more collaborative (Frost & Durrant, 2003b; Wasley, 1991).

It will come as little surprise to learn that teacher leadership strategies that feature community rather than hierarchy promote "norms of collective responsibility" (Smylie & Hart, 1999, p. 427) and "mutual accountability" (Frost & Durrant, 2003a, p. 174)—accountability that is more professionally grounded than bureaucratically anchored. In a similar vein, these shared and community-based strategies tend to be less discrete and less bound by time parameters. Rather, leadership here is an aspect of ongoing work; "teacher-leadership becomes a fluid role"

(Childs-Bowen et al., 2000, p. 28). As such, teacher leadership responsibilities are as much emergent as they are planned (Lieberman, 1992; Miller, 1992; Smylie, 1995). They often are "not prescribed a priori but are varied, flexible, and idiosyncratic to individual school[s]" (Darling-Hammond et al., 1995, p. 103). Work often evolves on an "ad hoc basis" (Conley, 1997, p. 334) as a "natural outgrowth of professional interests" (Boles & Troen, 1994, p. 11). Teacher leadership often has an "evolutionary and open nature" (Miller, 1992, p. 123). As such, it is often "unstructured" (Whitaker, 1995, p. 78).

Data on the impact of community-based teacher leadership strategies is limited. While there is a widespread belief "that teacher leadership can have a wide range of impacts" (Frost & Durrant, 2003a, p. 174), that it will "improve productivity conditions in schools" (Little, 1988, p. 84) and "lead to dramatic and permanent changes in American schools" (Kelley, 1994, p. 312) as well as recurring acknowledgments about the importance of evaluating teacher leadership positions (Wasley, 1991), the knowledge base on how teacher leadership is "really influencing change" (p. 150)—or not—is quite thin.

CONCLUSION

In this chapter, we examine the two broad-based pathways to teacher leadership—role-based strategies and community-based approaches. We outlined in some detail the scaffolding supporting each of these designs.

PART II

Overcoming Barriers and Capturing Opportunities

CHAPTER SIX

Confronting Organizational and Cultural Barriers

A . . . challenge is to introduce a new role to an institution and occupation. (Little, 1988, p. 103)

As theory and research on work redesign suggest, new opportunities for teacher participation in decision making may implicate a broad range of professional beliefs and working relationships within schools. (Smylie, 1992, p. 65)

Until spaces are made for teacher leadership and the culture is created to support teacher leadership, there will be few stories of successful . . . teacher leadership. (Silva et al., 2000, p. 802)

In Part II, we examine a collection of organizational conditions and cultural dynamics that can, paradoxically (Wasley, 1991), either promote or inhibit the growth of teacher leadership in schools. The focus is on the relationship between what Hart (1990) describes as "context dimensions" (p. 527) and teacher leadership—the "organizational environment and school contexts in which teachers can develop and be sustained in leadership roles" (Katzenmeyer & Moller, 2001, p. 124). We start the discussion in this chapter by providing a broad overview of organizational variables and cultural and professional norms. In Chapter 7, we address the special role principals play in ensuring the successful infusion of shared leadership in schools. In Chapter 8, the analytic spotlight is directed on the critical function of professional development for teacher leaders.

Our point of departure for Part II is that "the conventions of school contexts" (Griffin, 1995, p. 44) and school social conditions exert a dramatic influence on "conceptions of collegial leadership" (Rosenholtz, 1989, p. 64)—that "organizational components" (Doyle, 2000, p. 22) such as structure, support, and culture are explanatory variables in the teacher leadership equation. Or as Rosenholtz (1989) concluded in her landmark volume on teacher work, "teachers, like members of most organizations, shape their beliefs and actions largely in conformance with the structures, policies, and traditions of the workday world around them" (pp. 2–3).

The next link in our chain of analysis is that "crippling impediments" (Barth, 2001, p. 444), "barriers" (Mitchell, 1997, p. 2), and "myriad difficulties and obstacles confront the institutionalization of teacher leadership" (Boles & Troen, 1996, p. 61), and that these "barriers . . . exist at all levels" (Manthei, 1992, p. 17). These obstructions can be clustered into the broad categories of "structural conditions in schools" (Mitchell, 1997, p. 1), support for teacher leadership, and occupational and professional norms.

On a general front, the literature confirms that "the way [schools] are organized, structurally and normatively, is not amenable to experimentation . . . or rethinking" (Fullan, 1994, p. 243), "that organizations possess powerful conserving forces that often make persistence paramount to change" (Smylie, 1995, p. 6). More specifically, that "the culture and organization of many schools does not readily foster the spirit of collaboration" (Snell & Swanson, 2000, p. 13)—"that environments that support and nurture teacher leadership are not endemic to many schools" (Crowther et al., 2002, p. vii), and that "deep structures of symbols, routines, norms, and conventions" (Smylie, 1995, p. 6) and "tenacious habits of mind and deed make the achievement of strong collegial relations a remarkable accomplishment: not the rule, but the rare, often fragile exception" (Little, 1987, p. 493).

Scholars in the area of teacher leadership have consistently discovered that "teacher leadership activities have been thwarted by 'constraining contexts'" (Mitchell, 1997, p. 2). This is the case, as we recount below, because teacher leadership workplace reform proposals challenge long-standing and deeply rooted patterns of teacher isolation and autonomy. They defy most "cultural, institutional, and occupational precedents" (Little, 1988, pp. 80–81; Hart, 1990; Rosenholtz, 1989).

The final plank in our argument is that if it is true "that teacher leadership occurs most readily in supportive organizational environments" (Crowther et al., 2002, p. vii), in environments that permit and encourage teachers to lead (Lambert, 2003), then "we must change the culture and structure of schools so that they value developing teachers over developing efficient and effective structure" (Silva et al., 2000, p. 802). Success in instilling teacher leadership is dependent on "addressing the school as an organizational context into which new leadership is introduced and exercised" (Smylie & Denny, 1989, p. 3) and on "changing many components of the profession" (Manthei, 1992, p. 17). We must pay attention to the structural and cultural barriers and attend to the task of "designing a healthy context for teacher leadership" (Katzenmeyer & Moller, 2001, p. 124): "schools must be organized so the promise of this reform can be fulfilled" (Berry & Ginsberg, 1990, p. 619).

Our analysis unfolds under the three domains introduced above: structure, support, and culture.

ORGANIZATIONAL STRUCTURE

It is amazing that teacher leadership is possible in schools as they are currently structured. (Katzenmeyer & Moller, 2001, p. 81)

It is unlikely that these new approaches to teacher leadership will be effective if they are not supported by the broader organizational and institutional contexts in which they develop and function. (Smylie et al., 2002, p. 183)

Without a great deal of change in the workplace of schools, needed institutionalization of teacher leadership will not occur. (Yarger & Lee, 1994, p. 234)

Scholars who ply the domain of organizations have carefully documented how "the structure of the organization directs and defines the flow and pattern of human interactions in the organization" (B. L. Johnson, 1998, p. 13), how "the work-related attitudes, activities, and behaviors of teachers and principals are functions of the organizational contexts of the schools in which they work" (Smylie & Brownlee-Conyers, 1992, p. 155). Because "organizational contexts" (Doyle, 2000, p. 19) and "the actual organizational structure" (Katzenmeyer & Moller, 2001, p. 79) reflect important values and beliefs, they exercise considerable pull on shared leadership in a school, primarily through their "impact [on] school community and school change" (Doyle, 2000, p. 19). Indeed, there is plentiful evidence that organizational conditions are critical to the effectiveness, or lack thereof, of teacher leaders (Hatfield et al., 1986): "the organizational contexts of schools have substantial influence on the performance and outcomes of teacher leadership" (Smylie, 1996, p. 575).

Unfortunately, as we explore below, this context—"the organizational structure of schools" (Kowalski, 1995, p. 244)—with its "organizational and structural barriers" (Chrispeels, 1992, p. 75) has regularly "bedeviled . . . efforts to develop teacher leadership" (Smylie et al., 2002, p. 183). "Organizational characteristics [and] structural components can adversely impact the work of teacher leaders" (Silva et al., 2000, p. 790) and "impediments . . . found within . . . the organizational structures" (Duke, 1994, p. 269) of schools exercise a powerful dampening influence on shared leadership. The disheartening result is that "given the present structure of schools, it is difficult for teachers to view themselves as leaders or to view one another as leaders" (Coyle, 1997, p. 238).

In particular, analysts suggest that "the highly bureaucratic, axiomatic configuration of schools" (Suleiman & Moore, 1997, p. 3), with its "hierarchical culture of authority" (Lambert, 2003, p. 32), creates a framework that does not accommodate the behaviors associated with "new roles and norms" (Keedy, 1999, p. 787) and tends to "stifle . . . possibilities for teacher leaders to be effective change agents" (Wynne, 2001, p. 1). Specifically, reviewers maintain that with their emphasis on "the hierarchical nature of teaching . . . based on the nineteenth-century industrial model" (Boles & Troen, 1994, p. 9), "schools are not set up to accept teachers in leadership roles and often actually discourage teachers from taking on additional responsibility" (Smyser, 1995, p. 130). They conclude that "the traditional organizational setting of schools" (Rallis, 1990, p. 193) throws roadblocks in the way of developing distributed leadership.

A number of dimensions of the organizational dynamic merit attention. First, in a real sense, the current structure of schooling has worked—if not to educate all youngsters well, then at least to help meet the goal of universal access. Second, existing organizational arrangements benefit some people: actors who are not simply willing to promote the development of new structures and forms in which their deep-seated values are undermined and advantaged positions are negated (Crowther et al., 2002). For example, Little (1995) does an excellent job of exploring this issue in the context of the department structure at the high school level.

Third, for most educators, the current organizational system is the only one they have known. It is difficult to move to the unknown even when one can glimpse its contours. In addition, even if the change process can be engaged, there are strong inclinations to regress to the familiar. As Lieberman and Miller (1999) remind us, "new behaviors are difficult to acquire, and in the end it is easier to return to old habits than to embrace new ones" (p. 126); needed changes are often "abandoned in favor of more familiar and more satisfying routines" (Little, 1987, p. 493). Or as Heller (1994) observes, "people become used to a hierarchical structure which can be comforting. Someone else is responsible. Someone else takes the blame, finds the money, obtains the permission, and has the headaches" (p. 289).

Fourth, the current arrangements are not especially malleable (Donaldson, 2001). The "forces of organizational persistence" (Smylie & Hart, 1999, p. 421) and "institutional precedent" (Smylie, 1992, p. 55) are quite robust. Hierarchy has an extensive and deep root structure and enjoys a good deal of legitimacy (Murphy, Beck, Crawford, Hodges, & McGaughy, 2001). The system also displays considerable capacity to engage in the ritual of change (Meyer & Rowan, 1975) and to absorb new ideas and initiatives in ways that leave existing organizational structures largely unaffected (Cohen, 1988; Elmore, 1987; Weick, 1976). Finally, while some currents buoy concepts such as decentralization and professionalism that undergird shared leadership, equally powerful if not stronger currents support the movement to centralization and to the hardening of the hierarchical forms of schooling that "are having a challenging effect on the teaching profession and on the inclination and ability of teachers to assume broad leadership within their schools" (Barth, 2001, p. 445). Thus, while it is discouraging, it should not be surprising given the dynamics described above that "in many cases teachers and administrators have actively resisted the creation and implementation of these new [teacher leadership] roles" (Boles & Troen, 1994, p. 8).

Turning specifically to the dynamics of hierarchy, reviewers have observed that the "organizational structure makes it . . . inappropriate for a teacher to assume leadership" (Troen & Boles, 1994, p. 276), that "the school's bureaucratic structure makes it difficult for teachers to define and legitimate forms of leadership that are fully consistent with teaching's egalitarian culture" (Little, 1995, p. 55). Especially problematic for teacher leadership are the following ideas embedded in hierarchical structures: "the notion of a single leader" (Moller & Katzenmeyer, 1996, p. 6); "traditional patterns of relationships" (Conley, 1989, p. 2) featuring a boss and subordinates; the idea that the leader is "synonymous with boss" (Moller & Katzenmeyer, 1996, p. 4); and the metaphor of leader as supervisor (Myers, 1970).

Hierarchical organizations also define power and authority in ways that dampen the viability of shared leadership (Clark & Meloy, 1989; Sergiovanni, 1991b; Sykes & Elmore, 1989). Specifically, by defining authority in centralized (Fay, 1992a) and solitary terms (Barth, 1988b), the traditional structure of schools "simply does not support teacher decision making" (Rallis, 1990, p. 193). It leaves teachers "with very limited power in making decisions outside their own classrooms" (Smyser, 1995, p. 132). By configuring authority "as a 'zero-sum game'" (Boles & Troen, 1994, p. 10), "unyielding bureaucracies" (Suleiman & Moore, 1997, p. 3) make it "difficult for teacher leaders to emerge in schools" (Boles & Troen, 1994, p. 10). Simply put, "the hierarchical structure of schools works against multilevel access to policy debate and decision making" (Manthei, 1992, p. 15).

Bureaucracies also exert negative force on the health of shared leadership through the use of structures that isolate teachers, structures that reinforce core professional norms such as autonomy, equality, and privacy (Darling-Hammond, 1988) and that "work against the development of teacher leadership" (Urbanski & Nickolaou, 1997, p. 244). Two elements are featured in these structures: time schedules (Coyle, 1997) and systems for dividing up work responsibilities (Pellicer & Anderson, 1995; Printy, 2004). Both of these strands promote segmentation (Katzenmeyer & Moller, 2001). They slot teachers into self-contained classrooms (Buckner & McDowelle, 2000). All of this promotes the use of an "egg crate" (Boles & Troen, 1996, p. 59) structure that "buttress[es] teaching as a private endeavor" (Little, 1990, p. 530) that (1) "block[s] teachers' ability to work together" (Silva et al., 2000, p. 789)—that makes it "difficult for teachers to engage with other teachers" (Katzenmeyer & Moller, 2001, p. 67) and "makes genuine interdependence among teachers rare" (Little & McLaughlin, 1993b, p. 2)—and (2) promotes "individual rather than collective accountability" (Duke, 1994, p. 270). The consequence is "an assemblage of entrepreneurial individuals" (Little, 1990, p. 530) who "rather than work[ing] collectively on their problems . . . must struggle alone" (Lieberman et al., 1988, p. 151).

Unions as a piece of the organizational mosaic require attention here. At the macro level, unions can act as a brake on the development of teacher leadership throughout the profession (Pellicer & Anderson, 1995; Stone et al., 1997). This is most likely to occur when teacher leadership is seen as unsettling well-established patterns of collective bargaining (Wasley, 1991). At the micro level, "union contracts can be another challenge to teacher leadership" (Blegen & Kennedy, 2000, p. 5). By design, bureaucracy in general and labor relations in particular separate school administrators and teachers. And given that divide, it is not clear why teachers would gravitate to schoolwide leadership positions (Barth, 1988a, 1988b). More likely is the possibility that "the tension that exists between teacher unions and school district administrators [will] discourage teachers from engaging in roles beyond the classroom" (Killion, 1996, p. 75). And under existing structures and relationships, "the possibility that teacher leadership might actually mean union control" (Institute for Educational Leadership, 2001, p. 6) is not lost on school administrators. Clearly, if teacher leadership is to flourish, hierarchical perspectives of labor embedded in school organizations will need to experience a transformation, as will "labor-management relationships" (Boles & Troen, 1994, p. 8).

In the end, because (1) "new teacher leadership roles challenge the very structure of schools" (Whitaker, 1997, p. 2), (2) schools as currently organized have a "leadership resistant architecture" (Donaldson, 2001, p. 11), and (3) "the efforts of teacher leaders . . . will be only as successful as the bureaucracy allows them to be" (Pellicer & Anderson, 1995, p. 21), a direct attack on the prevailing organizational arrangements in schools is in order. Part of this assault will focus on helping "teacher leaders navigate the structure of schools" (Silva et al., 2000, p. 793). The major attack, however, will be shaped by the knowledge that "the organization itself [will] need to change" (Ainscow & Southworth, 1996, p. 235). It will necessitate the creation of "organizational structures [that] support efforts to make change" (Katzenmeyer & Moller, 2001, p. 82) and the provision of "organizational structures conducive to collegial interactions" (Keedy, 1999, p. 798).

We close this section on structure with a caveat that leads us into the last two parts of the chapter on support and culture. That is, while to be sure "organizational constraints continue to plague the promise of teacher leadership" (Katzenmeyer & Moller, 2001, p. 127) and "structural changes are needed to promote teacher leadership" (pp. 80–81), "changing structures . . . will not be enough" (Heller, 1994, p. 292; Murphy, 1991)—"structural change alone is not sufficient to broaden leadership" (Copland, 2003, p. 29). While "teacher leadership is enabled by structural changes" (Darling-Hammond et al., 1995, p. 94), developing the "revolutionary organizational structures needed to promote . . . teacher leadership" (Pellicer & Anderson, 1995, p. 19) must grow from the seedbed of changed norms and "changed social systems" (Odell, 1997, p. 121) we describe below.

SUPPORT SYSTEMS

Teachers are unlikely to be able to engage in such leadership without a framework of support. (Frost & Durrant, 2003b, p. 4)

The context in which teachers approach leadership is critical to their success. The type of support they receive can determine their ability to be effective as leaders. (Hart & Baptist, 1996, p. 96)

When teacher leaders are asked or aspire to take on leadership roles, they are seldom provided with the necessary support. (Katzenmeyer & Moller, 2001, p. 38)

Teacher leadership introduces important changes in the work of individuals and essential transformations in relationships in schools. In addition to new structures, it requires a web of supporting conditions to take root and blossom (Frost & Durrant, 2003a, 2003b)—"support for individual teacher's roles" (Hart, 1994, p. 495) and a reconceptualization of "the context in which they work" (Moller & Katzenmeyer, 1996, p. 7), that is, careful attention to "the organizational conditions necessary to function effectively" (Smylie et al., 2002, p. 166) is needed.

In their hallmark volume on teacher leadership, Katzenmeyer and Moller (2001) assert that "supporting teacher leadership means understanding the concept, awakening the understanding of teachers themselves to their leadership potential, and then providing for the development of teacher leadership" (pp. 123–124). Factors that hinder development include "a lack of time, unsatisfactory relationships with teachers and administrators, and a lack of money to get the job done" (Pellicer & Anderson, 1995, p. 8). Supportive factors, on the other hand, "enable [teachers] to engage in collaborative relationships" (Wasley, 1991, p. 136). According to Little (1987), they include (1) "symbolic endorsements and rewards that place value on cooperative work and make the sources of interdependence clear; (2) school-level organization of staff assignments and leadership; (3) latitude for influence on crucial matters of curriculum and instruction; (4) time; (5) training and assistance; and (6) material support" (p. 508). For Hart and Baptist (1996), supportive conditions cluster into three categories: (1) "interpersonal support," (2) "tangible support," and (3) "enlarged opportunities" (p. 97). Building on the work of colleagues in this area, we describe support for teacher leadership under six broad dimensions: (1) values and expectations, (2) structures, (3) training, (4) resources, (5) incentives and recognition, and (6) role clarity.

Values and Expectations

To begin with, because "the basic disposition of a school toward the value of leadership . . . ultimately determines whether and by what means teachers participate in the school community as leaders" (Barth, 2001, p. 446), there must be a vision about the significance of teacher leadership as well as an accompanying "set of values that accepts and expects teachers to participate in leadership" (Lieberman, 1992, p. 160). Vision and values can be traced to formal leaders, for, as Keedy (1999) maintains, "without . . . principals who value teacher leadership" (p. 797), the likelihood of teacher leadership emerging in schools is dim at best (Murphy & Datnow, 2003). Principals foster teacher leadership by "declaring that they value team efforts and by describing in some detail what they think it means" (Little, 1987, p. 508). Values are also linked to teachers themselves and to their professional associations (Hatfield et al., 1986; Wasley, 1991), particularly to their willingness to privilege community over autonomy and public work over norms of privacy. Values about shared leadership are built up from beliefs (Hart, 1994), shared interests (Little, 1988), shared expectations (Smylie, 1996), and shared purpose (Wasley, 1991). They are also about commitment, specifically about "organizational commitment to empowering teachers for leadership opportunities" (Fessler & Ungaretti, 1994, p. 218), for, as Lieberman and Miller (1999) recount, "a vision without accompanying commitment will have no chance of becoming a reality" (p. 11).

Because "prospects for teacher leadership will be directly influenced by district . . . practices" (Little, 1988, p. 102), values need to be buttressed by "enabling policies" (Lieberman & Miller, 1999, p. 28). Bishop and his colleagues (1997) outline the case as follows:

> Since policies usually guide the course of action of an organization, and their statements include objectives that guide the actions of a substantial portion of the total organization, teachers will believe that they are empowered when they feel that their actions are undergirded and protected by such formalized policy statements. (p. 78)

Little (1987) concurs, arguing that "at its strongest—most durable, most rigorously connected to problems of student learning, most commanding of teachers' energies, talents, and loyalties—cooperative work is a matter of school policy" (p. 512) and that "high levels of joint action are more likely to persist" (p. 508) when a supportive policy structure is in place.

Structures

In the first third of this chapter, we investigated how organizational structures, especially institutional and bureaucratic forms, inhibit the introduction and development of teacher leadership. We reported how, on the benign end of the problem continuum, school structures circumscribe the ability of "adults to work together in a routine, centrally coordinated fashion" (Donaldson, 2001, p. 19). We also revealed how, on the more troublesome end of that continuum, the tenets of hierarchy (e.g., separation of management and labor) often constrain initiatives to promote shared leadership. Here we present the obvious corollary; that is, "teacher leaders need to have a structure for their work" (Lieberman, 1992, p. 161) and "teacher leadership positions will require restructuring schools" (Manthei, 1992, p. 15). "Support for teacher leadership demands the creation of new leadership structures" (Katzenmeyer & Moller, 2001, p. 111), the absence of which makes the exercise of teacher leadership exceedingly difficult (Copland, 2003).

Scholars in the area of teacher leadership have identified an assortment of structural supports. Underlying all of them are the following two principles penned by Heller and Firestone (1994) and Lieberman (1992), respectively:

> When planning structural changes to promote teacher leadership, teachers should be considered as more than a possible source of resistance. Restructuring to make teacher leaders— like other kinds of change—is likely to benefit from leadership from many sources, including teachers themselves. (p. 32)

> Structure must enable teachers to experiment, to talk about what they are learning, and to rearrange resources to support student learning. (p. 161)

One key issue is the selection processes used to identify and tap teacher leaders. "To the extent that the selection problem remains at the forefront of discussions of teacher leadership" (Little, 1988, p. 101)—to the extent that "favoritism on the part of principals" (Hart, 1990, p. 515) is perceived, the resulting teacher resentment will likely severely undermine prospects for teacher leadership

(Hart, 1990; Little, 1988). A second aspect of supportive structure concerns the extent to which teacher leaders continue to teach or are pulled full time from their classrooms (Katzenmeyer & Moller, 2001; Wasley, 1991). It appears that structures that feature leadership at both the classroom and school levels enjoy greater legitimacy among teachers. In particular, dual structures allay general concerns about expansion of the bureaucracy (Crowther et al., 2002) and teacher worries about the creation of status differentials and a "new oligarchy among teachers" (Hart, 1995, p. 15).

In the narrative above, we recounted that existing school organizations provide "relatively rare occasions" (Fay, 1992a, p. 3) for teachers to perform "schoolwide leadership" (Barth, 1988b, p. 133) functions. New structures, on the other hand, will be supportive to the degree that they deepen opportunities for teachers to lead. Such forms provide for richer information networks and more robust vehicles for "deliberate exchange[s]" (Hart, 1994, p. 491). For example, "common planning periods, regularly scheduled team or subject-area meetings, and judicious use of release time" (Little, 1987, p. 511) are all examples of supportive structures. Finally, supportive structures need to be both flexible and enduring while encouraging continuity of stakeholders. Specifically, there needs to be "security for leadership roles" (Wasley, 1991, p. 27); they cannot be "subject to easy cancellation" (Troen & Boles, 1994, p. 276). The structure must also foster the capacity of the organization "to keep key people in those structures" (Copland, 2003, p. 29) over extended periods of time (Murphy & Datnow, 2003).

Training

While support in terms of structured learning opportunities consumes an entire later chapter, we offer a few introductory notes on its significance in our web of support here as well, highlighting three themes. To begin, there is ample evidence that teacher leaders are being asked to assume these roles with little or no training. As Smyser (1995) discovered,

> With a great need for leadership from teachers, and with lack of training a major obstacle in establishing this leadership, it would seem obvious that there is a need for teacher education programs

that specifically train teachers to take on leadership roles. Unfortunately these programs are rarely available. (p. 132)

And since "preservice programs often times omit leadership train- ing" (LeBlanc & Shelton, 1997, p. 34) for "assuming leadership roles outside the classroom" (Smyser, 1995, p. 134), most teachers enter the profession with few leadership skills (Buckner & McDowelle, 2000). When tapped for leadership roles, they "are expected to assume [them] with little or no preparation" (McCay et al., 2001, p. 137).

We also know that districts and schools are doing little to overcome these initial skill deficiencies. "Inservice programs have not prepared teachers for leadership roles outside the classroom" (Manthei, 1992, p. 1). Nor have they been supportive in helping potential teacher leaders become "aware of their leadership capabili- ties" (Crowther et al., 2002, p. 57) as individuals (Lieberman & Miller, 1999), as participants in groups (Crow & Pounder, 2000), or as members of political organizations (Katzenmeyer & Moller, 2001).

Given the points raised above, our third theme is that if teacher leadership is to become part of the culture of schools, much more support in terms of professional learning opportuni- ties is needed. Studies consistently demonstrate that "creating leadership roles without providing opportunities to learn how to enact these roles . . . leads to failure and despair" (Lieberman & Miller, 1999, p. 91). As a result, they "reinforce the importance . . . concerning the need for professional development to lay a foundation for teacher leadership and to support its function" (Smylie, 1996, p. 575), to "help teachers to more effectively assume leadership roles" (Mitchell, 1997, p. 13) by overcoming difficulties that arise "when teacher-leaders are recruited straight out of the classroom . . . with little preparation" (Little, 1988, p. 98). The crosscutting leitmotif on education for teacher leader- ship has been well penned by Forster (1997):

Commitment to leadership must be instilled as teachers are prepared to enter the profession and reinforced thereafter. It cannot be left to incidental learning or an assumption that the commitment exists simply because one chose teaching as a career. (p. 88)

Resources

Two additional resources—material and human capacity and time—are also critical planks in the support framework bracing teacher leadership. On the capacity issue, it is important to acknowledge that "teacher leadership requires more fiscal resources" (Katzenmeyer & Moller, 2001, p. 120). "Forms of material and human support appear to be crucial contributors" (Little, 1987, p. 512) to collaborative work and shared leadership. As is the case with changing organizational structures in general (Murphy & Hallinger, 1993), funding for teacher leadership is most effective when it is used to purchase other critical resources in the support framework such as time, training, and materials (Ainscow & Southworth, 1996) and to provide "added remuneration" (Engel, 1990, p. 45) for extra work.

Perhaps no element of the support framework has received more attention than time, especially the recognition that time is "at once a help and a hindrance" (Wasley, 1991, p. 137), that it "both supports and constrains teacher leadership" (Stone et al., 1997, p. 57; Walters & Guthro, 1992)—and in all cases it is a "critical [factor] in the development of programs for . . . teacher leadership" (Kahrs, 1996, p. 28) as well as a significant influence on the exercise of teacher leadership. Time becomes "the most important barrier to address in teacher leadership" (LeBlanc & Shelton, 1997, p. 45) and the "most needed" (p. 44) and "the most valuable resource of all" (Lieberman, 1992, p. 161).

Woven throughout the literature on teacher leadership is a collection of important findings on time, which acknowledge that (1) there is a scarcity of this critical resource (Wasley, 1991)—"time in schools is in finite supply and infinite demand" (Barth, 2001, p. 445); "that is, most teachers have no time or insufficient time each day for any sort of . . . leadership activity" (Donaldson, 2001, p. 12); (2) because "the plates of good teachers are full" (Blegen & Kennedy, 2000, p. 5), "an opportunity for leadership is an opportunity to deplete more time and energy" (Barth, 1988b, p. 133)—"for many teachers, leadership exists within the four walls of their classrooms, and the thought of anything beyond that is too time-consuming" (Coyle, 1997, p. 239)—and teacher leadership is equated with "long hours" (Katzenmeyer & Moller, 2001, p. 66); (3) because "teachers who wish to undertake new leadership positions end up spending more time than they are contracted for" (Wasley, 1991, p. 133), "teacher leaders report that finding time to accomplish all the work is the most stressful factor" (Katzenmeyer & Moller, 2001, p. 105); (4) time for teacher leadership often collides with classroom obligations (Hart & Baptist, 1996; Hatfield et al., 1986; Killion, 1996; Leithwood et al., 1997), time constraints pit different responsibilities against one another (Smylie, 1996, p. 548), and "few teachers report adequate time to perform their new roles well and to fulfill their other responsibilities, particularly working with students" (p. 549); (5) "the use of time in schools is a major explanation for the slow movement toward involving teachers in leadership roles" (Katzenmeyer & Moller, 2001, p. 119); (6) "the more people involved in [teacher leadership], the more time is required" (Blegen & Kennedy, 2000, p. 5); (7) even when "extra time is provided for leadership functions, it is usually not enough" (Leithwood et al., 1997, p. 5); (8) "finding time for teachers to assume leadership roles demands resources" (Katzenmeyer & Moller, 2001, p. 118); and (9) "time in the workday must be restructured so that it can become a resource, not one more reason why teachers are unable to assume leadership" (Boles & Troen, 1996, p. 59). In short, there is a realization that in the area of teacher leadership, time is the "biggest obstacle" (Doyle, 2000, p. 38), the most significant "barrier" (Blegen & Kennedy, 2000, p. 5; LeBlanc & Shelton, 1997, p. 44), and "the most pervasive problem" (Wasley, 1991, p. 137). "The problem of time in the teaching day present[s] the greatest deterrent to general teacher interest in assuming new roles" (Fay, 1992b, p. 77).

The literature also shows how "formal scheduled time for the role is essential to the definition" (Fay 1992a, p. 9) of teacher leadership and exposes an array of venues where time can support teacher leadership:

> time to learn; time to talk with one another; time to get new materials (or make them); time to experiment, reflect, talk about it; time to create; time to deal with the inevitable conflict that comes with a clash of values; time to build collegial relationships where there have been none. (Lieberman, 1992, p. 161)

Time is often needed to lift teacher leadership off the ground (Duke, 1994), to implement teacher leadership in ways that "barriers and obstacles can be resolved" (Whitaker, 1997, p. 15), and to prevent "the strains [that] are compounded when the pace of implementation is fast" (Little, 1988, p. 98). Time "to begin defining [one's] own set of values and beliefs" (Harrison & Lembeck, 1996, p. 108) is essential. Time is required for professional development (Blegen & Kennedy, 2000; Katzenmeyer & Moller, 2001), "for reflection and for opportunities to conduct professional inquiry" (Troen & Boles, 1994, p. 278)—time to be more "thoughtful" (Wasley, 1991, p. 138). Extra time is needed for teachers to take part in the leadership process (Wise, 1989), to perform leadership responsibilities (Katzenmeyer & Moller, 2001), and "to participate authentically in important conversations" (Silva et al., 2000, p. 802). Time for teachers to work together (Harrison & Lembeck, 1996; Wasley, 1991), "for teacher leaders to engage in collaborative relationships" (Katzenmeyer & Moller, 2001, p. 108) and "democratic decision making" (Kahrs, 1996, p. 28) is critical. Extra time for planning is also a requisite (Mitchell, 1997; Wasley, 1991). The theme throughout the storyline is quite distinct—until time is "made for teacher leadership . . . there will continue to be few stories of successful . . . teacher leadership" (Silva et al., 2000, p. 802).

Incentives and Recognition

"A school culture that celebrates teacher leadership" (Harrison & Lembeck, 1996, p. 111) is yet another indispensable element in the support portfolio. So, too, is a system of "incentives and rewards" (Little, 1988, p. 102) that motivates teachers to serve as leaders outside the classroom. In short, "meeting the monetary and non-monetary needs of teachers profoundly affects the chances of making a difference in teachers' willingness to serve as leaders" (Katzenmeyer & Moller, 2001, p. 127).

Currently, the picture that emerges from the literature is one in which "there are no real incentives for teachers to lead" (Pellicer & Anderson, 1995, p. 18). In fact, "there are substantial disincentives" (Little, 1988, p. 102) to change to collaborative work at the heart of teacher leadership. In many schools, there is limited recognition for the work of teacher leaders and there are "no rewards for extra effort" (Crowther et al., 2002, p. 34). In too many places, "the only rewards for teacher leadership are added responsibilities" (Moller & Katzenmeyer, 1996, p. 14).

Harrison and Lembeck (1996) remind us that "we have learned several ways to acknowledge teacher leadership" (p. 110). To begin with, as touched upon above, "recognition of leadership and credit for leadership among teachers is a key factor influencing teacher involvement and leadership" (Kahrs, 1996, p. 33): "Recognition was mentioned by all the participants. All of the teacher leaders desired respect, appreciation, and accolades for their work as teacher leaders. This emerged as an important need" (LeBlanc & Shelton, 1997, p. 41). One type of recognition is the acknowledgment of the importance of teacher leadership within the educational system writ large—what Katzenmeyer and Moller (2001) label "the widespread recognition of the development of teacher leaders as one of the catalysts that will propel school reform in the new century" (p. 124). In individual districts and schools, two types of recognition energize teacher leaders. First, the actions of persons of "status and influence" (Hart, 1994, p. 492) carry considerable weight. Administrators, union leaders, and well-respected veteran teachers here merit notice (Hart, 1994). Second, "peer acceptance and recognition" is important to teacher leaders, the absence of which can negatively affect the growth of shared leadership in a school (LeBlanc & Shelton, 1997).

While "rewarding teachers who are willing to move beyond their classrooms to lead is a complicated issue" (Moller & Katzenmeyer, 1996, p. 13) and a "challenge" (Harrison & Lembeck, 1996, p. 111; Hart, 1990, 1994, 1995), in the end school districts "must provide incentives and rewards for teachers who take the lead in tackling tasks and solving problems" (Boles & Troen, 1996, p. 60): "principals must identify meaningful ways to reward teachers in ways teachers value" (Harrison & Lembeck, 1996, p. 111). In addition to providing extra pay for leadership work, Moller and Katzenmeyer (1996) uncovered three ways in which principals

were able to provide real support and incentives for teachers engaged in both classroom teaching and teacher leadership responsibilities. First, the principals provided access to information and resources and gave their personal time to support the teacher leaders. Second, they honored teacher leaders' requests for professional development and sometimes initiated opportunities for them to attend conferences or represent the school at important meetings. Finally, they gave them the gift of time, covering classes for them, providing substitute teachers, or assigning support personnel to assist them. (pp. 13–14)

Role Clarity

Research on shared leadership exposes the fact that "the work of teachers acting as leaders . . . creates a number of potential difficulties" (Ainscow & Southworth, 1996, p. 243). For example, "role ambiguity, conflict, and overload are broadly reported negative side effects of teacher work redesign" (Hart, 1995, p. 12):

The research was clear, however, that these teacher leadership initiatives [can] cause serious problems. They [can] create work overload, stress, role ambiguity, and role conflict for teacher leaders as they [try] to balance their new school-level responsibilities with their classroom responsibilities. (Smylie et al., 2002, p. 166)

In his pathbreaking work on teacher leadership, Smylie has reported that

virtually without exception, teacher leaders and principals referred to ambiguities and uncertainties to describe the conditions in which they had to develop their new working relationships. These ambiguities and uncertainties concerned how teacher leadership roles were to be defined and performed as well as how these roles might affect principals' leadership roles, teacher leaders' ongoing classroom responsibilities, and the schools generally. They concerned how principals and teacher leaders would work together in the development and performance of these teacher leadership roles. They also concerned whether both teacher leaders and principals could trust each other and whether each possessed the requisite knowledge and skill to develop and perform successfully in new work roles and working relationships. (Smylie & Brownlee-Conyers, 1992, pp. 162–163)

The first piece of the problem that support is needed to address is the role ambiguity and conflict teachers almost always experience when they assume schoolwide leadership responsibilities. One dimension of this ambiguity emanates from confusion between the established role as classroom teacher and the new role as leader at the school level, over the question of "whether they are instructors of students or leaders of teachers" (Smylie, 1996, p. 548). Or, as Wasley (1991) found, "trying to both teach and lead creates its own tensions" (p. 144). Conflicts are especially likely to arise when teacher leaders themselves, or their peers, believe that schoolwide leadership responsibilities prevent teacher leaders from "fulfilling classroom obligations" (Clift et al., 1992, p. 901) and "interfere with teaching" (Crowther et al., 2002, p. 35). Especially damaging is the "perception that the responsibilities of teacher leaders remove them too frequently from the classroom" (Smylie & Denny, 1989, p. 11) and thus may "deter excellence in teachers' practices" (Crowther et al., 2002, p. 35) in classrooms and "delegitimize the roles of teacher leaders from the perspective of other classroom teachers" (Smylie, 1996, p. 548). The result has been that "left to define their roles for themselves, . . . teacher leaders have had difficulty separating their conventional classroom teacher roles from their extra-classroom teacher leadership roles" (Odell, 1997, p. 120).

Working with peers is a second source of role ambiguity and conflict, especially around issues of entering the work of colleagues and peer support for teacher leadership (Little, 1988; Smyser, 1995). The issue of "changed working relationships between teacher leaders and other teachers" (Whitaker, 1997, p. 10) is never far from the surface, neither is "the ambiguity associated with other teachers' perceptions" (Smylie & Denny, 1989, p. 16) of the role of teacher leaders, nor is the knowledge that "social relationships of teachers are powerful determiners of how teachers assuming leadership roles will be viewed" (Katzenmeyer & Moller, 2001, p. 13). Researchers have regularly discovered that peer teachers are unclear about the roles of teacher leaders (Smylie & Denny, 1989) and possess less-than-well-defined expectations for lead teachers (Odell, 1997). They often hold teacher leaders "suspect" (Walters & Guthro, 1992, p. 144) "and sometimes harbor resentment against them" (Odell, 1997, p. 120). This condition is most likely to materialize when there is evidence of "conflict between teacher leaders and the social and normative context of faculty relationships" (Smylie & Brownlee-Conyers, 1992, p. 156).

Locating and defining "the boundary between administration and teaching" (Hart, 1990, p. 518) only adds to role conflict for teacher leaders—and for other teachers and administrators (Little, 1988; Smylie & Brownlee-Conyers, 1992). In a real sense, teacher leaders experience "a netherworld that [is] neither that of the administrator nor that of the teacher" (Datnow & Castellano, 2002, p. 204). They enter "uncharted ground, not plain faculty, nor pure administration" (Wasley, 1991, p. 142),

> a kind of "no man's land" between their colleagues in the staff room and the senior management team. In acting in the interests of the whole school they may, on the one hand, be seen as agents of authority, whilst on the other hand, they are wanting to be perceived as acting on behalf of the staff. (Ainscow & Southworth, 1996, p. 243)

One of the most severe problems "experienced by these teacher-leaders [is that] of not being accepted by either the collegium of teachers or by the administration" (Whitaker, 1997, p. 11). These new roles "obscure previously clear boundaries" (Hart, 1990, p. 517) between teaching and managing. Of particular importance here are the findings that "suggest that ambiguities and uncertainties associated with new teacher leadership roles have significant implications for the development of new working relationships between teachers who assume those roles and their principals" (Smylie & Brownlee-Conyers, 1992, p. 179).

The consequences of role ambiguity and "role confusion" (LeBlanc & Shelton, 1997, p. 34) ribbon the research literature on teacher leadership. Most telling, "individuals have been left to carve out identities and build support from teachers and administrators on a case-by-case basis" (Little, 1988, p. 92). Personal identities are often blurred (Smylie, 1996). Fears often surface, especially around possible "social sanctions" (Hart, 1990, p. 519) and potential ostracism from peers—about "the chasm these new roles might place between [teacher leaders] and their colleagues" (Pellicer & Anderson, 1995, p. 13; Yarger & Lee, 1994). Mistrust sometimes emerges (Whitaker, 1997), confusion forms (Hart, 1994), and friendships are subject to "considerable strain" (Little, 1990, p. 513). As traditional norms and understandings change with the influx of teacher leadership roles, "conflicts increase" (LeBlanc & Shelton, 1997, p. 34), tensions rise (Collins & Sherrill, 1997; Smylie & Denny, 1989), congeniality declines, and jealousies increase (Smyser, 1995). For teacher leaders, feelings of loneliness and isolation often result.

In addition to the assistance needed to navigate through role conflicts, we know that considerable support is required to help teacher leaders negotiate the role overload that accompanies this new work (Broyles, 1991; Hart, 1995). Studies in this area conclude that "teacher-leaders essentially have two jobs" (Whitaker, 1997, p. 12), and because "the natural tendency of administrators, and even the teacher leaders themselves, is to expect . . . teacher leaders to take on additional roles, usually without eliminating other responsibilities" (Hart & Baptist, 1996, p. 97) or "compensating for the added demands made by engaging in school leadership" (Griffin, 1995, p. 44), it is not surprising that teachers assuming schoolwide leadership responsibilities often begin "experiencing overload" (Clift et al., 1992, p. 903) "associated with [these] new responsibilities" (Smylie, 1996, p. 550). While related to role ambiguity and conflict, role overload differs from these ideas "in that expectations do not clash; rather, they proliferate to the point at which the school runs out of time, energy, and resources" (Clift et al., 1992, p. 902).

There is an unwritten principle in the literature on teacher leadership that ferreting out problems illuminates solution paths as well. Here analysts have done an exceptional job in laying out needed avenues of support for teacher leadership. Work on compiling a portfolio of factors to eliminate obstacles and barriers to the successful practice of schoolwide leadership for teachers has been less forthcoming. When they do turn their attention in this direction, reviewers feature core strategies such as garnering "professional acceptance of the existence of teacher leaders in the profession and in the schools" (Crowther et al., 2002, p. 32) and deepening trust among teachers and between teachers and administrators (Blase & Blase, 2001; Crowther et al., 2002), especially through collaborative work (Katzenmeyer & Moller, 2001; Smyser, 1995). They also identify more concrete ideas, such as tightening expectations and clarifying roles by developing more specific job descriptions (Miller, 1992; Whitaker, 1997) and providing teachers "images of what is possible" (Darling-Hammond et al., 1995, p. 104) and "maps and reliable guides to follow" (Clift et al., 1992, p. 906).

CULTURE

> Proposals for teacher leadership challenge long-established and accepted values, beliefs, and norms of the teaching profession. (Hart, 1995, p. 12)

> The school culture is not conducive to the development of leadership skills of teachers, at least not outside the narrow confines of the individual classroom. (Smyser, 1995, p. 131)

Scholars investigating the nature of teacher work in general (Feiman-Nemser & Floden, 1986; Lortie, 1975; Rosenholtz, 1989) and teacher work redesign (Hart, 1990) and teacher leadership specifically (Katzenmeyer & Moller, 2001; Little, 1987, 1988) have uncovered a thick vein of knowledge about how "professional norms and school culture" (Wilson, 1993, p. 27)—"the occupational structure of teaching work itself" (Little, 1990, p. 511)—exert a powerful and often negative sway on the birth and development of shared leadership in schools. At the broadest level, it is argued that "teaching is not a profession that values or encourages leadership within its ranks" (Troen & Boles, 1994) and "that teachers who adhere to the current norms of the profession are . . . a barrier to changing the role of teachers in our schools" (Odell, 1997, p. 121). In particular, in the narrative that unfolds below, we reveal how norms of "privacy, autonomy, and egalitarianism" (Smylie, 1996, p. 576) define the teaching profession. We describe how these standards provide "the yardstick[s] most teachers use to measure . . . acceptability" (Whitaker, 1995, p. 80) and how "proposals for teacher leadership challenge [these] long-established . . . norms" (Hart, 1995, p. 12)—how "norms of equality, autonomy, cordiality, and privacy can counter interventions designed to redistribute leadership in schools and how these norms can neutralize teacher leader attempts to form new roles in providing support and collegial interaction for teachers" (Keedy,

1999, p. 788). We explain that because teacher leadership assaults the central "norms influencing working relationships among teachers" (Smylie, 1992, p. 56), it is "difficult for teachers in many schools to accept or display leadership" (Barth, 2001, p. 445). Too often, when opportunities for shared leadership are presented, professional norms stimulate teachers to resist new ways of doing business (Ainscow & Southworth, 1996; Barth, 2001) and cause those who accept schoolwide leadership responsibilities to "display caution toward their colleagues" (Little, 1988, p. 84) and "to tread lightly" (Smylie, 1996, p. 576).

Turning to "the many-headed hydras of school culture" (Griffin, 1995, p. 44), we learn that "each school's culture directly influences how willing its teachers will be to take on positive leadership roles" (Katzenmeyer & Moller, 2001, p. 71), that "teacher leadership can be encouraged or impeded depending on school culture and climate" (Snell & Swanson, 2000, p. 2). Indeed, it seems that "the specific social relationships and norms of individual schools [are] more influential . . . than the general professional norms" (Smylie, 1996, p. 555) that we introduced above. "The school social unit" (Hart, 1990, p. 526) also appears to "outweigh the strength of individual teachers' training, years of experience, effort, personal characteristics, and abilities, and the formal work structure and its impact on the functions of redesigned work" (p. 526). This appears to be the case because "the social and normative contexts of schools . . . define and govern teachers' professional relationships" (Smylie, 1996, p. 560), and "social system dynamics" (Hart, 1994, p. 493), in turn, exert considerable control over work redesign efforts such as teacher leadership.

Unfortunately, there is also a plentiful store of evidence that "something deep and powerful within school cultures seems to work against teacher leadership" (Barth, 2001, p. 443). That is, "the culture and social norms of schools conspire against leadership development . . . and bedevil . . . efforts to develop teacher leadership" (Smylie et al., 2002, p. 183). "Institutionalizing teacher leadership as a norm within the cultural fabric of an entire school is a . . . challenging task" (Keedy, 1999, p. 797). On one hand, efforts to cultivate shared leadership are hampered by the fact that there are "few meaningful precedents" (Little, 1990, p. 517) for introducing teacher leadership into the institution of schooling and the occupation of teaching (Little, 1990; Wasley, 1991). On the other hand, attempts to institutionalize teacher leadership are "influenced substantially by patterns of belief and practice that define old work roles and by socialization pressures from the workplace that resist new work roles or reshape them to conform to those prevailing practices and pressures" (Smylie & Brownlee-Conyers, 1992, p. 155). Not only are "established social patterns . . . resilient" (Hart, 1994, p. 477), but the tendency to regress to prevailing norms and practices is actually "height-ened" (p. 477) during periods of change such as those associated with work redesign. In "the absence of traditions for mutual work" (Little, 1988, p. 92), forays into teacher leadership often violate cultural foundations that define schools, foundations that are often "fatal to new work configurations" (Hart, 1990, p. 504). Too often, the end result is that "the behaviors and attitudes com-monly regarded as demonstrating leadership are not acceptable to . . . teachers" (Wilson, 1993, p. 27).

Not surprisingly, the literature in this area also helps us see that "the first element necessary in a successful guide to recogniz-ing and promoting teacher leaders is to establish an appropriate school culture" (Bishop et al., 1997, p. 78). While reculturing the organization to accommodate denser patterns of leadership must begin with knowledge about "how the concept [teacher leader-ship] fits into the existing culture" (Katzenmeyer & Moller, 2001, p. 80), it is also important to work from the understanding that "creating an appropriate culture to support teacher leadership establishes a new dimension" (Bishop et al., 1997, p. 78). What is required is "a school culture that is clearly committed to providing support for the learning of all its members" (Silva et al., 2000, p. 802), "a school culture in which classroom teachers are fully empowered partners in shaping policy, creating curriculum, man-aging budgets, improving practice, and bringing added value to the goal of improving education for children" (Boles & Troen, 1996, p. 42); that is, "settings in which teachers are encouraged to collaborate, to participate in school-site decision making, to engage in ongoing learning, and to reflect upon their pedagogy are the school sites that best foster the leadership of classroom practitioners" (Snell & Swanson, 2000, p. 2).

In the balance of this section, we fuse the concepts of profes-sional norms and organizational culture to explore potent dynamics that often obstruct efforts to grow teacher leadership in schools, keeping in mind that these forces often interact with the structural barriers and support impediments discussed in earlier sections. We collect these forces in two categories: norms about teaching and leading and norms about the nature of work.

Norms About Teaching and Leading

> Concerned with the problems of teaching and most interested in life in the classroom, teachers are reluctant to think of themselves as leaders. (Troen & Boles, 1994, p. 276)

> Teachers are socialized to be followers, not leaders. (Moller & Katzenmeyer, 1996, p. 3)

> While it is fine to talk about collaborative, participatory approaches to leadership in theory, there is still a great deal of work to do in defining, in a real-world context, what the common ground between teachers and administrators is. (Teitel, 1996, p. 149)

One value that is deeply entwined in the cultural tapestry of schools is what might best be labeled the *norm of legitimacy:* what counts as appropriate work for teachers. The literature confirms that authentic activity is what unfolds in classrooms (Doyle, 2000; Hinchey, 1997)—a "classroom-oriented, student-centered conception of work" (Smylie & Brownlee-Conyers, 1992, p. 156). For both the public and for teachers themselves, teaching is defined "almost exclusively by time spent in classrooms with children" (Little, 1988, p. 100). Because "time for leadership often equals time away from the classroom" (Fay, 1992b, p. 81), leadership work "can be stressful" (Katzenmeyer & Moller, 2001, p. 111) for individual teachers, especially if time away from teaching is seen as "compromising their effectiveness with children" (Smylie & Brownlee-Conyers, 1992, p. 164), and unsettling for the existing culture. Indeed, teacher leaders "take a lot of criticism from principals [and] fellow teachers . . . over 'missing school'" (Fay, 1992b, p. 81). It is not difficult to see how the norm of legitimacy could deter teachers from assuming schoolwide leadership responsibilities and how it could depress enthusiasm among the faculty for shared leadership.

A related standard is the *norm of the divide between teaching and administration*, a separation that "has been extensive and profound" (Rallis, 1990, p. 196; Murphy, 1999b). One dimension of this norm is the belief that the job of teachers is to teach and the task of school administrators is to manage and lead—"principals lead; teachers teach" (Barth, 2001, p. 445). A second aspect is that it is "the teacher's job to carry out plans developed by others higher up in the school hierarchy" (Boles & Troen, 1996, p. 43). This "strong us-them split" (Teitel, 1996, p. 149) is heavily buttressed by the structural elements of schooling we outlined earlier, especially the tenets of hierarchy. Where schoolwide leadership requires teachers to occupy territory traditionally held by administrators, to "cross the border" (p. 149) or "to change ranks" (Whitaker, 1997, p. 12) so to speak—that is, to violate the separation norm—formidable barriers are often erected (Little, 1988; Midgley & Woods, 1993).

The *norm of managerial prerogative*, or what Keedy (1999) calls the "norm of the authority and power of administrators" (p. 787), has a deep root structure in most schools and, as is the case with related norms discussed above, it casts a pall over the ideology of shared leadership. At the heart of the prerogative standard is the belief that school action outside of classrooms is the rightful domain of school administrators (Smylie, 1992). Given this culture, teachers are "reluctant to challenge traditional patterns of principals' authority" (Smylie, 1992, p. 55). Understandings have been forged over time between administrators and teachers (Murphy, Hallinger, Lotto, & Miller, 1987; Sizer, 1984). They often show considerable reluctance to overturn such negotiated arrangements, especially when doing so would undercut established patterns of "authority and autonomy" (Smylie, 1992, p. 55). Cast in less generous terms, the argument holds that teachers are powerless to influence activities beyond the classroom (Troen & Boles, 1994), that principals are resistant to actions that would alter this dynamic (Bishop et al., 1997; Brown & Sheppard, 1999; Little, 1988), and that efforts on the part of teachers to challenge the norm would produce unpleasant "repercussions" (Clift et al., 1992, p. 902).

Two related standards, the *norm of followership*—the belief that teachers are "followers, not leaders" (Moller & Katzenmeyer, 1996, p. 3)—and the *norm of compliance*—the belief that it is the job of teachers to comply with directives from above (Wasley, 1991)—also "undermine . . . the espoused theory of teacher leadership" (Clift et al., 1992, p. 906), hinder the emergence of teacher leaders, and complicate their work when they do emerge.

Norms About the Nature of Work

The norms of privacy, noninterference and nonjudgment, civility, equality, and individual autonomy generally characterize teachers' professional relationships. (Smylie, 1996, p. 560)

Analysts over the last quarter century have thrown considerable illumination on "the *autonomy norm* which defines the teaching profession" (B. L. Johnson, 1998, p. 18) and on the "deeply entrenched patterns of isolation and autonomy that define teachers' work" (Smylie & Hart, 1999, p. 430) and breed a "school culture of isolation" (Institute for Educational Leadership, 2001, p. 7). "Most teachers . . . work alone, in isolation from their colleagues" (Stigler & Hiebert, 1999, p. 157) and they prefer it that way (Griffin, 1995). Collaborative cultures are much in vogue in the educational literature but much less visible in schools.

Teachers see professional autonomy—"which is viewed as freedom from outside scrutiny and the right to make independent judgments" (Wasley, 1991, p. 26), to choose ends and means . . . to adopt for [one's] classroom" (Wilson, 1993, p. 27)—"as a contested right" (Uline & Berkowitz, 2000, p. 419). They also learn "not [to] meddle in the affairs of other teachers" (Teitel, 1996, p. 144), especially in matters dealing with how their colleagues work with youngsters in their classrooms. In short, "they do not wish to lead or be led" (Wilson, 1993, p. 27).

Perhaps no norm is more destructive to the health of teacher leadership than "this very strong standard of practice" (Wasley, 1991, p. 26); "the fundamental isolation of teachers in the classroom is a major barrier to their asserting a stronger leadership role" (Firestone, 1996, p. 413). It "inhibits teachers from extending their influence beyond their classroom doors" (Moller & Katzenmeyer, 1996, p. 8). The norm of autonomy and isolation "impedes productive relationships with . . . other [teachers] and with . . . administrators" (Uline & Berkowitz, 2000, p. 419) and "inhibit[s] the work of teacher leaders with their teaching colleagues" (Leithwood et al., 1997, p. 5). It "inhibit[s] professionalism" (Rallis, 1990, p. 194). It "stymies all attempts at reform" (Institute for Educational Leadership, 2001, p. 7). And, as Urbanski and Nickolaou (1997) assert, "for the sake of such autonomy in their own classrooms, teachers sacrifice their prospects for influence at the school level and beyond" (p. 245).

Tightly linked to professional and cultural values about autonomy are the *norms of privacy and noninterference* (Feiman-Nemser & Floden, 1986, p. 506) "that pervade most schools" (Smylie & Brownlee-Conyers, 1992, p. 156)—what Griffin (1995) calls "the privacy of practice" (p. 40). As Uline and Berkowitz (2000) document, the interaction rules in a culture of privacy parallel those found in highly autonomous climates and "include never interfering in another teacher's classroom affairs, and always being self-reliant with one's own" (p. 418), holding the classroom "inviolate" (Feiman-Nemser & Floden, 1986, p. 517). "The norm of professional privacy" (Smylie, 1992, p. 63) is construed "as freedom from scrutiny and the right of each teacher to make independent judgments about classroom practice" (Little, 1988, p. 94). While Little (1990) acknowledges that providing help to colleagues is acceptable within tight parameters, in a culture of noninterference and nonjudgmentalness there is a clear "boundary between offering advice when asked and interfering in unwarranted ways" (p. 515). "Offering . . . unsolicited advice runs counter to the valued, accepted collegial behavior of teachers" (Little, 1985, p. 36) and is a breach of the norm of privacy. Rather, "under the norm of noninterference . . . teachers are expected to work things out on their own" (Feiman-Nemser & Floden, 1986, p. 506). "Hands off" (p. 509) rules apply, especially on issues "that bear directly on classroom work" (Huberman, 1993, p. 34).

"The precedents of noninterference are powerful" (Little, 1987, p. 500), and the culture of privacy is potent. Both are toxic to shared leadership and to the culture of collaboration that supports it (Little, 1987) because "the more strongly that leaders are committed to the norm of professional privacy the less willing they are to participate in decisions concerning curriculum and instruction" (Smylie, 1992, p. 63). On the other hand, it is growing increasingly clear that "the prospects for school-based teacher leadership rest on displacing the privacy norm" (Little, 1988, p. 94) and on "teacher leaders abandon[ing] their private-ness" (McCay et al., 2001, p. 137; Carr, 1997).

"The culture of teaching [also] contends that all teachers are equal" (Childs-Bowen et al., 2000, p. 32), a condition that is widely cited as the *egalitarian norm* (Conley, 1989) or "the egalitarian ethic" (Boles & Troen, 1994, p. 9). Analysts consistently show that "egalitarian norms" (Katzenmeyer & Moller, 2001, p. 4) and "the culture of sameness" (Urbanski & Nickolaou, 1997, p. 245) have a long history within the profession (Lortie, 1975; Wasley, 1991) and "run deep in school buildings" (Huberman, 1993, p. 29): "egalitarianism is deeply rooted and with long-standing traditions" (Little, 1995, p. 55); "it is compelling" (Little, 1987, p. 510). As noted above, at its core, the egalitarian ethic of teaching—"the fact that all teachers hold equal position and rank, separated by number of years of experience and college credit earned" (Wasley, 1991, p. 166) "rather than function, skill, advanced knowledge, role, or responsibility" (Lieberman et al., 1988, p. 151)—"suggests that all teachers should be equal" (Katzenmeyer & Moller, 2001, p. 4).

Against this cultural backdrop, "teacher leadership . . . intro-duce[s] status differences based on knowledge, skill, and initiative" (Little, 1988, p. 98; Yarger & Lee, 1994). Teacher leadership positions "suggest superordinate and subordinate status differences that teachers may not view as socially and professionally legiti-mate" (Smylie & Brownlee-Conyers, 1992, p. 156). The consequence is not unexpected—"new responsibilities . . . clash with old expectations for equality" (Hart, 1990, p. 517). At a minimum, "the helping relationships that [are] central to [teacher leadership] challenge the norms of professional equality" (Smylie & Denny, 1989, p. 16). More severely, they "may compel violations of long-standing egalitarian norms among teachers" (Conley, 1989, p. 15). In effect, then, because "teacher leadership is incon-sistent with the egalitarian culture in most schools" (Moller & Katzenmeyer, 1996, p. 7) and "assaults the egalitarian norms that have long been in place in teaching" (Wasley, 1991, p. 147), norms of equality act as an "obstacle to teacher leadership" (Killion, 1996, p. 75) and as "an obstacle to designing meaningful teacher leadership roles" (Pellicer & Anderson, 1995, p. 20).

On the one hand, norms of equality "constrain teachers from the kinds of initiative, or exercise of authority, one typically associates with images of formal leadership responsibility" (Little, 1995, p. 55). They make help giving "problematic" (Little, 1990, p. 517). On the other hand, "they suggest a system of social costs associated with their violation" (Smylie & Denny, 1989, p. 15), social costs such as "collegial disfavor and sanction" (Smylie, 1992, p. 56) and "damag[ed] relationships with peers" (LeBlanc & Shelton, 1997, p. 43). The presence of such costs often produces reluctance on the part of teachers to assume the mantle of "leadership." Since they "fear the reactions of their colleagues and because they are hesitant to be singled out from the group in an environment that has valued treating everyone the same" (Bishop et al., 1997, p. 77), reticence to take on leadership roles is often the norm. In short, as Katzenmeyer and Moller (2001) confirm, "the egalitarian norms among teachers do not encourage a teacher to take leadership roles" (p. 79).

When teachers do accept schoolwide leadership responsibilities, they often "seem reluctant to challenge the norms of professional equality" (Smylie & Denny, 1989, p. 16). They sometimes "reject responsibility and role innovation . . . in favor of egalitarian norms" (Hart, 1990, p. 519). They are "hesitant to set themselves up as experts" (Little, 1985, p. 36). They avoid "drawing attention to themselves" (Katzenmeyer & Moller, 2001, p. 4) and "display a wondrous ability to diminish their new status and to downplay the leadership opportunities and obligations that (inescapably) accompany the title" (Little, 1988, p. 101). And, at times, in the face of "both covert and overt criticism [and] passive and/or active resistance [they] may relinquish their leadership role[s]" (Blegen & Kennedy, 2000, p. 4).

The research reveals that such reticence on the part of teacher leaders may be well founded because "attempts to assign formal leadership roles to teachers often place would-be teacher leaders in direct opposition to their colleagues" (Darling-Hammond et al., 1995, p. 90) and because teachers often are "not gentle with [colleagues] who violate egalitarian norms" (Hart, 1990, p. 521). And since in an egalitarian culture "the opinions of peers are important to teachers, . . . negative comments . . . may stop their initiatives" (Moller & Katzenmeyer, 1996, p. 7).

Teachers are known to "defend turf" (Boles & Troen, 1996, p. 44) in the face of teacher leadership and to distance themselves from colleagues who assume leadership roles (Johnson & Hynes, 1997). They often make it difficult for peers to be seen as experts (Wasley, 1991). They often resist the initiatives of teacher leaders (Hart, 1990; Little, 1988). More aggressively, they sometimes work to undermine the efforts of teacher leaders (LeBlanc & Shelton, 1997), to silence their voices (Dana, 1992), and to banish them from the ranks of the collegium (Stone et al., 1997; Wilson, 1993). In short, "teacher leaders . . . may . . . suffer rejection from peers" (Katzenmeyer & Moller, 2001, p. 80). And, as Duke (1994) observes, "teacher leadership hardly can thrive in such circumstances" (p. 270).

A final standard that often impedes the development of a culture of shared leadership and shackles the work of teacher leaders is the *norm of civility.* As Griffin (1995) reminds us, "schools are nonconfrontative social organizations, at least in terms of how teachers interact with one another" (p. 44). There is strong pressure for "cordiality" (Hart, 1990, p. 516) among teachers that often clashes with the function of teacher leadership (Hart, 1990). Coupled with this are accepted modes of interaction among teachers, such as contrived collegiality and "induced collaboration" (Little, 1990, p. 509), that promote the appearance of shared leadership while maintaining deeply ingrained norms of autonomy, privacy, and egalitarianism. And coupled to all these other standards are *norms of conservatism* and *aversion to risk taking* (Lortie, 1975; Rosenholtz, 1989) that privilege the status quo in the face of change, which is at the heart of teacher leadership.

CONCLUSION

In this chapter, we examined a collection of organizational conditions and a host of professional and cultural norms that can retard or promote the creation of a culture of shared leadership and constrain or enhance the activities of teacher leaders. We organized that analysis around the three broad topics of structure, support, and culture. In the remaining two chapters in this part of the book, we explore the special role that principals and professional development play in the birth and development of teacher leadership.

CHAPTER SEVEN

Promoting Teacher Leadership From the Principal's Office

The principal, it seems, has a disproportionate influence upon teacher leadership—for better or for worse. (Barth, 2001, p. 447)

We also recognize that teacher leaders cannot develop without consistent support and encouragement from their principal. Support from those persons in positions of power is of immeasurable value in bringing about change and developing future leaders. (Harrison & Lembeck, 1996, p. 102)

Because most new teacher leadership roles depend heavily on teacher leader-principal interaction and collaboration, principals are in first-order positions to block, to support and facilitate, and to shape the nature and function of teacher leadership in their schools. (Smylie & Brownlee-Conyers, 1992, p. 151)

We understand from the extensive literature on leadership that persons in formal leadership roles exercise considerable influence in determining the success of change initiatives in general and work redesign efforts in particular (Myers, 1970). An abundant body of scholarship confirms these conclusions in schools as well. This is the case because, as Slater and Doig (1988) remind us, "the energy for school reform must at some point flow through . . . school principals, who can enhance and direct it, permit it to dissipate, or—even worse—cut it off altogether" (p. 295). For our purposes here, we note that "principals . . . play a major role in teacher work redesign" (Whitaker, 1997, p. 5). In terms of shared leadership roles and functions specifically, "the success of teacher leadership initiatives" (Heller & Firestone, 1994, p. 4) and "the success of [teacher leaders] depends importantly on the active support of principals and district administrators" (Smylie, 1996, p. 575). "The greatest influence on teacher leadership is the principal" (Blegen & Kennedy, 2000, p. 4), or, as Barth (2001) succinctly captures it, "principals are crucial to the health and performance of teacher leaders" (p. 448).

This chapter begins with the understanding that in the area of teacher leadership good work does not stand on its own (Hart, 1994); "the most essential prerequisite for success is commitment from leaders" (Birnie & Lustgarten, 1996, p. 135), and the backing of principals is "critical to empowering teachers as leaders" (Katzenmeyer & Moller, 2001, p. 14) as well as to the growth and development of teacher leadership in schools (Brown & Sheppard, 1999; Hart, 1990; Miller, 1992). "Principals play a key role in developing teacher leadership" (Buckner & McDowelle, 2000, p. 36), and they have been "at the center of both successes and failures of teacher leadership" (Barth, 1988b, p. 137). Building from this knowledge, we examine principals' actions that encourage the development of leadership in the school and nurture the growth of individual teachers as leaders. At the organizational level, we explore the changing directions of teacher and principal roles in schools that are reshaping leadership patterns. We also discuss the importance of adjusting organizational structures to permit the emergence and growth of teacher leadership. In the second half of the chapter, we review functions that principals perform to help weave the thread of teacher leadership deeply into the cultural tapestry of the school.

DEVELOPING RELATIONSHIPS IN SUPPORT OF TEACHER LEADERSHIP

The school administrative role, with its various job tasks, appears to be in some conflict with the teacher leader role. (Hatfield et al., 1986, p. 19)

The creation of teacher leadership roles means that teachers and principals must forge new working relationships. (Wasley, 1991, p. 164)

Relationships between principals and teachers form the cauldron in which new understandings of leadership will be forged and new forms of teacher leadership will materialize. That is, in the area of teacher leadership "the social unit . . . significantly affect[s] the impact of the new work structure" (Hart, 1990, p. 516). What this means, of course, is that "new and different working relationships need to be established between teachers and administrators in order for any new leadership role to make a positive and lasting contribution" (Sherrill, 1999, p. 57) and that the nature of these relationships needs to be "jointly negotiated" (Datnow & Costellano, 2002, p. 26). Differences in perspectives need to be surfaced and addressed (Silva et al., 2000).

Teacher leadership changes the metric of work in schools. It often "bring[s] principals and teachers into collaborative working relationships for the first time" (Whitaker, 1997, p. 14); that is, "collaboration between administrators and teachers is a new rule of the game" (Wilson, 1993, p. 26). The changes accompanying the redefinition of working relationships are often difficult for educators to accept—for teachers in general who are comfortable with the traditional structures and ways of doing business in schools (Coyle, 1997); for teacher leaders who find the dual role of classroom instructor and school leader demanding and hard to negotiate (Smylie & Brownlee-Conyers, 1992); and especially for school administrators who often discern in teacher leadership the "potential for teacher leaders to challenge and reshape traditional prerogatives of principals" (Smylie & Brownlee-Conyers, 1992, p. 154) and "domains of influence" (Smylie, 1996, p. 549), to undermine "professional norms" (p. 549), and to threaten (Yarger & Lee, 1994) or "erode traditional realms of administrative authority" (Conley, 1989, p. 15). Thus while "teacher leadership need not conflict with principal leadership" (Rallis, 1990, p. 196), without concerted efforts to make the relationship work, teacher leadership may become "an occasion to renew the adversarial relationship that is often latent among teachers and principals" (Barth, 1988b, p. 142). The literature offers four lines of work to prevent this from happening and ensure that the relationships that form the cauldron of teacher leadership are productive. All four sets of activities center on linking new relations to "changes in the traditional roles of the principal" (Dana, 1992, p. 5): having principals examine and reset their understanding of their leadership role, building and reinforcing the "interpersonal dimensions" (Whitaker, 1997, p. 14) of the teacher-principal relationship, redefining power in the school, and reconfiguring structures to support the emergence of productive relationships and effective teacher leadership.

Recasting Leadership

Although principals' concerns . . . are multifaceted, most are evident in the dilemma of empowering others while maintaining a leadership presence. (Murphy, 1994b, p. 43)

The search for a redefined role for self must unfold as part of the growth of the school community. (Louis & Murphy, 1994, p. 272)

It is important to acknowledge that for many principals, championing teacher leadership necessitates a transformation of their own understanding of leadership and their own leadership roles (Murphy, 1994a, 1994b). "The implications for school principals are considerable" (Crowther et al., 2002, p. 64), and this repositioning "poses a significant challenge for principals" (p. 60)—"we cannot assume that [principals] . . . will be able to make shifts in leadership approach without effort or difficulty" (Brown & Sheppard, 1999, p. 17). As we have illustrated throughout this book, teacher leadership is in some essential ways "at odds with the dominant conceptions of the principalship that have been in place in most educational systems for decades" (Crowther et al., 2002, p. 6). Thus just as teacher leaders are being asked to step outside traditional perspectives of their roles, "so must the school principal think differently about his or her role" (Harrison & Lembeck, 1996, p. 111); "principals may have to change some of their behaviors and be comfortable as facilitators when teachers are leading" (Buckner & McDowelle, 2000,

p. 36). Or, as Blegen and Kennedy (2000) conclude, "accepting and encouraging teacher leadership requires a [new] knowledge and skill base" (p. 4) and a new set of performances that are not often highlighted in the education of school administrators (Childs-Bowen et al., 2000; Klecker & Loadman, 1998). New metaphors for the principalship emerge as well (Beck & Murphy, 1993; Sergiovanni, 1991a, 1991b)—metaphors that reflect the role of the principal not in terms of one's fit in the organizational structure but in terms of membership in a community of leaders (Beck & Murphy, 1993).

The point to be underscored here is that for many principals, a personal transformation in leadership must accompany the quest to rebuild schooling to cultivate teacher leadership and efforts to nurture the growth of teacher leaders. Absent this change, it is difficult to imagine that principals will develop the sense of security that is, as Barth (1988b) reminds us, "a precondition upon which development of a community of leaders rests" (p. 142). Likewise, cultivating teacher leadership in a hierarchical and bureaucratic organizational seedbed is problematic at best. New conceptions of organizations provide the foundations for developing the skills to foster teacher leadership. This is challenging work, but principals who do not begin here are not likely to be effective in making shared leadership a reality in their schools.

Building Strong Relationships With Teachers

Although relationships between teacher leaders and other teachers are clearly important, it is the relationship between teacher leaders and their principals that may be most crucial, especially in the early stages of leadership development. (Smylie & Brownlee-Conyers, 1992, p. 151)

Any teacher will be reluctant to take on a leadership role without being comfortable with the level of trust received from the school administration. (Kahrs, 1996, p. 36)

Scholarship in the area of leadership density has produced a rich trove of information about the significance of personal relationships to the health of teacher leadership. We know that "a relationship of trust, cooperation, and respect between identified teacher leaders and school administrators [is] critical to the success of [those] roles. . . . The dynamics of these relationships could be the greatest facilitator, or barrier, to change" (Sherrill, 1999, p. 59). For example, in a series of important studies, Smylie and his colleagues (Smylie, 1992, 1995, 1996; Smylie & Brownlee-Conyers, 1992; Smylie & Denny, 1989; Smylie & Hart, 1999) document that teachers' willingness to assume leadership roles is highly dependent on the relationships they have with their principals: "the principal-teacher relationship serves as a powerful precedent for teacher participation in new school decision-making structures" (Smylie, 1992, p. 63). In short, teacher leadership takes root and flourishes only when there is a healthy relationship between teachers and principals (Broyles, 1991).

We also have abundant evidence, unfortunately, that "one of the most enduring conditions of schools is that teachers and principals generally work in isolation and on different aspects of schooling" (Smylie & Brownlee-Conyers, 1992, p. 152; see Murphy, 1990a, 1999b). Thus there is "no history of trust on which to build new working relations" (Smylie & Brownlee-Conyers, 1992, p. 153). Absent opportunities to collaborate, the essential interpersonal dynamics that make shared leadership meaningful are often conspicuous by their absence in principal-teacher relationships.

Finally, we know that processes for developing the skills needed to build trust and to address the inevitable tensions that accompany the growth of teacher leadership must become part of the school culture. We turn to this learning work in the second half of the chapter.

Rethinking Conceptions of Power

Perhaps the most important item on a list of characteristics of effective principals, then, is the capacity to relinquish, so that the latent, creative powers of teachers can be released. (Barth, 1988a, p. 640)

The principal's willingness to share leadership with teacher leaders is a key to improving the climate of the workplace for emerging teacher leadership. (Yarger & Lee, 1994, p. 234)

As we discuss below, power is the DNA of leadership, both for administrators and for teacher leaders. One cannot lead without the resources and authority to influence others. Traditional models of school organization cede power to the principal. And principals operating from bureaucratic conceptions of schools and hierarchical understandings of leadership often show a "not surprising" (Barth, 2001, p. 447) "unwillingness to share power" (Brown & Sheppard, 1999, p. 17) with teachers. Indeed, as Barth (1988b) observes,

> many principals feel they already have too little power over a tottering building. To convey any to others is illogical. It is against human nature for us to relinquish power when we will probably be held accountable for what others do with it. One should accumulate and consolidate, not relinquish. (p. 138)

The problem is that because these traditional operating frames are inconsistent with the tenets of distributed leadership, institutional views of power stifle efforts to foster teacher leadership (Katzenmeyer & Moller, 2001; Silva et al., 2000; Wasley, 1991). Consequently, principals who want to cultivate denser patterns of leadership in their schools must learn to think about power differently and must be willing to share the playing field with a wider set of colleagues.

In a series of carefully crafted investigations, Leithwood (1992), Leithwood and Jantzi (1990), Leithwood et al. (1991), Leithwood et al. (1992), and Leithwood et al. (1994) exposed the two tasks that form the foundation of these redesigned power relationships: "delegating authentic leadership responsibilities" and developing "collaborative decision-making processes in the school" (Leithwood et al., 1992, p. 30). On the first issue, delegation of authority, initial studies convey both the importance and the difficulty of sharing power. First, they affirm that empowering others represents the biggest change (Prestine, 1991a) and poses "the greatest difficulties and problems for principals" (Prestine, 1991b, p. 15). As one principal astutely put it, "it's easy to set up a process, to delegate, but giving up control is hard" (Christensen, 1992, p. 24). At the same time, the studies impart a sense of how hard it can be for the organization and the community to permit the principal to let go. As we discussed in Chapter 6, existing routines, norms, and expectations are often solidly entrenched, while attempts to delegate control are often quite fragile indeed (Prestine, 1991a). These studies also underscore the centrality of a trusting relationship between principal and teachers in making teacher leadership come to life (Smylie & Denny, 1989). Furthermore, these studies reveal that principals in transformational reform efforts can be successful only by learning to delegate (Prestine, 1991a, 1994; Bredeson, 1991).

> Data indicated that the overwhelming change perceived as necessary in the principal's role was the ability to empower teachers by sharing authority and decision making. From the teachers' perspective, the sharing of decision making authority was seen as essential. (Prestine, 1991a, pp. 11–12)

Empirical investigations on the evolving role of school leaders indicate that even given the great difficulties involved, principals "have at their disposal activities which are reasonably effective" (Leithwood & Jantzi, 1990, p. 22) in "giv[ing] up hierarchical control" (Glickman, Allen, & Lunsford, 1992, p. 17) and empowering teachers to lead (Christensen, 1992; Goldman, Dunlap, & Conley, 1991; Short & Greer, 1993; Smith, 1993). There is also a thick line of analysis in the literature about the ways by which principals give meaning to these emerging shared leadership models through their words, actions, and interpersonal relationships.

Fashioning Supportive Organizational Structures

> Teacher leadership requires some coherent reordering of the workplace of schools. (Yarger & Lee, 1994, p. 234)

> If administrative bureaucrats do not provide the conditions . . . for leadership to flourish, then all educators fail. (Pellicer & Anderson, 1995, p. 21)

The cultivation of teacher leadership and the building of new principal-teacher relationships that encourage it to blossom "can only take place if principals and superintendents are willing to recommend and implement policies and procedures that institutionalize the practice of teachers being decision makers and leaders" (Bishop et al., 1997, p. 78). In Chapter 6, we devoted considerable space to "the organizational and administrative constraints [that make] it difficult to accommodate teacher leaders" (Yarger & Lee, 1994, p. 230). Here we add two points. First, the dimensions of the organizational culture (Moller & Katzenmeyer, 1996) and "the organizational context features" (Crow & Pounder, 2000, p. 244) that are most significant here are those linked to the principal. That is, principals "have both the power and the strategic position to create the internal structures and conditions that are conducive to teacher leadership" (Frost & Durrant, 2003a, p. 179). Second, if teacher leadership is to take root, principals must be aggressive in reshaping organizational structures and moving resources to support the goal of nurturing a deeper pool of leadership. Indeed, "here is where principals' leadership is crucial" (Moller & Katzenmeyer, 1996, p. 12).

In promoting teacher leadership, "the role of the principal is paramount in creating the infrastructures to support these roles" (Childs-Bowen et al., 2000, p. 29; Kahrs, 1996) as well as the policies that buttress the structures (Crowther & Olsen, 1997). The obvious starting point is for principals to "create opportunities for teachers to assume leadership roles" (Blegen & Kennedy, 2000, p. 5). That is, to provide them with the space and authority to engage the leadership work as well as with "the reason and the opportunity to lead" (Little, 1988, p. 99), including the furnishing of funds (Childs-Bowen et al., 2000) and the allocation of "time for . . . teacher leaders to carry out their leadership responsibilities" (Stone et al., 1997, p. 59).

WORKING TO PROMOTE TEACHER LEADERSHIP

It is a paradox of teacher leadership that it requires administrative leadership to be effective. (Smylie et al., 2002, p. 182)

Encouraging teacher leadership is intentional; it does not occur by chance. (Killion, 1996, p. 65)

> The growth in the teacher leaders can almost be gauged by
> the amount of interest, encouragement, and active support
> they receive from their principals. (Birnie & Lustgarten, 1996,
> p. 131)

As the title of this chapter suggests and the analysis throughout
the book reveals, principals occupy a central location in the teacher
leadership equation (Murphy & Datnow, 2003). It is the principal
who, in many ways, "must set the stage for teacher leadership and
allow teachers to seize the opportunity when they recognize the
need" (Kahrs, 1996, p. 27). As noted above, the principal is in a key
position to "set the climate that encourages or stifles teachers'
attempts to enter the circle of leadership" (Blegen & Kennedy,
2000, p. 4). It is the principal who must step to the forefront to
address the "issues that cause a reluctance among teachers to be
leaders" (Bishop et al., 1997, p. 77).

The principal also "plays a key role in how effectively the teacher
leader functions" (Feiler et al., 2000, p. 68). As Katzenmeyer and
Moller (2001) conclude from their extensive analysis, teacher leadership is not a chance organizational event. Where teacher leadership
thrives, administrators "make teacher leadership a priority and take
risks to provide teacher leaders what they need to succeed" (p. 85).
The message in the literature on teacher leadership is unambiguous:
"principals need to know how to develop, support, and manage these
new forms of leadership" (Smylie et al., 2002, p. 182). We devote
the remainder of this chapter to illustrating how principals can
meet this assignment, keeping in mind that part of the answer
was introduced in our earlier analysis of the building of productive principal-teacher relations.

As with most initiatives that work well in schools, vision,
goals, expectations, and "strategic intent" (Crowther et al., 2002,
p. 65) are at the center of efforts to operationalize teacher leadership. In schools where teacher leadership takes hold, principals
are active in conveying the expectation that teachers can lead
(Barth, 1988a; Blegen & Kennedy, 2000) and in creating goals
that help translate those expectations into concrete actions.

Principals nurture teacher leadership by actively identifying
teacher leaders, by matching them with leadership opportunities
(Harrison & Lembeck, 1996; Uline & Berkowitz, 2000), and by
"encourag[ing] them to accept [those] leadership opportunities"

(Buckner & McDowelle, 2000, p. 38): "Savvy principals learn early . . . who are the formal and informal leaders within the school and invite these people to help bring about change" (Katzenmeyer & Moller, 2001, p. 82). Productive principals also acknowledge that the identification of teacher leaders includes empowering teachers to tap colleagues whom they believe would be effective leaders (Whitaker, 1997). This dual strategy of "identifying and selecting teacher leaders" (Killion, 1996, p. 65) is richly illustrated in the research by Crowther and his associates (2002):

> In several instances, principals identified individual teachers, or small groups of teachers, for leadership of priority school projects and then made themselves available as mentors. In other instances, they encouraged staff members to nominate colleagues to develop innovative ideas and, subsequently, accorded the nominees wide responsibility in following through on those ideas. (p. 57)

Researchers from all domains of the teacher leadership field have consistently surfaced the significance of the legitimization role of principals (Lieberman, 1992). For example, in her studies Hart (1994) discovered that "the principals' attention . . . strongly affected the importance that teachers attached to new leadership roles" (p. 495). Moller and Katzenmeyer's (1996) research brought them to a similar position, that "the principal is the most important person to affect the willingness of the school community to accept teacher leaders" (p. 12). And Barth (2001) described the negative impact that ensues when principals "transmit forbidding, unwelcoming messages about teacher leadership" (p. 448).

The thread of legitimization takes on different hues throughout the tapestry of teacher leadership. Sometimes it means showing that the work of teacher leaders is valued, that it is seen as "meaningful" (Wasley, 1991, p. 138)—a type of "affirmation of teachers' leadership" (Clift et al., 1992, p. 904). At other times, it is about "demonstrat[ing] to teachers . . . that their leadership can make a difference in the operation of the school" (Kahrs, 1996, p. 27), "that teacher leadership produces positive school outcomes" (Crowther et al., 2002, p. 34). On still other occasions, legitimization means serving as an advocate for teacher leadership and teacher leaders (Katzenmeyer & Moller, 2001; Miller, 1992). And in still other places, because "teachers will not long go through the heroic efforts of leading schools . . . if the consequences of their work go unnoticed, unrecognized, or unvalued" (Barth, 2001, p. 448), legitimization is about "the recognition of teacher leaders" (Bishop et al., 1997, p. 78), about "recogniz[ing] and rewarding the efforts of those teachers willing to invest their time and energy in acting as leaders" (Katzenmeyer & Moller, 2001, p. 14). It is about finding ways to acknowledge effort and success (Blegen & Kennedy, 2000; Killion, 1996). It also includes "the frequent reinforcement of the real power of teachers" (Hart, 1994, p. 495). And, as Barth (1988a) recounts, it is about sticking with the concept even when the storyline is not especially rosy.

It may appear obvious, but it is nonetheless important to record that principals foster shared leadership by offering "active support" (Crowther et al., 2002, p. 33) to teachers who assume leadership responsibilities (Broyles, 1991; Feiler et al., 2000; Hart, 1990, 1994; Smyser, 1995). Indeed, as Killion (1996) asserts, inactivity on the part of administrators in this area is a recipe for failure. The lack of such support is "often associated with stress and conflict in role performance" (Smylie, 1996, p. 549). Or, obversely, from Crowther and his colleagues (2002), "where we have seen teacher leadership begin to flourish, principals have actively supported it, or at least encouraged it" (p. 33)—"supportive assistance of strategically-minded school administrators was essential to [teacher leaders'] success" (Crowther, 1997, p. 14); from Smylie and Brownlee-Conyers (1992), "principals' support is imperative to the successful performance of teacher leadership roles" (p. 164); and from Katzenmeyer and Moller (2001), "the actions of principals to provide supportive conditions is a key factor in encouraging shared leadership and nurturing teacher leadership roles" (p. 85).

While there is an extensive array of supportive actions that principals can take to cultivate teacher leadership, we illustrate here with specifics from the research literature. Helping everyone come to a clear understanding of the roles of teacher leaders is an especially helpful activity (Blase & Blase, 2001; Murphy & Datnow, 2003; Yarger & Lee, 1994). Allocating additional time can be beneficial (Harrison & Lembeck, 1996) as can making arrangements for common work time (Boles & Troen, 1996).

Furnishing needed resources is almost always viewed in a positive light (Whitaker, 1997). Principal mentoring can facilitate the growth of teachers in their new roles. Support in the form of encouragement can have a powerful impact (Wynne, 2001), especially when "things do not go as planned" (Blegen & Kennedy, 2000, p. 5). "Run[ning] interference and protect[ing]" (Barth, 2001, p. 448) teacher leaders from the bureaucracy and from "the assaults of their fellows" (Barth, 2001, p. 448) conveys an important message of support for teacher leaders. And perhaps no actions are seen as supportive as those that directly involve the principal in the work of teacher leaders (Harrison & Lembeck, 1996; Katzenmeyer & Moller, 2001).

Because "most teachers, like most principals, need assistance in becoming successful school leaders" (Barth, 1988b, p. 139), developing the skills and knowledge of teacher leaders is a central strategy in the portfolio of ideas to foster teacher leadership (Blase & Blase, 2001). Principals must not only ensure the availability of "professional development leadership and learning opportunities" (Doyle, 2000, pp. 39–40), "they must participate in teaching teachers how to be leaders" (Boles & Troen, 1996, p. 60). Indeed, while an assortment of colleagues can assist in the education of teacher leaders (Katzenmeyer & Moller, 2001), "the principal has primary responsibility for developing the leadership skills of . . . teacher leaders" (Feiler et al., 2000, p. 69). Three components of this responsibility merit special notice: (1) "model[ing] leadership strategies and skills that teacher leaders can use" (Katzenmeyer & Moller, 2001, p. 14), (2) participating in the training activities designed for teacher leaders (Hart & Baptist, 1996), and (3) coaching and mentoring around the elements of effective leadership (Barth, 1988b).

Finally, principals work to advance teacher leadership by managing the teacher leadership process. In their leadership toolbox are skills to facilitate the collective work of teacher leaders (Lieberman et al., 1988) and for "mak[ing] space for teacher leaders" (Crowther et al., 2002, p. 58) to undertake their work. Principals recognize the time and energy associated with assuming the extra responsibilities of the new role, and they are watchful to prevent teacher leaders from "wear[ing] themselves out" (Frost & Durrant, 2003a, p. 182; Barth, 1988a, 1988b). They are adept at managing the inevitable conflicts that emerge with teacher colleagues as teacher leaders emerge in schools, and they work to "help teacher leaders feel comfortable in conflict situations" (Buckner & McDowelle, 2000, p. 38). Principals manage teacher leadership at the building by monitoring the structures, both formal and informal, created to support more distributed patterns of leadership (Kahrs, 1996). They also monitor the work of these new leaders (Buckner & McDowelle, 2000), provide them with feedback (Whitaker, 1997), and craft strategies "for holding teacher leaders accountable" (Feiler et al., 2000, p. 69). In short, principals "have a crucial role to play in seeing that planning is followed through with effective monitoring and evaluation" (Frost & Durrant, 2003a, p. 182) and that when operations run smoothly the recognition spotlight is directed to the teacher leaders (Barth, 2001).

CONCLUSION

In this chapter, we explored in some detail the special role played by the building principal in locating, planting, and nurturing the seeds of teacher leadership. We reported that where the concept takes root and flourishes, supportive actions from the principal are almost always visible. We also revealed that through his or her actions the principal can be a significant obstacle to the emergence of teacher leadership.

We explored how the development of teacher leadership in general, and teacher leaders specifically, depends heavily on the quality of principal-teacher relationships. In this area, we emphasized the importance of principals arriving at new, nonhierarchical understandings of leadership, including the willingness to share power widely among their teacher colleagues. We also described how recast organizational structures can be employed in the service of teacher leadership.

In the final part of this chapter, we outlined six key functions in which principals engage to promote teacher leadership: crafting a vision and delineating expectations for teacher leadership in the school, identifying and selecting teacher leaders and linking them to leadership opportunities, legitimizing the work of teacher leaders, providing direct support, developing the leadership skill set of teacher leaders, and managing the teacher leadership process at the school level. In the next chapter, we provide a comprehensive review of what scholarship in this area tells us about how to structure the education of teacher leaders.

C H A P T E R   E I G H T

Developing Teacher Leaders

Clearly teacher leaders will have the most impact if they have the opportunity to benefit from professional development experiences. (Smith-Burke, 1996, p. 13)

If [we] hope to develop the critical mass of teachers who will be needed to reach challenging goals, an important place to start will be to provide all teachers with more opportunities to participate in rigorous, content-rich, collegial professional development. (Snell & Swanson, 2000, p. 20)

Teacher leadership thrives on meaningful professional development experiences, including leadership development. (Katzenmeyer & Moller, 2001, p. 37)

There is an abundance of evidence in the school reform literature that "the main link between policy and practice . . . is professional development" (Elmore, 1996, p. 4). In the area of teacher leadership, in particular, because "leading a group, a school, or an organization is not the same as teaching a class well" (Little, 1988, p. 102), professional development—that is, "providing [teachers] with the necessary support and training" (Fessler & Ungaretti, 1994, p. 218) "to develop new skills and abilities" (Katzenmeyer & Moller, 2001, p. 90)—is a key component in all efforts to deepen leadership in schools (Katzenmeyer & Moller, 2001;

Merchant, 1995; Smylie, 1996). "If we want teacher leaders, then we must work toward providing contexts which encourage learning" (Collinson & Sherrill, 1997, p. 55). Or, as Klecker and Loadman (1998) capture it, "practicing classroom teachers will need professional development to begin learning how to meaningfully take on these new roles" (p. 369), "to help other teachers grow as well" (Yarger & Lee, 1994, p. 223), and "to revitalize schools for all learners" (Keedy, 1999, p. 798; LeBlanc & Shelton, 1997). Indeed, "this is the point at which leadership and staff development intersect. Most teachers (like most principals) need assistance if they are to become successful school leaders" (Barth, 1988a, p. 641). "Professional development is the leverage point for building teacher quality through teacher leadership" (Childs-Bowen et al., 2000, p. 32).

At the same time, it is important to indicate that professional development should not be confined to the individuals assuming new roles or functions. To begin with, because "the amount of support from . . . other teachers will determine teacher leaders' success" (Katzenmeyer & Moller, 2001, p. 53), the peers of these teacher leaders "will also need to be socialized to accept leadership from one of their own" (Berry & Ginsberg, 1990, p. 619). Also, because (1) "educational leaders in the schools and school districts must be committed to taking action in support of teacher leadership" (Katzenmeyer & Moller, 2001, p. 123); (2) "many traditionally trained principals will have difficulty working effectively with teacher leaders" (Teitel, 1996, p. 150), and "challenges" (Katzenmeyer & Moller, 2001, p. 92) and "interpersonal tensions and conflicts [mark] new roles and relationships" (Smylie & Brownlee-Conyers, 1992, p. 180); and (3) "we cannot assume that principals and district administrators know how to do these things particularly well" (Smylie et al., 2002, p. 183), the provision of learning opportunities for school leaders in this area would seem to be essential (Sherrill, 1999; Smylie et al., 2002). The use of collective and collaborative professional development experiences that stretch across administrative and teaching roles may be an especially productive undertaking (Moller & Katzenmeyer, 1996).

THE STATE OF PREPAREDNESS

Teacher leaders often attribute their problems and lack of accomplishment to poor preparation. (Smylie, 1996, p. 549)

> Inservice and preservice programs, as well as the work site, do not promote experiences that enable teachers to develop in some areas that are basic to leadership. (Manthei, 1992, p. 9)

The need for much more thoughtful development of teacher leaders becomes most evident when we examine how existing arrangements leave teachers "ill-equipped" (Fessler & Ungaretti, 1994, p. 213) to exercise leadership outside their classrooms. Scholarship in the area of preservice activities reveals "that little in teacher education programs prepares teachers for such roles" (Carr, 1997, p. 241); that is, "teacher education programs do not regularly include preparation in assuming leadership roles outside of the classroom" (Creighton, 1997, p. 8). Specifically, they fail to facilitate the growth and refinement of the "diverse skills and expertise" (Killion, 1996, p. 70) in an array of areas that are crucial for exercising leadership at the school level (Fay, 1992a).

In a similar vein, "within the teaching profession there is little to nurture such potential" (Carr, 1997, p. 240). Likewise, school districts have largely failed to provide "information, practice, preparation, and support" (Manthei, 1992, pp. 14–15) to "address teacher leadership" (Moller & Katzenmeyer, 1996, p. 9) or to "experience . . . schoolwide leadership roles" (Teitel, 1996, p. 150). Even when such initial investments are forthcoming, they are often undermined by the failure of the district to have "teacher leaders . . . participate in ongoing professional development" (Smith-Burke, 1996, p. 4) to provide the "career-long" (Katzenmeyer & Moller, 2001, p. 125) support needed for teacher leaders to sustain their roles. Given that professional development opportunities have been shown to be "seminal in the development . . . of teacher leadership" (Snell & Swanson, 2000, p. 20), our conclusion that "many teachers have not been prepared for leadership roles in preservice education or staff development" (Johnson & Hynes, 1997, p. 115; Sherrill, 1999)—and "even the most accomplished teachers have had little preparation for an experience with roles outside their classrooms" (Urbanski & Nickolaou, 1997, p. 252)—is disheartening.

Concomitantly, there are important organizational dynamics that exacerbate the problem of teacher preparedness for leadership activities. Teachers in schools, as Swanson (2000) observes, too infrequently "have the benefit of effective leaders to guide their careers" (p. 14). Thus they often lack the informal mentoring as well as the formal staff development opportunities that support the exercise of leadership. Even more troubling is the fact that the work of teaching as currently defined in most schools, that is, "teaching students" (Killion, 1996, p. 73), does not furnish these educators with "the knowledge and skills to create and/or assume new teacher leadership roles" (Manthei, 1992, p. 1). Indeed, Lambert (2003) avers that to assume the mantle of teacher leader, many teachers will actually need to unlearn some of the dynamics of schooling and elements of organizational culture that define their lives as classroom instructors.

Equally important, research is confirming that organizational strategies, such as professionalization and school-based management, that endeavor to operationalize teacher leadership directly are generally ineffective (Murphy & Beck, 1995). As Smylie (1992, 1995, 1996) has consistently shown over the last decade, the goal of promoting teacher leadership is best approached "by designing and supporting professional learning and development opportunities" (1992, p. 65).

Further evidence that teachers are often ill equipped to handle the reigns of leadership outside the classroom comes from these educators themselves. As Stone et al. (1997), Smylie (1996), and Manthei (1992) have all discovered, teachers are "the first to admit that they lack some of the knowledge and skills needed to move into leadership roles with their colleagues" (Manthei, 1992, p. 16). Because they are often forced to "learn the new role just by doing it" (Gehrke, 1991, p. 1), they often express "high levels of frustration [as they] pilot new leadership roles" (McCay et al., 2001, p. 137).

PROFESSIONAL DEVELOPMENT: A GENERAL FRAMEWORK

Professional development will be effective to the extent that it centers on opportunities for staff members to work collaboratively on an ongoing basis. (Murphy & Hallinger, 1993, p. 263)

Elements of Effective Professional Development

Influential professional development offerings must provide teachers with the opportunity to acquire new knowledge, to practice applying this new knowledge, to solicit the feedback of their colleagues, and to have ongoing support in maintaining these newly adopted practices. (Snell & Swanson, 2000, p. 2)

Real learning occurs when one's current paradigms are challenged. (Swanson, 2000, p. 19)

Researchers who have examined the reasons why professional development serves to enhance teacher performance and student outcomes, and analysts who have traced the characteristics of professional development programs that are the most effective, have amassed a fruitful body of wisdom. To begin with, professional development is most efficacious when it is highly valued at the school by the teachers and the principal. Adult learning also works best when educators at the site have a "positive attitude toward staff growth and development" (Hoffman & Rutherford, 1984, p. 87) and a commitment to improvement.

Thinking about professional development from the perspective of structure or organization, we know that most staff development is free standing, short term, nonsystematic, and infrequent. We also understand that these characteristics make implementation of change problematic and do little to enhance performance. On the other hand, professional development is most effective when it is part of a thoughtful plan, is long term in nature, and employs frequent learning sessions for teachers. Inservice tends to be most influential when the "education programs involve teachers who choose to participate" (Anders, Hoffman, & Duffy, 2000, p. 730). Furthermore, because "achieving and sustaining . . . gains is often difficult when improvements are introduced on a classroom-by-classroom basis" (Snow, Burns, & Griffin, 1998, p. 11), schoolwide professional development often leads to more favorable results. The provision of sufficient time for learning is also a distinguishing characteristic of quality professional development. Finally, professional development in successful schools is defined by high levels of administrative support and involvement, especially "principal participation in training" (Samuels, 1981, p. 268).

Continuous and intensive support over time is an essential ingredient of inservice programs. Another critical point is "that teacher change needs support in the context of practice" (Anders et al., 2000, p. 730). The programs that are successful are practice anchored and job embedded; that is, they are context sensitive. "Context specificity" (Hiebert & Pearson, 1999, p. 13) contains a number of key ideas, but primarily it means "building from analysis of [one's] own setting" (p. 13). Sensitivity to context implies that "teachers learn in the classrooms and schools in which they teach" (Stigler & Hiebert, 1999, p. 135). Growth is "connected to and derived from teachers' work with children" (Askew & Gaffney, 1999, p. 87), and effectiveness comes to be defined in terms of "what works with the children [one is] teaching" (Duffy-Hester, 1999, p. 489). The center of gravity is real challenges in the classroom, that is, "resolving instructional problems" (Manning, 1995, p. 656). "All theory building is then checked against practice" (Askew & Gaffney, 1999, p. 85) and "application is direct and obvious" (Stigler & Hiebert, 1999, p. 165).

Concomitantly, professional learning is not insular. Effective programs are adept at bringing outside help to bear on local issues as appropriate. Schools with quality inservice programs are also likely to be part of a network of support of others engaged in learning efforts and to be part of "collaborative arrangements" (Fisher & Adler, 1999, p. 19) formed "among different role groups" (Anders et al., 2000, p. 730).

A trusting context for learning, especially the freedom to try out ideas in a safe environment, is also a key element of effective professional development. So too is the tendency to focus on growth rather than deficits. Finally, there is abundant support for the claim that reflection is a critical variable in the effective training equation. Lyons and Pinnell (1999) phrase this idea nicely when they explain that "teacher development is effective when there is a balance between demonstration of specific approaches and the reflection and analysis needed to build the process of thinking" (p. 210). The "teacher as inquirer" and "teacher as researcher" metaphors hold center stage in effective professional development.

Professional Development as Learning Community

The most powerful professional development opportunities were those where teachers . . . participated in some form of learning community. (Swanson, 2000, p. 15)

Over the past fifteen years, research on teaching, school improvement, and professional development has helped us deepen our understanding of teacher learning and its impact on schools and students. Specifically, this work has shown us that schools will benefit from becoming collaborative learning communities, or communities of practice. Explorations of "especially effective schools suggest that programs of professional development are most successful when several teachers from the same school . . . are involved" (Anderson, Hiebert, Scott, & Wilkinson, 1985, p. 111). In other words, "effective teacher development depends in large part on building a community of learners" (Lyons & Pinnell, 1999, p. 216). Two concepts that are difficult to bring to life in many American schools, collaboration and cooperation, are woven into the center of the community-of-practice tapestry.

Analysts have unearthed a number of elements of communities of practice as they relate to professional development. One is that staff development is cooperatively planned by teachers. Teachers' views are represented and taken seriously (Rutter, 1983). According to Allington and Walmsley (1995), teachers are regarded as "coprofessionals" (p. 261) rather than simply as employees. A second ingredient is shared conversations, what Askew and Gaffney (1999) label "a sharing of knowledge" (p. 87), and Samuels (1981) describes as the "cross-fertilization of ideas" (p. 264). According to Johnston (1999), this "openness of discussion maximizes the possibility of distributed cognition—the system of collective thought in which the whole is more than the sum of the parts" (p. 40). So too is cooperative problem solving a characteristic of professional learning communities. Shared information and shared resolution of problems undergird the growth of other pieces of the collaborative landscape—shared language, shared work, and focus on making historically self-contained and isolated teacher work open and public. From all of this flow two significant outcomes: shared ownership and collective responsibility.

Scholars have also documented tangible ways that communities of professional practice are energized and maintained. Some of the most referenced include the use of regularly scheduled meetings between regular classroom teachers and special teachers; the formation and the employment of grade-level teams as forums for discussion; the use of shared work time to attack challenges; the establishment of study groups and action research teams; creating interdependencies and establishing forums for teachers and administrators to work together; creating opportunities for teachers to observe colleagues in the act of leading; nurturing the development of informal consultations among teachers; and building formal mentoring strategies.

PROFESSIONAL DEVELOPMENT FOR TEACHER LEADERSHIP

Realizing the promise of teacher leadership requires careful attention to the continuous professional development of teachers' leadership knowledge, skills, and attitudes. (Killion, 1996, p. 74)

A more systematic approach to developing the requisite skills for assuming leadership roles may be helpful. (Gehrke, 1991, p. 1)

Support for teacher leadership must include more time and increased access to new knowledge and skills. (Urbanski & Nickolaou, 1997, p. 253)

Because "most professional development is superficial and violates what we know about how adults learn" (Katzenmeyer & Moller, 2001, p. 108), and because current learning opportunities tend to focus on the work that teachers and principals have traditionally performed (Klecker & Loadman, 1998), a good deal of thought must be directed to the structure and the content of learning experiences for teacher leaders.

Elements and Methods

Like other skills, leadership skills are fragile until the teacher leader practices them, gets feedback, and develops competence by using them. A hostile school environment can be an obstacle or can even prevent this growth and development. (Katzenmeyer & Moller, 2001, p. 53)

The literature on teacher leadership, building on the general framework for professional development outlined above, has surfaced key components of development work. To begin with, a quality program for teacher leadership development "recognizes a continuum of teacher growth and challenges participants to imagine larger roles for themselves as professionals" (Southwest Center for Teaching Quality [SCTQ], 2002, p. 1). "Continuous development" (Killion, 1996, p. 70) is a central theme in the learning story. That is, there are "opportunities for continued inquiry and learning" (Smith-Burke, 1996, p. 4), opportunities that unfold "over an extended period of time" (Swanson, 2000, p. 18).

Concentrating on the experiences themselves, it is important that they be "purposeful" (Swanson, 2000, p. 21), that they are anchored in learning and teaching and the desire to "improve schools for all students" (Katzenmeyer & Moller, 2001, p. 53). Learning activities should feature new challenges that push prospective teacher leaders "beyond their comfort zones" (Swanson, 2000, p. 20). They should reflect high expectations (SCTQ, 2002). Development experiences must provide teacher leaders with "the opportunity to acquire new knowledge" (Snell & Swanson, 2000, p. 2). Equally important, because "to learn new skills and not apply them within the school is nonproductive" (Katzenmeyer & Moller, 2001, p. 5), teacher leaders must be afforded opportunities "to apply what they learn in meaningful ways" (Swanson, 2000, p. 12; Rogus, 1988). The point is to provide opportunities "to develop and practice leadership skills" (Pellicer & Anderson, 1995, p. 13).

Given our focus on teacher leadership as an activity outside the classroom, that is, as adult-centered work, the collaborative framework described in the previous section assumes added significance (Smylie et al., 2002; Snell & Swanson, 2000), especially the importance of development within the context of a learning community. In particular, opportunities "to build collegial relationships with peers and mentors while working on collaborative projects" (Smyser, 1995, p. 133) provide an especially fertile seedbed for nurturing teacher leadership skills.

The literature on the development of teacher leadership features three strategies for promoting collaboration. Mentorship is often portrayed as crucial in the "career journeys" (Swanson, 2000, p. 7) of teacher leaders. So too is the concept of team and the importance of teamwork (Crow & Pounder, 2000), as opposed to leading alone. Finally, professional networks that encourage teachers to learn from a wide array of colleagues outside of their own schools are often depicted as an important piece of the collective professional development tapestry.

Turning to the vehicles of learning, scholars note that "professional development for teachers may be formal or informal" (Moller & Katzenmeyer, 1996, p. 9) and that what is most important is the use of a "wide range of methods" (Killion, 1996, p. 70) and a "network of . . . opportunities" (Swanson, 2000, p. 9) that spotlight both approaches. Within this broad framework, analysts point to the need for the creation of "a systematic program aimed at developing teacher leaders" (Killion, 1996, pp. 69–70; Fay, 1992b). They also underscore the importance of tailoring professional development to the specific "context of [a] system" (Smylie et al., 2002, p. 182). That is, "the specific program [of development] should be designed to meet the particular needs of a school district" (Yarger & Lee, 1994, p. 231).

Knowledge and Skills

We realize that there are specific skills that teachers need to be effective leaders. Teacher leaders need to develop reflective skills to examine their own beliefs and practices. They need to acquire communication and facilitation skills to orchestrate collaborative efforts with colleagues to implement change. But most important in becoming an effective leader is the development of sophisticated expertise in pedagogical content knowledge and a professional network to support ongoing learning. (Swanson, 2000, pp. 21–22)

As Forster (1997) has cogently asserted, "the right and responsibility of teachers to fulfill their role as educational leaders must be equally embraced by all segments of the education field and profession" (p. 93). Turning specifically toward professional development of teacher leaders, two segments stand out. First, efforts to develop teacher leaders must begin with teacher education programs (Carr, 1997; Hart, 1995; Stigler & Hiebert, 1999). "Colleges of education must recognize the importance of teacher leadership and strengthen their commitment to teaching those skills as a required component of teacher education" (Troen & Boles, 1994, p. 279). Because research suggests that failure to inculcate leadership skills early on impedes the development of teacher leadership later in one's career (Katzenmeyer & Moller, 2001), "teacher education institutions carry a particular responsibility" (Forster, 1997, p. 93) to help teachers "not only to understand and accept a leading role, but to be able to effectively function in that capacity" (p. 93). Second, districts need to underscore leadership training in their portfolios of ongoing professional development opportunities (Carr, 1997).

The obvious question, of course, is what skills and knowledge should be provided to teachers to help them assume the mantle of leadership? Analysts approach this question in two interrelated ways. They develop models and frameworks to capture best thinking and they examine specific skills. On the first issue, for example, Zimpher (1988) outlines five broad "knowledge domains" (p. 55) of teacher leadership development: "local district needs, interpersonal and adult development, classroom processes and school effectiveness, instructional supervision and observation, and a disposition toward inquiry" (p. 55). In the Katzenmeyer and Moller (2001) model, three categories are featured: teachers understanding themselves, their colleagues, and their schools. Wasley (1991), in turn, highlights five "categories of skills" (p. 25) in her framework of teacher leadership: "trust and rapport building, organizational diagnosis, dealing with process, managing the work, and building skills and confidence in others" (p. 25). Scanning these and related models and building inductively from the literature on the proficiencies required to exercise teacher leadership, we cluster important knowledge and skills into three groups: understanding and navigating the school organization, working productively with others, and building a collaborative enterprise.

Understanding and Navigating the School Organization

> We need to teach preservice and inservice teachers to walk in both the world of children and the world of the schools as organizations. (Silva et al., 2000, p. 800)

Scholarship on teaching and the profession of teaching reveals that many experienced teachers have little understanding of the "institutional structures and processes" (Manthei, 1992,

p. 14) of schools and have difficulty thinking outside the realm of their classrooms, or, as Howey (1988) remarks, "beyond their own teaching" (p. 29). That is, they tend not to "think about the larger context of the whole school or the whole school system" (Katzenmeyer & Moller, 2001, p. 100). Thus a key aspect of professional development for teacher leaders is helping teachers deepen their knowledge of schools as organizations, the development of what Manthei (1992) calls "institutional leadership skills" (p. 15). Teachers need a good deal of knowledge about "organizational theory and behavior" (Boles & Troen, 1996, p. 60), about how organizations beyond individual classrooms work (Manthei, 1992), and the ability "to navigate the organization" (Silva et al., 2000, p. 800) including the capacity "to adjust when they 'bump into' organizational structures" (p. 800). They require skills in "organizational diagnosis" (Gehrke, 1991, p. 1).

Districts will also need to help teacher leaders accumulate a deep understanding of the "politics of schools" (Pellicer & Anderson, 1995, p. 18), especially "organizational politics" (Silva et al., 2000, p. 795) and a good measure of what might best be described as administrative know how, that is, budgeting, finance, data analysis, law, and so forth (McCay et al., 2001; Teitel, 1996; Wasley, 1991). Finally, as part of the work of navigating the organization, teacher leaders will need professional development to master the "skills to function successfully in school reform efforts within their schools" (Katzenmeyer & Moller, 2001, p. 37). This includes an understanding of "the dynamics of the change process" (Clemson-Ingram & Fessler, 1997, p. 99) and "research on school change" (Kilcher, 1992, p. 110), including information on "the stages of change within the school" (Katzenmeyer & Moller, 2001, p. 48) and "knowledge about how to work for change within [the] educational and political system" (Snell & Swanson, 2000, p. 4; Troen & Boles, 1994).

Working Productively With Others

If teacher leaders are to be successful in helping teachers, . . . they must have a basic understanding of what it means to provide help in the context of the complexity of human relationships. (Pellicer & Anderson, 1995, p. 22)

As we studied how these teachers had developed their extensive knowledge and skills, . . . we found that in most cases we could trace these capabilities back to powerful professional development experiences. (Snell & Swanson, 2000, pp. 3–4)

For most teachers, working with students is a nearly all-consuming activity. Consequently, they have spent very little time working with other adults (Manthei, 1992). Not surprisingly, therefore, developing "managerial skills in dealing with people" (Ainscow & Southworth, 1996, p. 234)—the development of "robust interpersonal skills" (Buckner & McDowelle, 2000, p. 38)—is an essential component of professional development designed to help teachers become leaders outside the classroom. Or, as Little (1987) reports it, "the specific skills and perspectives of working with a colleague are critical" (p. 512) for teacher leaders—"teacher leaders need to develop . . . skills in maintaining their relationships with their colleagues" (Teitel, 1996, p. 150). "The importance of building relationships" (Silva et al., 2000, p. 795) cannot be overstated in the work of teacher leaders (Yarger & Lee, 1994); neither can the development of relationship-building capabilities (Lynch & Strodl, 1991): "critical to the development of teacher leaders is an understanding of their own interpersonal relationships with others, particularly their colleagues" (Zimpher, 1988, p. 57).

Scholars in the realm of teacher leadership have isolated an assortment of interpersonal capacities that promote productive working relationships with colleagues. They conclude that professional development should assist teachers in developing proficiencies around a number of "interpersonal issues" (Crow & Pounder, 2000, p. 248). For example, Katzenmeyer and Moller (2001) conclude that "the development of teacher leaders begins with personal knowledge" (p. 70). Professional development in this area builds from the assumption "that effective teacher leaders need to focus on increasing their own self awareness, identity formation, and interpretive capacity" (Zimpher, 1988, p. 57). It is this understanding that permits teacher leaders to (1) recognize the values, behaviors, philosophies, and professional concerns that underlie their personal performance and (2) understand their colleagues, especially those whose experiences and viewpoints do not mirror those of the teacher leaders (Katzenmeyer & Moller, 2001).

A particular aspect of self-understanding that needs exploration is professional development about the "role conflicts and contradictions inherent in assuming the dual roles of classroom teacher and school leader" (Clemson-Ingram & Fessler, 1997, p. 99) and the implications of that understanding for how one works with colleagues.

A bushel of competencies that lubricate effective working relations are often mentioned as candidates for inclusion in professional development for teacher leaders. For example, analysts assert that "skills that will make [teacher leaders] sensitive to seeing others' points of view" (Katzenmeyer & Moller, 2001, p. 67) and "sensitive to others' needs" (LeBlanc & Shelton, 1997, p. 38) are important ingredients in teacher leadership. Also, because teacher leaders often "report that they became more influential through using good listening techniques with peers" (Katzenmeyer & Moller, 2001, p. 93), gaining proficiency in the area of listening skills is important. In a similar view, because friction that sometimes surfaces in group interactions is greatly influenced by the form of those exchanges, teacher leaders are advantaged when they possess well-developed facilitation skills (Zimpher, 1988). According to analysts in this area, facilitation, in turn, "requires a repertoire of skills and strategies" (Kilcher, 1992, p. 110). In its broadest form, facilitation means "knowing how to help a group take primary responsibility for solving its problems and mitigat[ing] factors that hinder the group's ability to be effective" (Killion, 1996, p. 72; Crow & Pounder, 2000). More specifically, it includes the ability to establish trust and rapport and to navigate through problems (Kilcher, 1992). Likewise, there is agreement that teacher leaders need to develop consulting skills (Manthei, 1992) and proficiency in conferencing with colleagues (Zimpher, 1988) if they are to be effective in their new roles. The "principles and skills of advising" (Little, 1985, p. 34) are also key pieces in the portfolio of tools that help establish a productive context for teacher leaders to conduct their work. So too are influencing skills (Hart, 1995; Katzenmeyer & Moller, 2001).

In addition to the social lubrication skills just outlined, analysts assert that professional development for teacher leadership should address a variety of skills for attacking joint work endeavors and provide a set of "group process skills" (Kilcher, 1992, p. 110) for understanding and managing the "group dynamics"

(Pellicer & Anderson, 1995, p. 18) that accompany that work. Perhaps most important here is the broad array of communication skills needed to interact with colleagues (Broyles, 1991; Hart & Baptist, 1996; LeBlanc & Shelton, 1997). Indeed, it is almost an article of faith in the literature in this area that "teacher leaders benefit from ongoing learning and practice in effective communication" (Killion, 1996, p. 72). "Problem-solving techniques" (Hatfield et al., 1986, p. 18) and decision-making skills are also seen as quite important. As Killion (1996) reports, "knowing various decision-making methods, selecting the most appropriate method for a particular situation, and having a repertoire of strategies for helping others reach a decision with the chosen method are critical skills for teacher leaders" (p. 74). Finally, "because change inevitably brings conflict" (Killion, 1996, p. 73) and "teachers have not been adequately trained in conflict resolution techniques" (p. 73), teacher leaders generally benefit from professional development in "conflict management" (Hart, 1995, p. 24) and "conflict resolution" (Fay, 1992a, p. 7). "Change inevitably brings conflict. Teacher leaders who not only understand the factors that lead to conflict but also have a range of strategies for managing and resolving it will be more successful" (Killion, 1996, p. 73).

Building a Collaborative Enterprise

Teacher educators need to recognize the value of the collaborative role. This role needs to be addressed as one of the many [the] inservice teacher should develop in order to promote teacher leadership. (LeBlanc & Shelton, 1997, p. 44)

We must provide professional development experiences related to emerging models of team leadership and organizational learning. (Brown & Sheppard, 1999, p. 17)

While less is written directly on this topic, and to be sure a good deal of what we covered above could also apply here, there is an expanding sense that proficiency in promoting the development and effectiveness of teams or communities of practice is a distinct and an essential pattern in the tapestry of teacher leadership (Harrison & Lembeck, 1996; Smylie et al., 2002). There is also a consensus that even more so than with the two clusters of skills reviewed above, "teacher preparation programs rarely address the development of such skills" (McKeever, 2003, p. 81). Finally, there is a growing acknowledgment that "the realities of working collaboratively with others, especially in large groups with varied participants, require dramatically different skills" (Killion, 1996, p. 71) than those employed in working with youngsters in classrooms.

While there is an almost limitless number of skills needed to address "the collaborative role" (LeBlanc & Shelton, 1997, p. 44), some of the most essential include the ability "to facilitate . . . meetings of colleagues" (McKeever, 2003, p. 81; Harrison & Lembeck, 1996), "to develop relationships" (Sherrill, 1999, p. 58), "to use data" (Katzenmeyer & Moller, 2001, p. 531), "to facilitate joint action" (Forster, 1997, p. 85), and to promote learning in others (Lieberman et al., 1988; Smyser, 1995). In short, "it is helpful for teachers to understand group development and to have a repertoire of strategies for helping groups structure their work and techniques for building teams" (Killion, 1996, p. 73).

CONCLUSION

In these last few chapters, we have targeted the conditions that need to be energized to bring teacher leadership to life in schools. We addressed organizational and professional variables and discussed at some length the important role played by the school principal in ensuring the viability of teacher leadership. In this chapter, we targeted professional development. We began with an analysis of the state of teacher readiness to assume the mantle of teacher leadership. We concluded that many teachers are ill prepared to exercise leadership outside their classrooms. The remainder of the chapter was devoted to exploring the elements of successful models for educating teacher leaders and to unpacking the skills and knowledge that should anchor professional development experiences.

CHAPTER NINE

Conclusion

We must also be wary of the seductive nature of teacher empowerment rhetoric. (Rallis, 1990, p. 186)

However, shared leadership is not an end in itself. Rather, leadership that is shared by teachers and others is a means to accomplish other ends. (O'Hair & Reitzug, 1997, p. 70)

Empirical evidence concerning the actual effects of either formal or informal teacher leadership is limited in quantity and reports mixed results. (Leithwood & Jantzi, 1998, p. 5)

In these few remaining pages, we conclude with several analytic notes on the topic of teacher leadership. We revisit a few key issues, raise some questions, and surface some concerns.

SOME REMINDERS

We begin by reaffirming that the teacher leadership story is a complex narrative (Whitaker, 1997). There is considerable variability in what people mean by the concept, how it is implemented, and in what analysts suggest that it will accomplish. We also underscore again that context is "critically important" (Wasley, 1991, p. 151) in understanding teacher leadership and its effects. Each leadership initiative is "firmly rooted in a particular context and takes into account the school and its participants, the community, the state and the region" (Wasley, 1991, p. 151).

Within context, local history seems to be especially relevant (Little, 1988). Complexity also materializes because teacher leadership is a fluid concept undergoing regular shifts (Uline & Berkowitz, 2000)—changes that because of its short life on the reform stage are neither well understood nor well documented. Or as Silva and his colleagues (2000) disclose, this is often "uncharted territory" (p. 802).

We also acknowledge again that certain essential ingredients are required for teacher leadership to function effectively. Preparation for teacher leadership at the school site seems to be especially important (Copland, 2003), and here clear goals are critical (Barth, 2001). Time to undertake the work and time to "cultivat[e] teacher leadership" (Stone et al., 1997, p. 59) are also necessary elements in the implementation equation. And, as we detailed in Chapters 7 and 8, absent professional development to prepare educators to assume the mantle of teacher leadership and without the backing of those in formal administration positions, this avenue to school improvement will lay fallow (Katzenmeyer & Moller, 2001; Wasley, 1991).

A SKEPTICAL NOTE

It is difficult to digest the literature on teacher leadership without probing into the motives of its supporters. Our analysis into this topic surfaces two nagging concerns connected to issues of power and control. On the one hand, beneath all the rhetoric the possibility that teacher leadership is, for some, little more than an attempt to shift the calculus of control from management to teachers needs to be considered. Even more troubling is the possibility that teacher leadership is a rear-guard effort to reduce teacher autonomy by loosening teacher control over operations in individual classrooms. While one hand is offering greater influence over school-level decisions, the other hand is snatching away control over "classroom policy—what to teach, how to use time, how to assess programs" (Boles & Troen, 1996, p. 44) and so forth. A careful analysis of the preliminary evidence on this point suggests that teachers could end up losing much more than they gain in this "exchange." What is especially intriguing here is the fact that earlier and more blunt efforts to "break the bounds of privacy in teaching" (Little & McLaughlin, 1993b, p. 1) via policy were largely ineffective. An especially skeptical person might view teacher leadership as a type of Trojan horse that allows certain reformers to take over from the inside what they have consistently failed to achieve by direct assaults.

A PARADOX

If one were inclined to undertake the assignment, an interesting parable could be constructed around the role of structure in the teacher leadership narrative. To begin with, there is abundant evidence to show that emphasizing structure in teacher leadership work often results in new rungs in the hierarchical system of school management. In these cases, rather than being loosened, the bureaucratic tentacles of schools are actually tightened. Given this conclusion, not surprisingly, over the last decade much of the energy supporting role-based and other structural strategies to capture leadership responsibilities for teachers has been withdrawn. The focus has shifted to culture building, community development, and the more informal aspects of teacher leadership.

Unfortunately, we also know that "formal policy and structure stand as safety nets for teacher leaders" (Hart, 1995, p. 13). Operating outside the protection of structure is a recipe for limited traction and ultimate failure. As Katzenmeyer and Moller (2001) discovered, reformers in the area of teacher leadership "have come to understand, however, that role differentiation in terms of titles, responsibilities, and pay can hasten the movement of teachers into roles in which they can support their colleagues to affect student outcomes" (p. 126). A reasonable conclusion to draw at this stage in the development of teacher leadership is that more structure, not less, is in order. The quest must be not to find ways to eliminate structure but rather to use structures in the service of deeper conceptions of teacher leadership.

GAPS IN THE LANDSCAPE

There are a few obvious thin spots in the tapestry of teacher leadership that merit consideration. To begin with, even in a profession that has historically turned a blind eye to the assessment of reform initiatives, the lack of evaluation in the area of teacher leadership is noteworthy. In a similar vein, the assumptions supporting teacher leadership endeavors are rarely scrutinized. We return to these issues below.

In the era of the most stringent accountability in the history of education, the near absence of attention to accountability issues in the teacher leadership literature is difficult to justify. This conclusion is especially salient in light of the following caution provided by Katzenmeyer and Moller (2001): "Simply opening leadership roles for teachers may not make a difference in improving student performance. Only when teachers have both the chance to be involved and the accountability for progress will teacher-led change be meaningful" (p. 30).

Likewise, in a period of unparalleled concern for social justice, especially around experiences unfolding for youngsters, the failure, or unwillingness, of teacher leadership scholars to weave moral threads into the technical and community dimensions of the teacher leadership chronicle is somewhat unexpected. Given this, while it may not be surprising, it is still disappointing that the teacher leadership movement has done so little to address what O'Hair and Reitzug (1997) label its "underside" (p. 71)—an insular and singular focus by reform advocates on teachers at the expense of empowering students and families as well.

Perhaps the most surprising gap in the teacher leadership literature is the relatively small number of teachers who are involved in providing the chronicle. As Hinchey (1997) observes, "many of the efforts to professionalize teaching and to offer teachers a voice in how the business of a school is conducted have been designed, implemented, and critiqued without significant input from teachers themselves" (p. 234). Teachers have simply often "not been included in the current discussion about teacher leadership" (Wasley, 1991, p. 161).

SOME CAVEATS AND CONCERNS

Three embedded themes in the teacher leadership literature merit scrutiny. To begin with, there is an underlying current in the scholarship in this area that leadership that is exercised by teachers is better than leadership enacted by school administrators. This is a problematic assumption. If there are any clues on this issue, they lead to the conclusion that yoking teacher and administrator leadership in the service of a worthy end is the most productive leadership architecture. Likewise, there is a sense in this work that shared leadership is better than concentrated leadership. While there is support for this conclusion based on democratic values, it enjoys considerably less support when organizational impact criteria are employed. As Donaldson (2001) informs us, "what the group does as a result of the leadership relationship is of the utmost importance" (p. 42). Finally, there is a presumption throughout the corpus of work here that more leadership is to be preferred, that the goal is to get as many teachers as possible in a school to become teacher leaders. Additional empirical evidence may support this point. However, Leithwood and Jantzi (1998) remind us that the research available to date suggests the exercise of prudence in uncritically following this path. Their results "call for considerable caution on the part of those who argue that everyone should become a leader. However attractively egalitarian and democratic that may seem, perhaps schools benefit most from the leadership of a small number of easily identified sources" (p. 27).

In addition, there are a host of concerns that can be raised about the teacher leadership movement. Here we focus on the one that seems most important. Specifically, given the narrative produced to date, there is good reason to worry that teacher leadership is being forged using a surfeit of administrative material as opposed to a generous supply of instructional material. A number of scholars have unearthed this troubling theme; that is, "rather than being instructional in nature" (Whitaker, 1997, p. 14), the central dynamic of teacher leadership is administration (Bliss et al., 1995; Little, 1995; Smylie, 1996). Analyses of the work of guidance counselors and department heads only reinforce this concern. Given the dominance of bureaucratic and hierarchical organizational frames in schools and the strong managerial imperative in school leadership roles, the continued managerialization of teacher leadership seems to be an especially likely scenario. If alternative narratives are to be developed, ones that highlight the teaching dimensions of teacher leadership, advocates will need to be considerably more proactive than they have been to date.

A QUESTION OF EVIDENCE

Perhaps no issue is more critical in the area of teacher leadership than documenting the ways this reform functions and the outcomes it produces. There are few investigations of the engines that are supposed to power distributed leadership (Ingersoll, 1996; see Copland, 2003, for an exception). Nor have researchers accumulated information on the theory in action or "assumptions that undergird most of the teacher leadership initiatives" (Zimpher, 1988, p. 54); "we know relatively little about the specific mechanisms by which collegial relations among teachers operate to the benefit of students" (Little, 1987, p. 494). Finally, we have only "skimpy insights" (Leithwood & Jantzi, 1998, p. 7) into the effects or outcomes of teacher leadership. Data on teacher leadership are "limited in quantity" (Leithwood et al., 1997, p. 4). In particular, evidence that teacher leadership "makes schools richer or more productive for students" (Schmoker & Wilson, 1994, p. 148) is in short supply.

The research we do have on the impact question has "produced mixed results" (Little, 1988, p. 87). "Research concerning the relationship of teacher leadership to student learning is . . . equivocal" (Smylie, 1996, p. 576), as is the evidence on the connections between teacher leadership and classroom instruction (Griffin, 1995; Smylie, 1996).

While there is a sense that individual educators assigned leadership responsibilities may benefit from teacher leadership initiatives (Katzenmeyer & Moller, 2001), there are concerns that these benefits may not be spreading to the larger community of teachers (Darling-Hammond et al., 1995; O'Hair & Reitzug, 1997; Wasley, 1991). These concerns, as Odell (1997) observes, apply especially to role-based approaches to teacher leadership: "While these formal role assignments have empowered teachers as leaders and have served to deregulate the teaching process from direct administrative control, in general these role assignments have not led to a pervasive enhancement of teachers" (p. 120). These roles simply may "not spread benefits to the larger teaching force" (Wasley, 1991, p. 25).

The limited evidence available also reveals "a very modest connection between school redesign and shared decision making and individual teachers' pedagogical practice" (Griffin, 1995,

p. 38). Indeed, there is a thin line of evidence showing that an "increase on time spent on schoolwide issues" (Kahrs, 1996, p. 29) "diminish[es] the time teachers have with children" (LeBlanc & Shelton, 1997, p. 34) and "reduces their effectiveness in the classroom" (Kahrs, 1996, p. 29).

Despite the well-ingrained proposition that "the linchpin to creating professional leadership for teachers" (Schmoker & Wilson, 1994, p. 137) must rest upon "a commitment to making connections between professional knowledge and activity and educational results" (p. 137) and the widely acknowledged argument that "the ultimate measure of the contributions of teacher leaders . . . is the impact of teacher leaders on student academic performance" (Wynne, 2001, p. 1), this linkage has been largely unstudied. In short, to date "there is little evidence that these roles improve the quality of education experience . . . students receive" (Wasley, 1991, p. 27; Crow & Pounder, 2000; Leithwood & Jantzi, 1998).

A NOTE ON RESEARCH

Katzenmeyer and Moller (2001) maintain that a "change that could profoundly advance the cause of teacher leadership is more research on the concept itself" (p. 128). Given the analysis provided above, it should come as no surprise that we echo this call for additional study on teacher leadership—on its contours, operations, and impacts. It is especially important as we accept this charge that we deepen the richness of the investigatory work, moving beyond a near exclusive relevance on descriptive studies while paying more attention to formal theory and "strong conceptual definition[s]" (Smylie, 1996, p. 574). We need to acknowledge that distributed leadership is more difficult to isolate and to assess than individual leadership (Crowther et al., 2002). We require studies that are sufficiently nuanced to explore informal leadership roles (Moller & Katzenmeyer, 1996). There is a demand for studies that follow the thread of leadership generally rather than leadership within specific roles (Leithwood & Jantzi, 1998). In this regard, research that tracks leadership in change initiatives and across areas of school operations may prove to be especially productive.

CONCLUSION

In this final chapter, we completed a number of assignments. We reintroduced some key issues raised in earlier chapters that must be kept in mind as we move forward in our quest to understand teacher leadership. We revisited the complex nature of this reform initiative and emphasized again important supporting conditions such as principal leadership and professional development. We also raised some concerns and provided some challenges that, if met, could significantly enhance the viability of teacher leadership. Finally, we teased out some dilemmas associated with the motives that inform and the structures that buttress the teacher leadership movement, pointed out some thin spots in the teacher leadership tapestry, introduced a few caveats, and outlined ways research on teacher leadership could be strengthened.

References

Achilles, C. M., Brubaker, D., & Snyder, H. (1990, October). *Organizing for leading and learning: The interplay of school reform and restructuring with preparation program reform and restructuring.* Paper presented at the annual meeting of the University Council for Educational Administration, Pittsburgh, PA.

Ainscow, M., & Southworth, G. (1996). School improvement: A study of the roles of leaders and external consultants. *School Effectiveness and School Improvement, 7*(3), 229–251.

Allington, R. L., & Walmsley, S. A. (1995). No quick fix: Where do we go from here? In R. L. Allington & S. A. Walmsley (Eds.), *No quick fix: Rethinking literacy programs in America's elementary schools* (pp. 253–264). New York: Teachers College Press.

American Association of Colleges for Teacher Education. (1988). *School leadership preparation: A preface for action.* Washington, DC: Author.

Anders, P. L., Hoffman, J. V., & Duffy, G. G. (2000). Teaching teachers to teach reading: Paradigm shifts, persistent problems, and challenges. In M. L. Kamil, P. B. Mosenthal, P. D. Pearson, & R. Barr (Eds.), *Handbook of Reading Research* (Vol. 3, pp. 719–742). Mahwah, NJ: Lawrence Erlbaum.

Anderson, R. C., Hiebert, E. H., Scott, J. A., & Wilkinson, I. A. G. (1985). *Becoming a nation of readers: The report of the commission on reading.* Washington, DC: The National Institute of Education, US Department of Education.

Angus, L. B. (1988, April). *School leadership and educational reform.* Paper prepared for the annual meeting of the American Educational Research Association, New Orleans, LA.

Askew, B. J., & Gaffney, J. S. (1999). Reading recovery: Waves of influence on literacy education. In J. S. Gaffney & B. J. Askew (Eds.), *Stirring the waters: The influence of Marie Clay* (pp. 75–98). Portsmouth, NH: Heinemann.

Association for Supervision and Curriculum Development. (1986, September). *School reform policy: A call for reason.* Alexandria, VA: Association for Supervision and Curriculum Development.

Astuto, T. A. (1990, September). *Reinventing school leadership* (pp. 2–5). Working memo prepared for the Reinventing School Leadership Conference. Cambridge, MA: National Center for Educational Leadership.

Banathy, B. H. (1988). An outside-in approach to design inquiry in education. In Far West Laboratory for Educational Research and Development (Ed.), *The redesign of education: A collection of papers concerned with comprehensive educational reform* (Vol. 1, pp. 51–71). San Francisco: Far West Laboratory.

Barth, R. S. (1986, December). On sheep and goats and school reform. *Phi Delta Kappan, 68*(4), 293–296.

Barth, R. S. (1988a). Principals, teachers, and school leadership. *Phi Delta Kappan, 69*(9), 639–642.

Barth, R. S. (1988b). School: A community of leaders. In A. Lieberman (Ed.), *Building a professional culture in schools* (pp. 129–147). New York: Teachers College Press.

Barth, R. S. (2001, February). Teacher leader. *Phi Delta Kappan, 82*(6), 443–449.

Bates, R. J. (1984). Toward a critical practice of educational administration. In T. J. Sergiovanni & J. E. Corbally (Eds.), *Leadership and organizational culture: New perspectives on administrative theory and practice* (pp. 260–274). Urbana: University of Illinois Press.

Beare, H. (1989, September). *Educational administration in the 1990s.* Paper presented at the national conference of the Australian Council for Educational Administration, Armidale, New South Wales, Australia.

Beck, L. G. (1994). *Reclaiming educational administration as a caring profession.* New York: Teachers College Press.

Beck, L. G., & Foster, W. (1999). Administration and community: Considering challenges, exploring possibilities. In J. Murphy & K. S. Louis (Eds.), *Handbook of Research on Educational Administration* (pp. 337–358). San Francisco: Jossey-Bass.

Beck, L. G., & Murphy, J. (1993). *Understanding the principalship: A metaphorical analysis, 1920s–1990s.* New York: Teachers College Press.

Beck, L. G., & Murphy, J. (1994). *Ethics in educational leadership programs: An expanding role.* Thousand Oaks, CA: Corwin Press.

Beck, L. G., Murphy, J., & Associates. (1996). *Ethics in educational leadership programs: Emerging models.* Columbia, MO: University Council for Educational Administration.

Berends, M., Bodilly, S., & Kirby, S. N. (2002). District and school leadership for whole-school reform. In J. Murphy & A. Datnow (Eds.), *Leadership for school reform: Lessons from comprehensive school reforms* (pp. 109–131). Thousand Oaks, CA: Corwin Press.

Berliner, D. L. (1986, October). On the expert teacher: A conversation with David Berliner. *Educational Leadership, 44*(2), 4–9.

Berry, B., & Ginsberg, R. (1990, April). Creating lead teachers: From policy to implementation. *Phi Delta Kappan, 71*(8), 616–621.

Birnie, B. F., & Lustgarten, C. (1996). SUNRAYS: Cultivating teacher leaders in an urban community. In G. Moller & M. Katzenmeyer (Eds.), *Every teacher as a leader: Realizing the potential of teacher leadership* (pp. 117–138). San Francisco: Jossey-Bass.

Bishop, H. L., Tinley, A., & Berman, B. T. (1997, Fall). A contemporary leadership model to promote teacher leadership. *Action in Teacher Education, 19*(3), 77–81.

Blackman, M. C. (1990, September). *Reinventing school leadership* (pp. 8–11). Working memo prepared for the Reinventing School Leadership Conference. Cambridge, MA: National Center for Educational Leadership.

Blase, J., & Blase, J. (2001). *Empowering teachers: What successful principals do* (2nd ed.). Thousand Oaks, CA: Corwin Press.

Blegen, M. B., & Kennedy, C. (2000, May). Principals and teachers, leading together. *NASSP Bulletin, 84*(616), 1–6.

Bliss, T., Fahrney, C., & Steffy, B. (1995, October). *Secondary department chair roles: Ambiguity and change in systemic reform.* Lexington: University of Kentucky, Institute on Educational Reform.

Boles, K., & Troen, V. (1994). *Teacher leadership in a professional development school.* Paper presented at the annual meeting of the American Educational Research Association, New Orleans, LA.

Boles, K., & Troen, V. (1996). Teacher leaders and power: Achieving school reform from the classroom. In G. Moller & M. Katzenmeyer (Eds.), *Every teacher as a leader: Realizing the potential of teacher leadership* (pp. 41–62). San Francisco: Jossey-Bass.

Bolin, F. S. (1989, Fall). Empowering leadership. *Teachers College Record, 91*(1), 81–96.

Boyd, W. L. (1987, Summer). Public education's last hurrah? Schizophrenia, amnesia, and ignorance in school politics. *Educational Evaluation and Policy Analysis, 9*(2), 85–100.

Bredeson, P. V. (1989, March). *Redefining leadership and the roles of school principals: Responses to changes in the professional work life of teachers.* Paper presented at the annual meeting of the American Educational Research Association, Seattle, WA.

Bredeson, P. V. (1991, April). *Letting go of outlived professional identities. A study of role transition for principals in restructured schools.* Paper presented at the annual meeting of the American Educational Research Association, Chicago, IL.

Brown, D. J. (1992, September). The recentralization of school districts. *Educational Policy, 6*(3), 289–297.

Brown, J., & Sheppard, B. (1999, April). *Leadership, organizational learning, and classroom change.* Paper presented at the annual meeting of the American Educational Research Association, Montreal, Quebec.

Brownlee, G. D. (1979, Spring). Characteristics of teacher leaders. *Educational Horizons, 57*(3), 119–122.

Broyles, I. L. (1991, April). *Transforming teacher leadership through action research.* Paper presented at the annual meeting of the New England Educational Research Association, Portsmouth, NH.

Brunner, C. C., Grogan, M., & Björk, L. (2002). Shifts in discourse defining the superintendency: Historical and current foundations of the positions. In J. Murphy (Ed.), *The educational leadership challenge: Redefining leadership for the 21st century* (pp. 211–238). Chicago: University of Chicago.

Bryk, A. S. (1993, July). *A view from the elementary schools: The state of reform in Chicago.* Chicago: Consortium on Chicago School Research.

Buckner, K. G., & McDowelle, J. O. (2000, May). Developing teacher leaders: Providing encouragement, opportunities, and support. *NASSP Bulletin, 84*(616), 35–41.

Burke, C. (1992). Devolution of responsibility to Queensland schools: Clarifying the rhetoric critiquing the reality. *Journal of Educational Administration, 30*(4), 33–52.

Caine, G., & Caine, R. N. (2000, May). The learning community as a foundation for developing teacher leaders. *NASSP Bulletin, 84*(616), 7–14.

Campbell, R. F., Fleming, T., Newell, L., & Bennion, J. W. (1987). *A history of thought and practice in educational administration.* New York: Teachers College Press.

Candoli, J. C. (1991). *School system administration: A strategic plan for site-based management.* Lancaster, PA: Technomic.

Carnegie Forum on Education and the Economy. (1986, May). *A nation prepared: Teachers for the 21st century.* Washington, DC: Carnegie Forum on Education and the Economy.

Carnoy, M., & MacDonnell, J. (1990). School district restructuring in Santa Fe, New Mexico. *Educational Policy, 4*(1), 49–64.

Carr, D. A. (1997, May/June). Collegial leaders: Teachers who want more than just a job. *The Clearing House, 70*(5), 240–242.

Chapman, J. (1990). School-based decision making and management: Implications for school personnel. In C. Chapman (Ed.), *School-based decision making and management* (pp. 221–244). London: Falmer.

Chapman, J., & Boyd, W. L. (1986, Fall). Decentralization, devolution, and the school principal: Australian lessons on statewide educational reform. *Educational Administration Quarterly, 22*(4), 28–58.

Cheng, Y. C. (1994). Teacher leadership style: A classroom-level study. *Journal of Educational Administration, 32*(3), 54–71.

Chenoweth, T. G., & Everhart, R. B. (2002). *Navigating comprehensive school change: A guide for the perplexed.* Larchmont, NY: Eye on Education.

Childs-Bowen, D., Moller, G., & Scrivner, J. (2000, May). Principals: Leaders of leaders. *NASSP Bulletin, 84*(616), 27–34.

Chrispeels, J. H. (1992). *Purposeful restructuring: Creating a culture for learning and achievement in elementary schools.* Bristol, PA: Falmer.

Christensen, G. (1992, April). *The changing role of the administrator in an accelerated school.* Paper presented at the annual meeting of the American Educational Research Association, San Francisco, CA.

Christensen, J. C. (1987). Roles of teachers and administrators. In P. R. Burden (Ed.), *Establishing career ladders in teaching: A guide for policy makers* (pp. 88–110). Springfield, IL: Charles C. Thomas.

Chubb, J. E. (1988, Winter). Why the current wave of school reform will fail. *Public Interest, 90,* 28–49.

Clark, D. L. (1987, August). *Thinking about leaders and followers: Restructuring the roles of principals and teachers.* Paper presented at the conference on Restructuring Schooling for Quality Education, Trinity University, San Antonio, TX.

Clark, D. L., & Meloy, J. M. (1989). Renouncing bureaucracy: A democratic structure for leadership in schools. In T. J. Sergiovanni & J. A. Moore (Eds.), *Schooling for tomorrow: Directing reform to issues that count* (pp. 272–294). Boston: Allyn & Bacon.

Clemson-Ingram, R., & Fessler, R. (1997, Fall). Innovative programs for teacher leadership. *Action in Teacher Education, 19*(3), 95–106.

Clift, R., Johnson, M., Holland, P., & Veal, M. L. (1992, Winter). Developing the potential for collaborative school leadership. *American Educational Research Journal, 29*(4), 877–908.

Clune, W. H., & White, P. A. (1988, September). *School-based management: Institutional variation, implementation, and issues for further research.* New Brunswick, NJ: Rutgers University, Eagleton Institute of Politics, Center for Policy Research in Education.

Cohen, D. K. (1988, September). *Teaching practice: Plus ça change . . .* (Issue paper 88-3). East Lansing: Michigan State University, The National Center for Research on Teacher Education.

Collins, J. (1990, September). *Reinventing school leadership* (pp. 31–35). Working memo prepared for the Reinventing School Leadership Conference. Cambridge, MA: National Center for Educational Leadership.

Collinson, V., & Sherrill, J. (1997, Winter/Spring). Changing contexts for changing roles: Teachers as learners and leaders. *Teaching Education, 8*(2), 55–63.

Conley, D. T. (1991, March). Lessons from laboratories in school restructuring and site-based decision making. *Oregon School Study Council Bulletin, 34*(7), 1–61.

Conley, D. T. (1997). *Roadmap to restructuring: Charting the course of change in American education.* Eugene, OR: ERIC Clearinghouse on Educational Management.

Conley, S. C. (1989, March). *"Who's on first?": School reform, teacher participation, and the decision-making process.* Paper presented at the annual meeting of the American Educational Research Association, San Francisco, CA.

Conley, S., & Muncey, D. E. (1999, Winter). Teachers talk about teaming and leadership in their work. *Theory Into Practice, 38*(1), 46–55.

Copland, M. A. (2003). Building the capacity to lead: Promoting and sustaining change in an inquiry-based model of school reform. Draft copy of a manuscript (pp. 1–34) that later appeared in J. Murphy & A. Datnow (Eds.), *Leadership for school reform: Lessons from comprehensive school reform designs* (pp. 159–183). Thousand Oaks, CA: Corwin Press.

Corbett, H. D., & Rossman, G. B. (n.d.). *How teachers empower superordinates: Running good schools.* Philadelphia: Research for Better Schools. (ERIC Document Reproduction Service No. ED374540)

Corcoran, T. B. (1989). Restructuring education: A new vision at Hope Essential High School. In J. M. Rosow & R. Zager (Eds.), *Allies in educational reform* (pp. 243–274). San Francisco: Jossey-Bass.

Coyle, M. (1997, May/June). Teacher leadership vs. school management: Flatten the hierarchies. *Teacher Leadership, 70*(5), 236–239.

Creighton, T. B. (1997, March). *Teachers as leaders: Is the principal really needed?* Paper presented at the Annual Conference on Creating Quality Schools, Oklahoma City, OK. (ERIC Document Reproduction Service No. ED411117)

Crow, G. M., Hausman, C. S., & Scribner, J. P. (2002). Reshaping the role of the school principal. In J. Murphy (Ed.), *The educational leadership challenge: Redefining leadership for the 21st century* (pp. 162–188). Chicago: University of Chicago Press.

Crow, G. M., & Pounder, D. G. (2000, April). Interdisciplinary teacher teams: Context, design, and process. *Educational Administration Quarterly, 36*(2), 216–254.

Crowther, F. (1997). The William Walker oration, 1996: Unsung heroes: The leaders in our classrooms. *Journal of Educational Administration, 35*(1), 5–17.

Crowther, F., Kaagan, S. S., Ferguson, M., & Hann, L. (2002). *Developing teacher leaders: How teacher leadership enhances school success.* Thousand Oaks, CA: Corwin Press.

Crowther, F., & Olsen, P. (1997). Teachers as leaders—an exploratory framework. *International Journal of Educational Management, 11*(1), 6–13.

Cuban, L. (1984, November). School reform by remote control: SB 813 in California. *Phi Delta Kappan, 66*(3), 213–215.

Cuban, L. (1989). The "at-risk" label and the problem of urban school reform. *Phi Delta Kappan, 70*(10), 780–784, 799.

Culbertson, J. A. (1988). A century's quest for a knowledge base. In N. J. Boyan (Ed.), *Handbook of research on educational administration* (pp. 3–26). New York: Longman.

Cunningham, L. L. (1990). Educational leadership and administration: Retrospective and prospective views. In B. Mitchell & L. L. Cunningham (Eds.), *Educational leadership and changing contexts of families, communities, and schools* (Eighty-ninth NSSE Yearbook, Part II, pp. 1–18). Chicago: University of Chicago Press.

Dana, N. F. (1992, October). *Teacher leadership through collaborative action research: Implications for teachers, principals, and university researchers/teacher educators.* Paper presented at the annual meeting of the Pennsylvania Association for Colleges of Teacher Educators, Grantsville, PA.

Darling-Hammond, L. (1988). Policy and professionalism. In A. Lieberman (Ed.), *Building a professional culture in schools* (pp. 55–77). New York: Teachers College Press.

Darling-Hammond, L., Bullmaster, M. L., & Cobb, V. L. (1995, September). Rethinking teacher leadership through professional development schools. *The Elementary School Journal, 96*(1), 87–107.

Datnow, A., & Castellano, M. (2002). Leadership and success for all. Draft copy of a manuscript (pp. 1–32) that later appeared in J. Murphy & A. Datnow (Eds.), *Leadership for school reform: Lessons from comprehensive school reforms* (pp. 187–208). Thousand Oaks, CA: Corwin Press.

David, J. L. (1989, May). Synthesis of research on school-based management. *Educational Leadership, 46*(8), 45–53.

Deck, L. (1990, September). *Reinventing school leadership* (pp. 48–51). Working memo prepared for the Reinventing School Leadership Conference. Cambridge, MA: National Center for Educational Leadership.

Dellar, G. B. (1992, April). *Connections between macro and micro implementation of educational policy: A study of school restructuring in Western Australia.* Paper presented at the annual meeting of the American Educational Research Association, San Francisco, CA.

Donaldson, G. A. (2001). *Cultivating leadership in schools: Connecting people, purpose, and practice.* New York: Teachers College Press.

Doyle, M. (2000, April). *Making meaning of teacher leadership in the implementation of a standards-based mathematics curriculum.* Paper presented at the annual meeting of the American Educational Research Association, New Orleans, LA.

Driscoll, M. E. (1990). The formation of community in public schools: Findings and hypotheses. *Administrator's Notebook, 34*(4), 1–4.

Duffy-Hester, A. M. (1999, February). Teaching struggling readers in elementary school classrooms: A review of classroom reading programs and principles for instruction. *The Reading Teacher, 52*(5), 480–495.

Duke, D. L. (1994). Drift, detachment, and the need for teacher leadership. In D. R. Walling (Ed.), *Teachers as leaders: Perspectives on the professional development of teachers* (pp. 255–273). Bloomington, IN: Phi Delta Kappa.

Duttweiler, P. C., & Mutchler, S. E. (1990). *Organizing the educational system for excellence: Harnessing the energy of people.* Austin, TX: Southwest Educational Development Laboratory.

Early, P., Baker, L., & Weindling, D. (1990). *"Keeping the raft afloat": Secondary leadership five years on.* Slough, UK: National Foundation for Educational Research in England and Wales.

Elmore, R. F. (1987, November). Reform and the culture of authority in schools. *Educational Administration Quarterly, 23*(4), 60–78.

Elmore, R. (1990a). Introduction: On changing the structure of public schools. In R. Elmore & Associates (Eds.), *Restructuring schools: The next generation of educational reforms* (pp. 1–29). San Francisco: Jossey-Bass.

Elmore, R. F. (1990b, September). *Reinventing school leadership* (pp. 62–65). Working memo prepared for the Reinventing School Leadership Conference. Cambridge, MA: National Center for Educational Leadership.

Elmore, R. F. (1993). School decentralization: Who gains? Who loses? In J. Hannaway & M. Carnoy (Eds.), *Decentralization and school improvement* (pp. 33–54). San Francisco: Jossey-Bass.

Elmore, R. F. (1996, March). *Staff development and instructional improvement: Community District 2, New York City.* Draft paper presented to the National Commission on Teaching and America's Future.

Elmore, R. F. (2000). *Building a new structure for school leadership.* Washington, DC: The Albert Shanker Institute.

Elmore, R. (2003). Accountability and capacity. In M. Carnoy, R. Elmore, & L. S. Siskin (Eds.), *High schools and the new accountability* (pp. 195–209). New York: Routledge.

Elmore, R. F., Peterson, P. L., & McCarthey, S. J. (1996). *Restructuring in the classroom: Teaching, learning, and school organization.* San Francisco: Jossey-Bass.

Engel, D. E. (1990, May). Pittsburgh's teacher-administrator partnership: A new relationship. *Educational Leadership, 47*(8), 44–45.

Epps, E. G. (1992). School-based management: Implications for minority parents. In J. J. Lande & E. G. Epps (Eds.), *Restructuring the schools: Problems and prospects* (pp. 146–163). Berkeley, CA: McCutchan.

Etheridge, C. P., Valesky, T. C., Horgan, D. D., Nunnery, J., & Smith, D. (1992, April). *School-based decision making: An investigation into effective and ineffective decision making processes and the impact on school climate variables.* Paper presented at the annual meeting of the American Educational Research Association, San Francisco, CA.

Evans, R. (1991, April). *Ministrative insight: Educational administration as pedagogic practice.* Paper presented at the annual meeting of the American Educational Research Association, Chicago, IL.

Fay, C. (1992a, April). *The case for teacher leadership: Toward definition and development.* Paper presented at the annual meeting of the American Educational Research Association, San Francisco, CA.

Fay, C. (1992b). Empowerment through leadership: In the teachers' voice. In C. Livingston (Ed.), *Teachers as leaders: Evolving roles* (pp. 57–90). Washington, DC: National Education Association.

Feiler, R., Heritage, M., & Gallimore, R. (2000, April). Teachers leading teachers. *Educational Leadership, 57*(7), 66–69.

Feiman-Nemser, S., & Floden, R. F. (1986). The cultures of teaching. In C. W. Wittrock (Ed.), *Handbook of research on teaching* (3rd ed., pp. 505–526). New York: Macmillan.

Fessler, R., & Ungaretti, A. (1994). Expanding opportunities for teacher leadership. In D. R. Walling (Ed.), *Teachers as leaders: Perspectives on the professional development of teachers* (pp. 211–222). Bloomington, IN: Phi Delta Kappa.

Firestone, W. A. (1996). Leadership roles or functions. In K. Leithwood, J. Chapman, D. Corson, P. Hallinger, & A. Hart (Eds.), *International handbook of educational leadership and administration* (pp. 395–418). Dordrecht: Boston: Kluwer Academic.

Fisher, C., & Adler, M. A. (1999, December). *Early reading programs in high-poverty schools: Emerald Elementary beats the odds.* Ann Arbor: University of Michigan, Center for the Improvement of Early Reading Achievement.

Forster, E. M. (1997, Fall). Teacher leadership: Professional right and responsibility. *Action in Teacher Education, 19*(3), 82–94.

Foster, R., & Suddards, C. (1999, April). *Leadership within high school communities: A multiple study perspective.* Paper presented to the American Educational Research Association, Montreal, Quebec.

Foster, W. P. (1984). Toward a critical theory of educational administration. In T. J. Sergiovanni & J. E. Corbally (Eds.), *Leadership and organizational culture: New perspectives on administrative theory and practice* (pp. 240–259). Urbana: University of Illinois Press.

Foster, W. (1986). *Paradigms and promises: New approaches to educational administration.* Buffalo, NY: Prometheus.

Foster, W. (1988). Educational administration: A critical appraisal. In D. E. Griffiths, R. T. Stout, & R. B. Forsyth (Eds.), *Leaders for America's schools* (pp. 68–81). Berkeley, CA: McCutchan.

Foster, W. (1989, March). *School leaders as transformational intellectuals: A theoretical argument.* Paper presented at the annual meeting of the American Educational Research Association, San Francisco, CA.

Frank, L. (1990, September). *Reinventing school leadership* (pp. 67–71). Working memo prepared for the Reinventing School Leadership Conference. Cambridge, MA: National Center for Educational Leadership.

Fraser, J. M. (1991). Walking the tightrope of teacher leadership. *Kappa Delta Pi Record, 27*(3), 80–83.

Frost, D., & Durrant, J. (2003a, May). Teacher leadership: Rationale, strategy, and impact. *School Leadership & Management, 23*(2), 173–186.

Frost, D., & Durrant, J. (2003b). *Teacher-led development work: Guidance and support.* London: David Fulton.

Frymier, J. (1987). Bureaucracy and the neutering of teachers. *Phi Delta Kappan, 69*(1), 9–14.

Fullan, M. (1994). Teacher leadership: A failure to conceptualize. In D. R. Walling (Ed.), *Teachers as leaders: Perspectives on the professional development of teachers* (pp. 241–254). Bloomington, IN: Phi Delta Kappa.

Fullan, M. (2004). *The moral imperative of school leadership.* Thousand Oaks, CA: Corwin Press.

Furman, G. C., & Starratt, R. J. (2002). Leadership for democratic community in schools. In J. Murphy (Ed.), *The educational leadership challenge: Redefining leadership for the 21st century* (pp. 105–133). Chicago: University of Chicago Press.

Fusarelli, L. D., & Scribner, J. D. (1993, October). *Site-based management and the critical democratic pluralism: An analysis of promises, problems, and possibilities.* Paper presented at the annual conference of the University Council for Educational Administration, Houston, TX.

Gehrke, N. (1991). *Developing teachers' leadership skills.* Washington, DC: ERIC Clearinghouse on Teacher Education. (ERIC Document Reproduction Service No. ED330691)

Giroux, H. A. (1988). *Teachers as intellectuals: Toward a critical pedagogy of learning.* Granby, MA: Bergin & Garvey.

Glickman, C. D. (1990, September). Pushing school reform to a new edge: The seven ironies of school empowerment. *Phi Delta Kappan, 71*(1), 68–75.

Glickman, C. D., Allen, L., & Lunsford, B. (1992, April). *Facilitation of internal change: The league of professional schools.* Paper presented at the annual meeting of the American Educational Research Association, San Francisco, CA.

Goldman, P., Dunlap, D. M., & Conley, D. T. (1991, April). *Administrative facilitation and site-based school reform projects.* Paper presented at the annual meeting of the American Educational Research Association, Chicago, IL.

Goldring, E., & Greenfield, W. (2002). Understanding the evolving concept of leadership in education: Roles, expectations, and dilemmas. In J. Murphy (Ed.), *The educational leadership challenge: Redefining leadership for the 21st century* (pp. 1–19). Chicago: University of Chicago Press.

Goldring, E., & Rallis, S. F. (1993). *Principals of dynamic schools: Taking charge of change.* Newbury Park, CA: Corwin Press.

Goodlad, J. I. (1984). *A place called school: Prospects for the future.* New York: McGraw-Hill.

Greenfield, T. B. (1988). The decline and fall of science in educational administration. In D. E. Griffiths, R. T. Stout, & P. B. Forsyth (Eds.), *Leaders for America's schools* (pp. 131–159). Berkeley, CA: McCutchan.

Greenfield, W. D. (1988). Moral imagination, interpersonal competence, and the works of school administrators. In D. E. Griffiths, R. T. Stout, & P. B. Forsyth (Eds.), *Leaders for America's schools* (pp. 207–232). Berkeley, CA: McCutchan.

Greenfield, W. D. (1990, September). *Reinventing school leadership* (pp. 73–74). Working memo prepared for the Reinventing School Leadership Conference. Cambridge, MA: National Center for Educational Leadership.

Greenfield, W. D. (1995). Toward a theory of school administration: The centrality of leadership. *Educational Administration Quarterly, 31*(7), 61–85.

Greer, J. (1989, January). Another perspective and some immediate proposals on "teacher empowerment." *Exceptional Children, 55*(4), 294–297.

Griffin, G. A. (1995, September). Influences of shared decision making on school and classroom activity: Conversations with five teachers. *The Elementary School Journal, 96*(1), 29–45.

Guthrie, J. W. (1986, December). School-based management: The next needed education reform. *Phi Delta Kappan, 68*(4), 305–309.

Hallinger, P. (1990). *Reinventing school leadership* (pp. 75–78). Working memo prepared for the Reinventing School Leadership Conference. Cambridge, MA: National Center for Educational Leadership.

Hallinger, P. (2003, November). Leading educational change: Reflections on the practice of instructional and transformational leadership. *Cambridge Journal of Education, 33*(3), 329–351.

Hallinger, P., & Richardson, D. (1988, Winter). Models of shared leadership: Evolving structures and relationships. *The Urban Review, 20*(4), 229–245.

Hannaway, J. (1992, March). *Decentralization in education: Technical demands as a critical ingredient.* (ERIC Document Reproduction Service No. ED345362)

Hanson, E. M. (1991). *School-based management and educational reform: Cases in the USA and Spain.* (ERIC Document Reproduction Service No. ED336832)

Harlow, J. G. (1962). Purpose-defining: The central function of the school administrator. In J. A. Culbertson & S. P. Hencley (Eds.), *Preparing administrators: New perspectives* (pp. 61–71). Columbus, OH: University Council for Educational Administration.

Harrison, J. W., & Lembeck, E. (1996). Emergent teacher leaders. In G. Moller & M. Katzenmeyer (Eds.), *Every teacher as a leader: Realizing the potential of teacher leadership* (pp. 101–116). San Francisco: Jossey-Bass.

Hart, A. W. (1990, Fall). Impacts of the school social unit on teacher authority during work redesign. *American Educational Research Journal, 27*(3), 503–532.

Hart, A. W. (1994, November). Creating teacher leadership roles. *Educational Administration Quarterly, 30*(4), 472–497.

Hart, A. W. (1995, September). Reconceiving school leadership: Emergent view. *The Elementary School Journal, 96*(1), 9–28.

Hart, R., & Baptist, B. (1996). Developing teacher leaders: A state initiative. In G. Moller & M. Katzenmeyer (Eds.), *Every teacher as a leader: Realizing the potential of teacher leadership* (pp. 85–100). San Francisco: Jossey-Bass.

Harvey, G., & Crandall, D. P. (1988). A beginning look at the what and how of restructuring. In C. Jenks (Ed.), *The redesign of education: A collection of papers concerned with comprehensive educational reform* (pp. 1–37). San Francisco: Far West Laboratory.

Hatfield, R. C. (1989, December). *Redesigning faculty curriculum leader roles.* (ERIC Document Reproduction Service No. ED319677)

Hatfield, R. C., Blackman, C. A., & Claypool, C. (1986). *Exploring leadership roles performed by teaching faculty in K–12 schools.* Paper presented at the annual conference of the American Association of Colleges of Teacher Education, Chicago, IL.

Heifetz, R. A., & Laurie, D. L. (1997, January/February). The work of leadership. *Harvard Business Review, 75*(1), 124–135.

Heller, D. A. (1994). The problem with power. In D. R. Walling (Ed.), *Teachers as leaders: Perspectives on the professional development of teachers* (pp. 287–297). Bloomington, IN: Phi Delta Kappa.

Heller, M. F., & Firestone, W. A. (1994, January). *Heroes, teams, and teachers: A study of leadership for change.* (ERIC Document Reproduction Service No. ED371445)

Hiebert, E., & Pearson, P. D. (1999). *Building on the past, budgeting to the future: A research agenda for the Center on the Improvement of Early Reading Achievement.* Ann Arbor: University of Michigan, Center for the Improvement of Early Reading Achievement.

Hill, P. T., & Bonan, J. (1991, September). *Decentralization and accountability in public education.* Santa Monica, CA: Rand.

Hinchey, P. H. (1997, May/June). Teacher leadership: Introduction. *The Clearing House, 70*(5), 233–236.

Hoffman, J. V., & Rutherford, W. L. (1984, Fall). Effective reading programs: A critical review of outlier studies. *Reading Research Quarterly, 20*(1), 79–92.

The Holmes Group. (1986). *Tomorrow's teachers: A report of the Holmes group.* East Lansing, MI: Author.

Houston, H. M. (1989, March). *Professional development for restructuring: Analyses and recommendations.* Paper presented at the annual meeting of the American Educational Research Association, San Francisco, CA.

Howey, K. R. (1988, January/February). Why teacher leadership? *Journal of Teacher Education, 39*(1), 28–31.

Huberman, M. (1993). The model of the independent artisan in teachers' professional relations. In J. W. Little & M. W. McLaughlin (Eds.), *Teachers' work: Individuals, colleagues, and contexts* (pp. 9–50). New York: Teachers College Press.

Hynes, J. L., Summers, P., & Socoski, P. (1992, Fall/Winter). Making the lead teacher concept work: The Southeastern Teacher Leadership Center. *Teacher Education, 5*(1), 43–49.

Imber, M. (1983, April). Increased decision-making involvement for teachers: Ethical and practical implications. *Journal of Educational Thought, 17*(1), 36–42.

Ingersoll, R. M. (1996, April). Teachers' decision-making power and school conflict. *Sociology of Education, 69*(2), 159–176.

Institute for Educational Leadership. (2001, April). *Leadership for student learning: Redefining the teacher as leader.* Washington, DC: Author.

Jandura, D. M., & Burke, R. J. (1989). *Differentiated career opportunities for teachers.* Bloomington, IN: Phi Delta Kappa Educational Foundation.

Johnson, B. L. (1998). Organizing for collaboration: A reconsideration of some basic organizing principles. In D. G. Pounder (Ed.), *Restructuring schools for collaboration: Promises and pitfalls* (pp. 9–25). Albany: State University of New York Press.

Johnson, J., & Hynes, M. C. (1997, Fall). Teaching/learning/leading: Synonyms for change. *Action in Teacher Research, 19*(3), 107–119.

Johnson, S. M. (1989). Schoolwork and its reform. In J. Hannaway & R. Crowson (Eds.), *The politics of reforming school administration. 1989 Yearbook of the Politics of Education Association* (pp. 95–112). New York: Falmer Press.

Johnston, P. (1999). Unpacking literate achievement. In J. S. Gaffney & B. J. Askew (Eds.), *Stirring the waters: The influence of Marie Clay* (pp. 27–46). Portsmouth, NH: Heinemann.

Kahrs, J. R. (1996). Principals who support teacher leadership. In G. Moller & M. Katzenmeyer (Eds.), *Every teacher as a leader: Redefining the potential of teacher leadership* (pp. 19–40). San Francisco: Jossey-Bass.

Kanter, R. M. (1983). *The change masters.* New York: Simon & Schuster.

Katzenmeyer, M., & Moller, G. (2001). *Awakening the sleeping giant: Helping teachers develop as leaders.* Newbury Park, CA: Corwin Press.

Keedy, J. L. (1999, October). Examining teacher instructional leadership within the small group dynamics of collegial groups. *Teaching and Teacher Education, 15*(7), 785–799.

Keiser, N. M., & Shen, J. (2000, Summer). Principals' and teachers' perceptions of teacher empowerment. *Journal of Leadership Studies, 7*(13), 115–122.

Kelley, J. A. (1994). The National Board for Professional Teaching Standards: Toward a community of teacher leaders. In D. R. Walling (Ed.), *Teachers as leaders: Perspectives on the professional development of teachers* (pp. 299–313). Bloomington, IN: Phi Delta Kappa.

Kilcher, A. (1992). Becoming a change facilitator: The first-year experience of five teacher leaders. In C. Livingston (Ed.), *Teachers as leaders: Evolving roles* (pp. 91–113). Washington, DC: National Education Association.

Killion, J. P. (1996). Moving beyond the school: Teacher leaders in the district office. In G. Moller & M. Katzenmeyer (Eds.), *Every teacher as a leader: Realizing the potential of teacher leadership* (pp. 63–84). San Francisco: Jossey-Bass.

Klecker, B. J., & Loadman, W. E. (1998, Spring). Defining and measuring the dimensions of teacher empowerment in restructuring public schools. *Education, 118*(3), 358–371.

Kochan, F. K., Bredeson, P., & Riehl, C. (2002). Rethinking the professional development of school leaders. In J. Murphy (Ed.), *The educational leadership challenge: Redefining leadership for the 21st century* (pp. 289–306). Chicago: University of Chicago Press.

Kotter, J. P. (1996). *Leading change.* Boston: Harvard Business School Press.

Kowalski, T. J. (1995). Preparing teachers to be leaders: Barriers in the workplace. In M. J. O'Hair & S. J. Odell (Eds.), *Educating teachers for leadership and change* (pp. 243–256). Thousand Oaks, CA: Corwin Press.

Lam, D. (1990, September). *Reinventing school leadership* (pp. 85–87). Working memo prepared for the Reinventing School Leadership Conference. Cambridge, MA: National Center for Educational Leadership.

Lambert, L. (2003). *Leadership capacity for lasting school improvement.* Alexandria, VA: Association of Supervision and Curriculum Development.

Larkin, R. W. (1973, Fall). Contextual influences on teacher leadership styles. *Sociology of Education, 46,* 471–479.

Larson, C. L., & Murtadha, K. (2002). Leadership for social justice. In J. Murphy (Ed.), *The educational leadership challenge: Redefining leadership for the 21st century* (pp. 134–161). Chicago: University of Chicago Press.

Lawton, S. B. (1991, September). *Why restructure?* Revision of paper presented at the annual meeting of the American Educational Research Association, Chicago, IL.

LeBlanc, P. R., & Shelton, M. M. (1997, Fall). Teacher leadership: The needs of teachers. *Action in Teacher Education, 19*(3), 32–48.

Leithwood, K. A. (1992). The move toward transformational leadership. *Educational Leadership, 49*(5), 8–12.

Leithwood, K., & Jantzi, D. (1990). *Transformational leadership: How principals can help reform school cultures.* Paper presented at the annual meeting of the Canadian Association for Curriculum Studies, Victoria, British Columbia.

Leithwood, K., & Jantzi, D. (1998, April). *Distributed leadership and student engagement in school.* Paper presented at the annual meeting of the American Educational Research Association, San Diego, CA.

Leithwood, K., Jantzi, D., & Dart, B. (1991, February). *How the school improvement strategies of transformational leaders foster teacher development.* Paper presented at the sixth annual conference of the Department of Educational Administration and Centre for Educational Leadership, Ontario Institute for Studies in Education, Toronto, Ontario.

Leithwood, K., Jantzi, D., & Fernandez, A. (1994). Transformational leadership and teachers' commitment to change. In J. Murphy & K. S. Louis (Eds.), *Reshaping the principalship: Insights from transformational reform efforts* (pp. 77–98). Thousand Oaks, CA: Corwin Press.

Leithwood, K., Jantzi, D., Ryan, S., & Steinbach, R. (1997, March). *Distributed leadership in secondary schools.* Paper presented at the annual meeting of the American Educational Research Association, Chicago, IL.

Leithwood, K. A., Jantzi, D., Silins, H., & Dart, B. (1992, January). *Transformational leadership and school restructuring.* Paper presented at the International Congress for School Effectiveness and Improvement, Victoria, British Columbia.

Lieberman, A. (1987, Spring). Teacher leadership. *Teachers College Record, 88*(3), 400–405.

Lieberman, A. (1992). Teacher leadership: What are we learning? In C. Livingston (Ed.), *Teachers as leaders: Evolving roles* (pp. 159–165). Washington, DC: National Educational Association.

Lieberman, A., & Miller, L. (1999). *Teachers—transforming their world and their work.* New York: Teachers College Press.

Lieberman, A., Saxl, E. R., & Miles, M. B. (1988). Teacher leadership: Ideology and practice. In A. Lieberman (Ed.), *Building a professional culture in schools* (pp. 148–166). New York: Teachers College Press.

Lindelow, J. (1981). School-based management. In S. C. Smith, J. A. Mazzarella, & P. K. Piele (Eds.), *School leadership: Handbook for survival* (pp. 94–129). Eugene: University of Oregon, ERIC Clearing House on Educational Management.

Little, J. W. (1985, November). Teachers as teacher advisors: The delicacy of collegial leadership. *Educational Leadership, 43*(3), 34–36.

Little, J. W. (1987). Teachers as colleagues. In V. Richardson-Koehler (Ed.), *Educators' handbook: A research perspective* (pp. 491–518). White Plains, NY: Longman.

Little, J. W. (1988). Assessing the prospects for teacher leadership. In A. Lieberman (Ed.), *Building a professional culture in schools* (pp. 78–105). New York: Teachers College Press.

Little, J. W. (1990, Summer). The perspective of privacy: Autonomy and initiative in teachers' professional relations. *Teachers College Record, 91*(4), 509–536.

Little, J. W. (1995, September). Contested ground: The basis of teacher leadership in two restructuring high schools. *The Elementary School Journal, 96*(1), 47–63.

Little, J. W., & McLaughlin, M. W. (1993a). Conclusion. In J. W. Little & M. W. McLaughlin (Eds.), *Teachers' work: Individuals, colleagues, and contexts* (pp. 185–190). New York: Teachers College Press.

Little, J. W., & McLaughlin, M. W. (1993b). Introduction. Perspectives on cultures and contexts of teaching. In J. W. Little & M. W. McLaughlin (Eds.), *Teachers' work: Individuals, colleagues, and contexts* (pp. 1–8). New York: Teachers College Press.

Livingston, C. (1992). Teacher leadership for restructured schools. In C. Livingston (Ed.), *Teachers as leaders: Evolving roles* (pp. 9–17). Washington, DC: National Education Association.

Lortie, D. (1975). *School teacher.* Chicago: University of Chicago Press.

Louis, K. S., & Miles, M. B. (1990). *Improving the urban high school: What works and why.* New York: Teachers College Press.

Louis, K. S., & Murphy, J. (1994). The evolving role of the principal: Some concluding thoughts. In J. Murphy & K. S. Louis (Eds.), *Reshaping the principalship: Insights from transformational reform efforts* (pp. 265–281). Newbury Park, CA: Corwin Press.

Lynch, M., & Strodl, P. (1991, February). *Teacher leadership: Preliminary development of a questionnaire.* Paper presented at the annual conference of the Eastern Educational Research Association, Boston. MA.

Lyons, C. A., & Pinnell, G. S. (1999). Teacher development: The best investment in literacy education. In J. S. Gaffney & B. J. Askew (Eds.). *Stirring the waters: The influence of Marie Clay* (pp.197–220). Portsmouth, NH: Heinemann.

Maccoby, M. (1989, December). *Looking for leadership now.* Paper presented at the National Center for Educational Leadership Conference, Harvard University, Cambridge, MA.

Maeroff, G. (1988). *The empowerment of teachers: Overcoming the crisis of confidence.* New York: Teachers College Press.

Malen, B., Ogawa, R. T., & Krantz, J. (1989, May). *What do we know about school-based management? A case study of the literature—a call for research.* Paper presented at the Conference on Choice and Control in American Education, University of Wisconsin, Madison.

Manning, J. C. (1995). Ariston metron. *The Reading Teacher, 48*(8), 650–659.

Manthei, J. (1992). *The mentor teacher as leader: The motives, characteristics and needs of seventy-three experienced teachers who seek a new leadership role.* Paper presented at the annual meeting of the American Educational Research Association, San Francisco, CA. (ERIC Document Reproduction Service No. ED346042)

Marks, H. M., & Printy, S. M. (2003, August). Principal leadership and school performance: An integration of transformational and instructional leadership. *Educational Administration Quarterly, 39*(3), 370–397.

Martin, B., & Crossland, B. J. (2000, October). *The relationships between teacher empowerment, teachers' sense of responsibility for student outcomes and student achievement.* Paper presented at the annual meeting of the Midwestern Educational Research Association, Chicago, IL.

McCarthy, S. J., & Peterson, P. L. (1989, March). *Teacher roles: Wearing new patterns in classroom practice and school organization.* Paper presented at the annual meeting of the American Educational Research Association, San Francisco, CA.

McCay, L., Flora, J., Hamilton, A., & Riley, J. F. (2001, Spring). Reforming schools through teacher leadership: A program for classroom teachers as agents of change. *Educational Horizons, 79*(3) 135–142.

McKeever, B. (2003). *Nine lessons of successful school leadership teams: Distilling a decade of innovation.* San Francisco: West Ed.

McLaughlin, M. W., & Yee, S. M. L. (1988). School as a place to have a career. In A. Lieberman (Ed.), *Building a professional culture in schools* (pp. 23–44). New York: Teachers College Press.

McNeil, L. M. (1988, January). Contradictions of control, part 1: Administrators and teachers. *Phi Delta Kappan, 69*(5), 333–339.

Merchant, B. (1995). From hierarchical to distributed leadership. In R. T. Clift & P. W. Thurston (Eds.), *Distributed leadership: School improvement through collaboration* (pp. 121–153). Greenwich, CT: JAI Press.

Meyer, J., & Rowan, B. (1975). *Notes on the structure of educational organizations: Revised version.* Paper presented at the annual meeting of the American Sociological Association, San Francisco, CA.

Midgley, C., & Woods, S. (1993, November). Beyond site-based management: Empowering teachers to reform schools. *Phi Delta Kappan, 75*(3), 245–252.

Miller, B., Moon, J., & Elko, S. (2000). *Teacher leadership in mathematics and science: Casebook and facilitator's guide.* Portsmouth, NH: Heinemann.

Miller, L. (1988). Unlikely beginnings: The district office as a starting point for developing a professional culture for teaching. In A. Lieberman (Ed.), *Building a professional culture in schools* (pp. 167–184). New York: Teachers College Press.

Miller, L. (1992). Teacher leadership in a renewing school. In C. Livingston (Ed.), *Teachers as leaders: Evolving roles* (pp. 115–130). Washington, DC: National Education Association.

Mitchell, A. (1997, Fall). Teacher identity: A key to increased collaboration. *Action in Teacher Education, 19*(3), 1–14.

Mojkowski, C., & Fleming, D. (1988). *School-site management: Concepts and approaches.* Andover, MA: Regional Laboratory for the Educational Improvement of the Northeast and Islands.

Moller, G., & Katzenmeyer, M. (1996). The promise of teacher leadership. In G. Moller & M. Katzenmeyer (Eds.), *Every teacher as a leader: Realizing the potential of teacher leadership* (pp. 1–18). San Francisco: Jossey-Bass.

Monson, M. P., & Monson, R. J. (1993, October). Who creates curriculum? New roles for teachers. *Educational Leadership, 51*(2), 19–21.

Moorman, H. (1990, September). *Reinventing school leadership* (pp. 98–103). Working memo prepared for the Reinventing School Leadership Conference. Cambridge, MA: National Center for Educational Leadership.

Morris, V. G., & Nunnery, J. A. (1994, January). *A case study of teacher empowerment in a professional development school.* Memphis, TN: Memphis State University, Center for Research in Educational Policy, College of Education. (ERIC Document Reproduction Service No. ED404293)

Mulkeen, T. A. (1990). *Reinventing school leadership.* Working memo prepared for the Reinventing School Leadership Conference. Cambridge, MA: National Center for Educational Leadership.

Murphy, J. (1990a). The educational reform movement of the 1980s: A comprehensive analysis. In J. Murphy (Ed.), *The reform of American public education in the 1980s: Perspectives and cases* (pp. 3–55). Berkeley, CA: McCutchan.

Murphy, J. (1990b). Principal instructional leadership. In L. S. Lotto & P. W. Thurston (Eds.), *Advances in educational administration: Changing perspectives on the school* (Volume 1, Part B, pp. 163–200). Greenwich, CT: JAI Press.

Murphy, J. (1991). *Restructuring schools: Capturing and assessing the phenomenon.* New York: Teachers College Press.

Murphy, J. (1992). *The landscape of leadership preparation: Reframing the education of school administrators.* Newbury Park, CA: Corwin Press.

Murphy, J. (1994a). The changing role of the teacher. In M. J. O'Hair & S. J. Odell (Eds.), *Educating teachers for leadership and change* (pp. 311–323). Newbury Park, CA: Corwin Press.

Murphy, J. (1994b). Transformational change and the evolving role of the principalship: Early empirical evidence. In J. Murphy & K. S. Louis (Eds.), *Reshaping the principalship: Insights from transformational reform efforts* (pp. 20–53). Newbury Park, CA: Corwin Press.

Murphy, J. (1996). *The privatization of schooling: Problems and possibilities.* Newbury Park, CA: Corwin Press.

Murphy, J. (1999a). New consumerism: The emergence of market-oriented governing structures for schools. In J. Murphy & K. S. Louis (Eds.), *The handbook of research on school administration* (pp. 405–419). San Francisco: Jossey-Bass.

Murphy, J. (1999b). Reconnecting teaching and school administration: A call for a unified profession. *UCEA Review, 40*(2), 1–3, 6–7.

Murphy, J. (1999c). *The quest for a center: Notes on the state of the profession of educational leadership.* Columbia, MO: University Council for Educational Leadership.

Murphy, J. (2000, February). Governing America's schools: The shifting playing field. *Teachers College Record, 102*(1), 57–84.

Murphy, J. (2002, April). Reculturing the profession of educational leadership: New blueprints. *Educational Administration Quarterly, 38*(3), 176–191.

Murphy, J. (in press). Uncovering the foundations of the ISLLC *Standards* and addressing concerns from the academic community. *Educational Administration Quarterly.*

Murphy, J., & Adams, J. E. (1998). Reforming America's schools 1980–2000. *Journal of Educational Administration, 36*(5), 426–444.

Murphy, J., & Beck, L. G. (1995). *School-based management as school reform: Taking stock.* Thousand Oaks, CA: Corwin Press.

Murphy, J., Beck, L., Crawford, M., Hodges, A., & McGaughy, C. L. (2001). *The productive high school: Creating personalized academic communities.* Thousand Oaks, CA: Corwin Press.

Murphy, J., & Datnow, A. (2003). Leadership lessons from comprehensive school reform designs. In J. Murphy & A. Datnow (Eds.), *Leadership for school reform: Lessons from comprehensive school reform designs* (pp. 263–278). Thousand Oaks, CA: Corwin Press.

Murphy, J., & Hallinger, P. (1992). The principalship in an era of transformation. *Journal of Educational Administration, 30*(2), 77–88.

Murphy, J., & Hallinger, P. (1993). Restructuring schooling: Learning from ongoing efforts. In J. Murphy & P. Hallinger (Eds.), *Restructuring schooling: Learning from ongoing efforts* (pp. 251–271). Newbury Park, CA: Corwin Press.

Murphy, J., Hallinger, P., Lotto, L. S., & Miller, S. K. (1987, December). Barriers to implementing the instructional leadership role. *Canadian Administrator, 27*(3), 1–9.

Murphy, J., & Louis, K. S. (Eds.). (1994). *Reshaping the principalship: Insights from transformational reform efforts.* Thousand Oaks, CA: Corwin Press.

Murphy, J., & Louis, K. S. (1999, October). Understanding the *Handbook:* Notes from the editors. *Educational Administration Quarterly, 35*(4), 472–476.

Murphy, J., & Shipman, N. J. (1999, September). The Interstate School Leaders Licensure Consortium: A standards-based approach to strengthening educational leadership. *Journal of Personnel Evaluation in Education, 13*(3), 205–224.

Murphy, J. T. (1989, June). The paradox of decentralizing schools: Lessons from business, government, and the Catholic church. *Phi Delta Kappan, 70*(10), 808–812.

Murphy, J. T. (1991, March). Superintendents as saviors: From the Terminator to Pogo. *Phi Delta Kappan, 72*(7), 507–513.

Myers, M. S. (1970). *Every employee a manager: More meaningful work through job enrichment.* New York: McGraw-Hill.

National Association of Elementary School Principals. (1990). *Principals for 21st century schools.* Alexandria, VA: Author.

National Commission on Teaching and America's Future. (1996, September). *What matters most: Teaching for America's future.* New York: Author.

Odell, S. J. (1997, Fall). Preparing teachers for teacher leadership. *Action in Teacher Education, 19*(3), 120–124.

Ogawa, R. T., & Bossert, S. T. (1995, May). Leadership as an organizational quality. *Educational Administration Quarterly, 31*(2), 224–243.

O'Hair, M. J., & Reitzug, W. C. (1997, Fall). Teacher leadership: In what ways? For what purposes? *Action in Teacher Education, 19*(3), 65–76.

Olson, L. (1992). A matter of choice: Minnesota puts "charter schools" idea to test. *Education Week, 12*(12), 10–11.

Parker, D. C. (1986). From conventional wisdom to concept: School administration texts 1934–1945. In T. E. Glass (Ed.), *An analysis of texts on school administration 1820–1985* (pp. 39–75). Danville, IL: Interstate.

Pellicer, L. O., & Anderson, L. W. (1995). *A handbook for teacher leaders*. Thousand Oaks, CA: Corwin Press.

Perry, N. J. (1988, July). The education crisis: What business can do. *Fortune, 118*(1), 70–81.

Petrie, H. G. (1990). Reflecting on the second wave of reform: Restructuring the teaching profession. In S. L. Jacobson & J. A. Conway (Eds.), *Educational leadership in an age of reform* (pp.14–29). New York: Longman.

Pounder, D. G., Ogawa, R. T., & Adams, E. A. (1995, November). Leadership as an organization-wide phenomena: Its impact on school performance. *Educational Administration Quarterly, 31*(4), 564–588.

Prestine, N. A. (1991a, April). *Completing the essential schools metaphor: Principal as enabler*. Paper presented at the annual meeting of the American Educational Research Association, Chicago, IL.

Prestine, N. A. (1991b, October). *Shared decision making in restructuring essential schools: The role of the principal*. Paper presented at the annual conference of the University Council for Educational Administration, Baltimore, MD.

Prestine, N. A. (1994). Ninety degrees from everywhere: New understandings of the principal's role in restructuring an essential school. In J. Murphy & K. S. Louis (Eds.), *Reshaping the principalship: Insights from transformational reform efforts* (pp. 123–153). Thousand Oaks, CA: Corwin Press.

Printy, S. M. (2004, Winter). The professional impact of communities of practice. *UCEA Review, 46*(1), 2023.

Rallis, S. F. (1990). Professional teachers and restructured schools: Leadership challenges. In B. Mitchell & L. L. Cunningham (Eds.), *Educational leadership in changing contexts of families, communities, and schools* (Eighty-ninth Yearbook of the National Society for the Study of Education, Part II, pp. 184–209). Chicago: National Society for the Study of Education.

Reinoso, M. (2002, Winter). Teacher leadership: The reorganization of room 15. *Preventing School Failure, 46*(12), 70–74.

Retallick, J., & Fink, D. (2002). Framing leadership: Contributions and impediments to educational change. *International Journal of Leadership in Education, 5*(2), 91–104.

Riehl, C. J. (2000, Spring). The principal's role in creating inclusive schools for diverse students: A review of normative, empirical, and critical literature on the practice of educational administration. *Review of Educational Research, 70*(1), 55–81.

Rinehart, J. S., Short, P. M., Short, R. J., & Eckley, M. (1998, December). Teacher empowerment and principal leadership: Understanding the influence process. *Educational Administration Quarterly, 34*, 630–649.

Roberts, L. (1990, September). *Reinventing school leadership* (pp. 132–136). Working memo prepared for the Reinventing School Leadership conference. Cambridge, MA: National Center for Educational Leadership.

Robertson, P. J., & Buffett, T. M. (1991, April). *The move to decentralize: Predictors of early success*. Paper presented at the annual meeting of the American Educational Research Association, Chicago, IL.

Rogus, J. F. (1988, January/February). Teacher leader programming: Theoretical underpinnings. *Journal of Teacher Education, 39*(1), 46–52.

Rosenholtz, S. J. (1989). *Teachers' workplace: The social organization of schools.* White Plains, NY: Longman.

Rothstein, R. (1990, November). *Shared decision making—the first year.* Los Angeles: Los Angeles Unified School District, Independent Analysis Unit.

Rowley, J. (1988, May/June). The teacher as leader and teacher educator. *Journal of Teacher Education, 39*(3), 13–16.

Rungeling, B., & Glover, R. W. (1991, January). Educational restructuring—the process for change? *Urban Education, 25*(4), 415–427.

Rutter, M. (1983, February). School effects on pupil progress: Research findings and policy implications. *Child Development, 54*(1), 1–29.

Sackney, L. E., & Dibski, D. J. (1992, August). *School-based management: A critical perspective.* Paper presented at the Seventh Regional Conference of the Commonwealth Council for Educational Administration, Hong Kong.

Samuels, S. J. (1981). Characteristics of exemplary reading programs. In J. T. Guthrie (Ed.), *Comprehension and teaching: Research reviews* (pp. 255–273). Newark, DE: International Reading Association.

Sanford, R. A. L. H. (1990, September). *Reinventing school leadership* (pp. 144–145). Working memo prepared for the Reinventing School Leadership Conference. Cambridge, MA: National Center for Educational Leadership.

Schlechty, P. C. (1990). *Schools for the 21st century: Leadership imperatives for educational reform.* San Francisco: Jossey-Bass.

Schmoker, M. J., & Wilson, R. B. (1994). Redefining results: Implications for teacher leadership and professionalism. In D. R. Walling (Ed.), *Teachers as leaders: Perspectives on the professional development of teachers* (pp. 137–150). Bloomington, IN: Phi Delta Kappa.

Sedlak, M. W., Wheeler, C. W., Pullin, D. C., & Cusik, P. A. (1986). *Selling students short: Classroom bargains and academic reform in the American high school.* New York: Teachers College Press.

Seeley, D. (1988, February). A new vision for public education. *Youth Policy, 10*(2), 34–36.

Sergiovanni, T. J. (1984). Developing a relevant theory of administration. In T. J. Sergiovanni & J. E. Corbally (Eds.), *Leadership and organizational culture: New perspectives on administrative theory and practice* (pp. 275–291). Urbana: University of Illinois Press.

Sergiovanni, T. J. (1989). Value-driven schools: The amoeba theory. In H. J. Walberg & J. J. Lane (Eds.), *Organizing for learning: Toward the 21st century* (pp. 31–40). Reston, VA: National Association of Secondary School Principals.

Sergiovanni, T. J. (1990). *Value-added leadership: How to get extraordinary performance in schools.* San Diego: Harcourt, Brace, & Jovanovich.

Sergiovanni, T. J. (1991a). The dark side of professionalism in educational administration. *Phi Delta Kappan, 72*(7), 521–526.

Sergiovanni, T. J. (1991b). *The principalship: A reflective practice perspective* (2nd ed.). Boston: Allyn & Bacon.

Sergiovanni, T. J. (1992, February). Why we should seek substitutes for leadership. *Leadership, 49*(5), 41–45.

Sergiovanni, T. J. (1994). Organizations or communities? Changing the metaphor changes the theory. *Educational Administration Quarterly, 30*(2), 214–226.

Shakeshaft, C. (1990, September). *Reinventing school leadership* (pp. 147–150). Working memo prepared for the Reinventing School Leadership Conference. Cambridge, MA: National Center for Educational Leadership.

Shakeshaft, C. (1999). The struggle to create a more gender-inclusive profession. In J. Murphy & K. S. Louis (Eds.), *The handbook of research on educational administration* (2nd ed., pp. 99–118). San Francisco: Jossey-Bass.

Sherrill, J. A. (1999,Winter). Preparing teachers for leadership roles in the 21st century. *Theory Into Practice, 38*(1), 56–61.

Short, P. M., & Greer, J. T. (1989, March). *Increasing teacher autonomy through shared governance: Effects on policy making and student outcomes.* Paper presented at the annual meeting of the American Educational Research Association, San Francisco, CA.

Short, P. M., & Greer, J. T. (1993). Restructuring schools through empowerment. In J. Murphy & P. Hallinger (Eds.), *Restructuring schooling: Learning from ongoing efforts* (pp. 165–187). Newbury Park, CA: Corwin Press.

Silva, D. Y., Gimbert, B., & Nolan, J. (2000, August). Sliding the doors: Locking and unlocking possibilities for teacher leadership. *Teachers College Record, 102*(4), 779–804.

Sirotnik, K. A. (1989). The schools as the center of change. In T. J. Sergiovanni & J. H. Moore (Eds.), *Schooling for tomorrow: Directing reforms to issues that count* (pp. 89–113). Boston: Allyn & Bacon.

Sisken, L. S. (1994). *Realms of knowledge: Academic departments in secondary schools.* Washington, DC: Falmer.

Sizer, T. R. (1984). *Horace's compromise: The dilemma of the American high school.* Boston: Houghton Mifflin.

Slater, R. O., & Doig, J. W. (1988, May). Leadership in education: Issues of entrepreneurship and environment. *Education and Urban Society, 20*(3), 294–301.

Smith, W. E. (1993, April). *Teachers' perceptions of role change through shared decision making: A two-year case study.* Paper presented at the annual meeting of the American Educational Research Association, Atlanta, GA.

Smith-Burke, M. T. (1996, Winter). Professional development for teacher leaders: Promoting program ownership and increased success. *Reading Recovery Council Network News, 1–4, 13, 15.*

Smylie, M. A. (1992, Spring). Teacher participation in school decision making: Assessing willingness to participate. *Educational Evaluation and Policy Analysis, 14*(1), 53–67.

Smylie, M. A. (1995, September). New perspectives on teacher leadership. *The Elementary School Journal, 96*(1), 3–7.

Smylie, M. A. (1996). Research on teacher leadership: Assessing the state of the art. In B. J. Biddle, T. L. Good, & I. F. Goodson (Eds.), *International handbook of teachers and teaching* (pp. 521–592). Dordrecht: Boston: Kluwer Academic.

Smylie, M. A., & Brownlee-Conyers, J. (1992, May). Teacher leaders and their principals: Exploring the development of new working relationships. *Educational Administration Quarterly, 28*(2), 150–184.

Smylie, M. A., Conley, S., & Marks, H. M. (2002). Exploring new approaches to teacher leadership for school improvement. In J. Murphy (Ed.), *The educational leadership challenge: Redefining leadership for the 21st century* (pp. 162–188). Chicago: University of Chicago Press.

Smylie, M. A., & Denny, J. W. (1989, March). *Teacher leadership: Tensions and ambiguities in organizational perspective.* Paper presented at the annual meeting of the American Educational Research Association, San Francisco, CA.

Smylie, M. A., & Hart, A. W. (1999). School leadership for teacher learning: A human and social capital development perspective. In J. Murphy & K. S. Louis, *Handbook of research on educational administration* (2nd ed., pp. 421–441). San Francisco: Jossey-Bass.

Smylie, M. A., Wenzel, S. A., & Fendt, C. R. (2003). The Chicago Annenberg Challenge: Lessons on leadership for school development. In J. Murphy & A. Datnow (Eds.), *Leadership for school reform: Lessons from comprehensive school reforms* (pp. 135–158). Thousand Oaks, CA: Corwin Press.

Smyser, S. O. (1995, Autumn). Developing the teacher leader. *Teacher Education, 31*(2), 130–137.

Snauwaert, D. T. (1993). *Democracy, education, and governance: A developmental conception.* Albany: State University of New York Press.

Snell, J., & Swanson, J. (2000, April). *The essential knowledge and skills of teacher leaders: A search for a conceptual framework.* Paper presented at the annual meeting of the American Educational Research Association, New Orleans, LA.

Snow, C. E., Burns, M. S., & Griffin, P. (Eds.) (1998). *Preventing reading difficulties in young children.* Washington, DC: National Academy Press.

Southwest Center for Teaching Quality. (2002, October). *Teacher leadership for teaching quality: The teachers network policy institute model.* Chapel Hill, NC: Author.

Spaedy, M. (1990, September). *Reinventing school leadership* (pp. 156–159). Working memo prepared for the Reinventing School Leadership Conference. Cambridge, MA: National Center for Educational Leadership.

Spillane, J. P., Diamond, J. B., & Jita, L. (2000, April). *Leading classroom instruction: A preliminary explanation of the distribution of leadership practice.* Paper presented at the annual meeting of the American Educational Research Association, New Orleans, LA.

Spillane, J. P., Halverson, R., & Diamond, J. B. (n.d.). *Toward a theory of leadership practice: A distributed perspective.* Evanston, IL: Northwestern University, Institute for Policy Research.

Starratt, R. J. (1991, May). Building an ethical school: A theory for practice in educational leadership. *Educational Administration Quarterly, 27*(2), 185–202.

Stigler, J. W., & Hiebert, J. (1999). *The teaching gap: Best ideas from the world's teachers for improving education in the classroom.* New York: The Free Press.

Stone, M., Horejs, J., & Lomas, A. (1997, Fall). Commonalities and differences in teacher leadership at the elementary, middle, and high school level. *Action in Teacher Education, 19*(3), 49–64.

Strodl, P. (1992, March). *A model of teacher leadership.* Paper presented at the annual meeting of the Eastern Research Association, Hilton Head, SC.

Suleiman, M., & Moore, R. (1997). *Teachers' roles revisited: Beyond classroom management.* Paper presented at the ATE summer workshop, Tarpon Springs, FL.

Swanson, J. (2000, April). *What differentiates an excellent teacher from a teacher leader?* Paper presented at the annual meeting of the American Educational Research Association, New Orleans, LA.

Sykes, G., & Elmore, R. F. (1989). Making schools manageable. In J. Hannaway & R. Crowson (Eds.), *The politics of reforming school administration. 1988 Yearbook of the Politics of Education Association* (pp. 77–94). New York: Falmer Press.

Teitel, L. (1996). Finding common ground: Teacher leaders and principals. In G. Moller & M. Katzenmeyer (Eds.), *Every teacher as a leader: Realizing the potential of teacher leadership* (pp. 139–154). San Francisco: Jossey-Bass.

Timar, T. B., & Kirp, D. L. (1988, Summer). State efforts to reform schools: Treading between a regulatory swamp and an English garden. *Educational Evaluation and Policy Analysis, 10*(2), 75–88.

Troen, V., & Boles, K. (1994). Two teachers examine the power of teacher leadership. In D. R. Walling (Ed.), *Teachers as leaders: Perspectives on the professional development of teachers* (pp. 275–286). Bloomington, IN: Phi Delta Kappa.

Tyack, D. (1993). School governance in the United States: Historical puzzles and anomalies. In J. Hannaway & M. Carnoy (Eds.), *Decentralization and school improvement* (pp. 1–32). San Francisco: Jossey-Bass.

Uline, C. L., & Berkowitz, J. M. (2000). Transforming school culture through teaching teams. *Journal of School Leadership, 10*(1), 416–444.

Urbanski, A., & Nickolaou, M. B. (1997, June). Reflections on teacher leadership. *Educational Policy, 11*(2), 243–254.

Vazquez, A. (1990, September). *Reinventing school leadership* (pp. 172–174). Working memo prepared for the Reinventing School Leadership Conference. Cambridge, MA: National Center for Educational Leadership.

Vertiz, V., Fortune, J. C., & Hutson, B. A. (1985, Winter). Teacher leadership styles as they relate to academic gain for unsuccessful students. *Journal of Research and Development in Education, 18*(3), 63–67.

Wagstaff, L. H., & Reyes, P. (1993, August). *School site-based management* (Report presented to the Educational Economic Policy Center). Austin: University of Texas, College of Education.

Wall, R., & Rinehart, J. S. (1997, April). *School-based decision making and the empowerment of secondary school teachers.* Paper presented at the annual meeting of the American Educational Research Association, Chicago, IL.

Walters, S., & Guthro, C. (1992). Leading, learning, and leaving. In C. Livingston (Ed.), *Teachers as leaders: Evolving roles* (pp. 131–155). Washington, DC: National Education Association.

Wasley, P. A. (1991). *Teachers who lead: The rhetoric of reform and realities of practice.* New York: Teachers College Press.

Wasley, P. A. (1992). Working together: Teacher leadership and collaboration. In C. Livingston (Ed.), *Teacher leaders: Evolving roles* (pp. 21–55). Washington, DC: National Education Association.

Watkins, J. M., & Lusi, S. F. (1989, March). *Facing the essential tensions: Restructuring from where you are.* Paper presented at the annual meeting of the American Educational Research Association, San Francisco, CA.

Weick, K. E. (1976, March). Educational organizations as loosely coupled systems. *Administrative Science Quarterly, 21*(1), 1–19.

Weick, K. E., & McDaniel, R. R. (1989). How professional organizations work: Implications for school organization and management. In T. J. Sergiovanni & J. H. Moore (Eds.), *Schooling for tomorrow: Directing reforms to issues that count* (pp. 330–355). Boston: Allyn & Bacon.

Weiss, C. H. (1993, February). *Interests and ideologies in educational reform: Changing the venue of decision making in the high school* (Occasional Paper #19). Cambridge, MA: National Center for Educational Leadership.

Weiss, C. H., Cambone, J., & Wyeth, A. (1991, April). *Trouble in paradise: Teacher conflicts in shared decision making* (Occasional Paper #8). Cambridge, MA: Harvard University, National Center for Educational Leadership.

Whitaker, K. S. (1997, Summer). Developing teacher leadership and the management team concept: A case study. *Teacher Education 33*(1), 1–16.

Whitaker, T. (1995, January). Informed teacher leadership—the key to successful change in the middle level school. *NASSP Bulletin, 79*(567), 76–81.

Wigginton, E. (1992). A vision of teacher leadership. In C. Livingston (Ed.), *Teachers as leaders: Evolving roles* (pp. 167–173). Washington, DC: National Education Association.

Wilson, M. (1993, March). The search for teacher leaders. *Educational Leadership, 50*(6), 24–27.

Wimpelberg, R. K. (1990, September). *Reinventing school leadership* (pp. 176–178). Working memo prepared for the Reinventing School Leadership Conference. Cambridge, MA: National Center for Educational Leadership.

Wise, A. E. (1978, February). The hyper-rationalization of American education. *Educational Leadership, 35*(5), 354–361.

Wise, A. E. (1989). Professional teaching: A new paradigm for the management of education. In T. S. Sergiovanni & J. H. Moore (Eds.), *Schooling for tomorrow: Directing reforms to issues that count* (pp. 301–310). Boston: Allyn & Bacon.

Wohlstetter, P. (1990, April). *Experimenting with decentralization: The politics of change.* (ERIC Document Reproduction Service No. ED337861)

Wohlstetter, P., & McCurdy, K. (1991, January). The link between school decentralization and school politics. *Urban Education, 25*(4), 391–414.

Wynne, J. (2001, November). *Teachers as leaders in education reform.* ERIC Clearinghouse on Teaching and Teacher Education. (EDO-SP-2001–5)

Yarger, S. J., & Lee, O. (1994). The development and sustenance of instructional leadership. In D. R. Walling (Ed.), *Teachers as leaders: Perspectives on the professional development of teachers* (pp. 223–237). Bloomington, IN: Phi Delta Kappa.

Yukl, G. (2002). *Leadership in organizations* (5th ed.). Upper Saddle River, NJ: Prentice-Hall.

Zeichner, K. M., & Tabachnich, B. R. (1991). Reflections on reflective teaching. In B. R. Tabachnich & K. M. Zeichner (Eds.), *Issues and practices in inquiry-oriented teacher education* (pp. 1–37). London: Falmer Press.

Zimpher, N. L. (1988, January/February). A design for the professional development of teacher leaders. *Journal of Teacher Education, 39*(1), 53–60.

Index

**CORWIN
PRESS**

The Corwin Press logo—a raven striding across an open book—represents the union of courage and learning. Corwin Press is committed to improving education for all learners by publishing books and other professional development resources for those serving the field of K–12 education. By providing practical, hands-on materials, Corwin Press continues to carry out the promise of its motto: **"Helping Educators Do Their Work Better."**